GETTING IT RIGHT

Also by James F. Dunnigan

How to Stop War (with William Martel)

How to Make War

Dirty Little Secrets (with Al Nofi)

Shooting Blanks (with Al Nofi)

A Quick and Dirty Guide to War (with Austin Bay)

From Shield to Storm (with Austin Bay)

The Complete Wargames Handbook

GETTING IT RIGHT

American Military Reforms After Vietnam to the Persian Gulf and Beyond

James F. Dunnigan
and
Raymond M. Macedonia

William Morrow and Company, Inc.
New York

Library of Congress Cataloging-in-Publication Data

Dunnigan, James F.
   Getting it right : American military reforms after Vietnam to the Gulf War and beyond / James F. Dunnigan and Raymond M. Macedonia.
      p.   cm.
   Includes index.
   ISBN 0-688-12096-2
   1. United States—Armed Forces—History—20th century.   2. United States.   Army—History—20th century.   I. Macedonia, Raymond.
II. Title.
UA23.D834   1993
355'.00973'0904—dc20   93-19751
                                                                                                          CIP

Printed in the United States of America

First Edition

1   2   3   4   5   6   7   8   9   10

BOOK DESIGN BY BRIAN MOLLOY / CIRCA 86

To the Memory of
GENERAL WILLIAM E. DEPUY, U.S. ARMY

He led the way in "breaking the mold by creating an Army trained and ready to win its first battles quickly, decisively, and with minimum casualties."

ACKNOWLEDGMENTS

We are indebted to a large number of people for helping us gather the information for this book and contributing ideas, data, insights, and comments. The following list is not exhaustive. We may have missed a few. But you know who you are.

General Gordon Sullivan, General Charles Gabriel, General Jack Merritt, Brigadier General Harold Nelson, Ed Josephson, Albert A. Nofi, Major Michael Macedonia, John Macedonia, Captain Christian Macedonia, Captain David Macedonia, Susan Leon, Bob Shuman, Austin Bay, Evan Brooks, Mark Herman, Mike Garrombone, Sterling S. Hart, Thomas Molina, Christopher H. Baumgartner, Trent J. Telenko, Mark F. Hennessey, Steve Plegge, Tom Trinko.

CONTENTS

	Introduction		9
Chapter	1	Never Quite Got It Right	23
Chapter	2	Lessons Learned—and Forgotten	39
Chapter	3	The Army Gets Nuked	50
Chapter	4	The Central Front Fixation	61
Chapter	5	Vietnam: False Confidence	68
Chapter	6	The Hollow Army	96
Chapter	7	Reform	113
Chapter	8	Reeducation	130
Chapter	9	The Volunteers	143
Chapter	10	New Ideas	157
Chapter	11	Innovative Training	170
Chapter	12	The Fat 80s	190
Chapter	13	Proof of Performance	205
Chapter	14	The Other Services	213
Chapter	15	An Uncertain Future	237
	Appendices		261
	Index		314

INTRODUCTION

This is a book about a little-understood subject, the dramatic reform of the American military, and particularly the U.S. Army, between the end of the Vietnam War and the Persian Gulf War of 1990–1991. We cover a number of subjects that few Americans are familiar with. While the book was written for a general audience, we know that many military professionals will read it. We have, however, purposely avoided using a lot of military jargon in explaining what the military had to do and how they did it. The military professionals who read this may find it jarring when we use common civilian terms in place of the more familiar (to soldiers) jargon. For example, a popular buzzword in the military these days is "synchronization." This term is used to describe the successful team effort among all the weapons, equipment, tasks, and units in achieving a result so that there is no wasted effort. We use the word "coordination," which is more comprehensible to the average civilian and still gets the point across.

You will also find some subjects coming up in several different chapters, each time being explained a little differently. This was done partially for the benefit of civilian readers. The "NCO (noncommissioned officers, or sergeants) Problem" after the Vietnam War is an example. Since the problem was attacked from several different angles, we explain it thoroughly, despite some seeming repetition, in the several chapters where it is a factor. This makes it easier for civilians who have only a vague idea what an NCO is, and gives the military reader a multifaceted look at this key issue.

To further assist civilian readers, we include in the Appendices a description of the military rank structure, life in the peacetime military, and sundry other details that most nonmilitary people are unfamiliar with. For the military personnel reading this, take comfort in the fact that once civilians have read this, they will have a much better appreciation of what soldiers do and how they do it.

Although we have excised many of the purely military terms, some of this technobabble is unavoidable. Below is a glossary containing the terms you will most frequently encounter and, if you are a civilian, be mystified by.

GLOSSARY

AC—Active Component. Also known as "the regulars." Troops and units that are on active duty, as opposed to reserve troops and units that train only part time.

ACC—Air Combat Command. New streamlined organization formed by the Air Force to provide more effective bomber and fighter support to meet regional conflicts in a new security environment where most of the U.S. military forces are stationed in the United States. In practical terms, this means putting bomber and fighter squadrons (12 to 24 planes each) together in units that train together and would be quickly sent overseas together. Previously, the bomber and fighter units were quite separate organizations that rarely operated together except in wartime.

AD—Active Defense. A flexible and elastic defense used by mechanized and armored forces. Instead of just digging in and waiting for the attacking enemy, the Active Defense has the defending units using their mobility to outmaneuver the attacker.

AFQT—Armed Forces Qualification Test. An aptitude test given to potential recruits to determine their suitability for military service. There are five categories, with category 1 being the recruits most likely to succeed in uniform and categories 4 and 5 usually not allowed to enlist (because they would be likely to fail in training or otherwise have problems doing their military jobs).

ALB—AirLand Battle. Name given the Army's warfighting doctrine, published in 1982, that emphasized a closer coordination between air power and Army ground units in extending the battlefield by attacking the enemy deep in his rear and also by balancing attrition (destroying the enemy's forces and equipment) with maneuver (fancy footwork).

AMC—Air Mobility Command or **Army Material Command.**

AOE—Army of Excellence. A program in the 1980s to make the Army more efficient so that it could do more with less.

ARTEP—Army Training and Evaluation Program. The basic system the Army uses to train the troops and test the effectiveness of that training.

ASW—Antisubmarine Warfare (by aircraft, ships, subs, and land-based equipment).

ATO—Air Tasking Order. An Air Force computer program for assigning all available aircraft to their tasks in an efficient manner. During combat, a new one is generated for every twenty-four hours of operations.

ATTRITION. The reduction of the effectiveness of military forces caused by loss of personnel or material. Not just casualties, but also lost and worn-out equipment as well as fatigue of the troops.

AWACS—Airborne Warning and Control System. Air surveillance and control provided by airborne early-warning aircraft equipped with radar and communications equipment for controlling aircraft.

AWC—Army War College (in Carlisle, Pennsylvania). Where up-and-coming lieutenant colonels spend a year learning how to think like generals. Selection for going to the Army War College is based on a general officers' board (committee) recommendation that the student has the potential to become a general officer. Most students do not become generals only because of the relatively small number of generals on duty, as well as the fact that some of these positions require special skills and training (medical, scientific, legal). The officers who attend the AWC (and the other services' war colleges) are the best officers available. In wartime, with larger armed forces, the AWC graduates would be the primary source of promotions to general.

BAI—Battlefield Air Interdiction. Attacking enemy ground forces who are not involved in the ongoing close battle with U.S. ground forces, but close enough to be a threat to U.S. forces in the battle. It is the position of the Army that BAI should be closely coordinated with the ground commander and BAI targets should be selected by the ground commander. This is so because air power is the primary weapon for the Army to hit enemy targets deep in enemy territory. The Air Force wants to keep control over

BAI missions, if only because Air Force planes are flying most of the missions. The purpose of BAI is to destroy, delay, or disrupt enemy reserves before they can enter the battle. BAI missions also include isolating the enemy in the close battle by preventing their movement or reinforcement by other enemy units. BAI missions can take place on either side of the fire-support coordination line (FSCL, the line separating areas where you might encounter friendly forces, and the area where you won't). Missions that take place short of the FSCL require close coordination because friendly forces may be in the area. BAI missions beyond the FSCL do not require continuous coordination during the execution phase of the mission (friendly forces crossing the FSCL).

BCTP—Battle Command Training Program. A program established by the Army in the 1980s to help division (and larger unit) commanders and their staffs develop and maintain competence at running their units in combat. This was done utilizing computerized combat simulations.

BLITZKRIEG ("Lightning War"). Coordinating air and ground forces in swift, offensive attacks. The Germans, during World War II, were the first to integrate the use of the airplane and the tank for rapid attacks.

BVR—Beyond Visual Range. Refers to distant targets, beyond what any of the troops can see with their own eyes.

C^2—Command and Control. A function in which the commander controls the battlefield interaction of his weapons with the terrain and enemy.

C^3I—Command, Control, Communications, and Intellience. All those things that a commander needs to sort out the progress of a battle and make the best decisions.

CAMPAIGN. A connected series of military operations forming a distinct phase of war to accomplish a long-range major strategic objective.

CAS—Close Air Support. Air attacks against hostile targets near friendly forces, which require detailed cooperation of each air mission with the fire and movement of friendly ground forces in order to avoid friendly-fire casualties.

CASSS—Combined Arms and Service Staff School (where Army officers go to learn how to be staff officers and commanders).

CEM—Combined Effects Munition. Shells that are designed to efficiently damage more than one kind of target. For example, an antitank shell that also does a lot of damage to troops in the vicinity (older antitank shells didn't).

CIA—Central Intelligence Agency.

CINC—Commander in Chief (usually refers to a U.S. commander who commands one of the regional commands). There is one of these regional commands for most parts of the world where there are U.S. troops or U.S. military responsibilities.

CINCCENT—Commander in Chief, Central Command (the regional command for U.S. forces in the Middle East).

CINCLANT—Commander in Chief, Atlantic Command.

CINCSOC—Commander in Chief, Special Operations Command (Special Forces and the like).

CJCS—Chairman, Joint Chiefs of Staff.

CMTC—Combat Maneuver Training Center. A large area where the troops can move around in their armored vehicles and fire their weapons.

CNO—Chief of Naval Operations. Commander of the U.S. Navy.

COMBINED ARMS TEAM. Two or more arms mutually supporting one another. A team usually consists of tanks, infantry, cavalry, aviation, artillery, air defense, and engineers.

COMBINED OPERATION. An operation conducted by forces of two or more allied nations acting together for the accomplishment of a single mission.

COME AS YOU ARE. As in "Be prepared to go to war with what you've got and still win." An official Army slogan in the 1980s. The U.S. Army historically has been unprepared for its first battle in a war. It achieved its victories eventually with the sheer weight of material and troops brought to bear after the onset of the war. "Come as you are" means that the United States would often have to fight and win with the material and forces it had on hand at the beginning of the war because the war might be very short and intense and the outcome of the war decided by the results of the initial battles.

CONARC—Continental Army Command. A now-defunct command for all Army forces stationed in the United States.

CONCEPT OF OPERATION. A concise graphic, verbal, or written statement that gives an overall picture of a commander's scheme with regard to a military operation or series of operations.

COUNTERINSURGENCY. Military, paramilitary, political, economic, psychological, and civil actions taken by a country to defeat actions to undermine its rule. In other words, fighting guerrillas.

CP—Contingency Plan. A plan for major events that can reasonably be anticipated. It is not "spur of the moment" planning.

CSAF—Chief of Staff, United States Air Force.

CSS—Combat Services Support. The assistance provided to sustain combat forces, primarily in the fields of administration and logistics.

CVA—Aircraft Carrier.

CVBG—Carrier Battle Group.

DARPA—Defense Advance Research Project Agency. Supplies money and encouragement to research projects that are too off-the-wall for anyone else to touch. Very successful in turning many of these ideas into useful items. In 1993, DARPA's name has been changed to ARPA to reflect President Clinton's policy of placing emphasis on civilian as well as military research.

DAS—Direct Air Support. Aircraft attacking enemy ground forces that are fighting friendly ground forces.

DEEP ATTACK. Using airpower, long-range artillery, and fast-moving armored units to isolate enemy units from each other so that the defender may be eliminated one piece at a time. Deep attack depends on good communications and fast movement to keep the enemy off balance while not losing control of one's own forces.

DEFEAT DISEASE. An affliction that is often caught by armies that suffer a defeat. It is characterized by a self-defeating tendency to search for scapegoats to blame for the defeat. Armies normally blame it on politicians. The U.S. military did not fall victim to this disease after the Vietnam War.

DESERT ONE. This was the name given to the designated refueling point for the helicopters used in the 1980 effort to rescue the U.S. Embassy staff taken hostage in Iran. The name is also used to refer to the entire event, including its tragic failure.

DOCTRINE. In its traditional meaning, this is the written guide that the military services have developed for fighting the next war. It is authoritative but requires judgment in its application. To be successful, doctrine has to be close enough to the actual requirements of the war so that it can be easily adapted. In the post–Cold War environment, doctrine is beginning to include guides for military procedures short of war (counter-drug activities, humanitarian efforts).

DPICM—Dual Purpose, Improved Conventional Munitions. Rounds containing shaped-charge antimaterial and antipersonnel bomblets.

ECM—Electronic Countermeasures. Actions taken to prevent or reduce the enemy's effective use of the electronic spectrum (radios, radars, etc.)

EW—Electronic Warfare. ECM (above) as well as any electronic tool that will give you an edge over the enemy.

FM 100-5, OPERATIONS (usually just referred to as "100-5"; the "FM" stands for "Field Manual"). This is the Army's key "how to make war" manual. (There are many others, covering all the details.) It explains how Army forces plan and conduct campaigns, major operations, and battles in conjunction with the Air Force, Navy, and Marines, and with allied forces.

It also is the foundation for subordinate doctrine, force design, material acquisition, professional military education, and individual and unit training.

FORSCOM—Army Forces Command. Established by the Army in 1973 as part of a reform movement to streamline the Army (Project Steadfast). It was given the responsibility for unit training and readiness. As part of the Department of Defense Reorganization Act of 1986 (reform movement of the military initiated by Congress), FORSCOM was given the mission in 1987 of providing combat-ready forces to overseas commands and land defense of the CONUS (Continental United States), as well as military support to civil defense.

FRIENDLY FIRE. Losses to your troops in combat because, during the chaos of battle, some of your units accidentally fired on each other. Such losses have been known to be as high as 20 percent of all losses.

GDP—General Defense Plan. An overall defense plan for the positioning of units in West Germany during the Cold War was the largest GDP, although there were GDPs for other areas as well.

GNA—Goldwater-Nichols Department of Defense Reorganization Act of 1986. This law was a major effort by Congress to reform the military. The law had a major impact on many aspects of the military, including giving more authority to the Chairman of the Joint Chiefs of Staff and the major warfighting commanders, improving joint doctrine, and giving more clout to special operating forces.

GPS—Global Positioning System. A system that uses satellites to assist in determining location. U.S. forces used GPS to navigate in the desert during the Gulf War.

HE—High Explosive (usually refers to a type of artillery shell that contains just HE, rather than bomblets, poison gas, or whatever).

HOLLOW ARMY. A phrase used to indicate a condition of lack of readiness by the Army to perform its wartime mission because of inadequate funding for training, maintenance, ammunition, etc.

ICBM—Intercontinental Ballistic Missile.

INTEL—Intelligence, as in information about the enemy.

JCS—Joint Chiefs of Staff. The uniquely American version of the traditional "General Staff of the Armed Forces" found in most other nations. The JCS is a committee composed of the heads of the three services (Army, Air Force, and Navy) plus the head of the Marine Corps (which belongs to the Navy, thus giving the Navy two people on the JCS, but that's another story). The fifth member of the JCS is the Chairman, who is selected by the president from among the senior generals of the armed forces to serve a three-year term. Note that the Coast Guard, in wartime, becomes, like the Marines, another part of the Navy, but in peacetime it is part of the Department of Transportation. Part of this has to do with U.S. law, which prohibits members of the armed forces from arresting civilians. This, in turn, goes back to the American Revolution, which began in part because British troops were often used as police. Since the Coast Guard has to enforce laws on American waterways, its members have to be able to arrest American citizens. Navy personnel cannot do that.

JOINT OPERATIONS. One or more military services working together.

JRTC—Joint Readiness Training Center.

JS—Joint Staff. The staff that supports the JCS. Since the Goldwater-Nichols Act, the Joint Staff has begun to operate more like a traditional General Staff. However, unlike most General Staffs in the world, America's has no "Chief of the General Staff" who serves as the commander of the armed forces. In America, the president is the commander of the armed forces at all times. This is why U.S. troops always salute the president, as he is the senior commander in the armed forces.

JSTARS—Joint Surveillance and Target Attack Radar System. A large aircraft that uses a special radar to keep track of friendly and enemy vehicles on the ground.

JTFME—Joint Task Force Middle East. Formed in 1987 to escort re-flagged tankers in the Persian Gulf (during the Iran-Iraq war).

LIC—Low Intensity Conflict. Guerrilla wars, and other conflicts that do not involve all-out war (like the situations in Yugoslavia and Somalia during the early 1990s).

MILES—Military Integrated Laser Engagement System. A training device, similar to the civilian "laser tag."

MILITARY STRATEGY. This is the art and science of employing the armed forces of a nation to secure the objectives of national policy by application of force or the threat of force.

MLRS—Multiple Rocket Launcher. A U.S. weapon that fires rockets.

MOS—Military Occupation Specialties. Job descriptions and job code.

MTM—McClintic Theater Model. Computer wargame developed at the Army War College in the late 1970s. Named after the programmer, Fred McClintic.

NATIONAL STRATEGY. This is the art and science of developing and using the political, economic, and psychological powers of a nation together with its armed forces, during peace and war, to secure national objectives.

NATO—North Atlantic Treaty Organization.

NCO—Noncommissioned Officer (sergeants and petty officers).

NFRP—Navy Fleet Readiness Program.

NTC—National Training Center, Fort Irwin, CA. A TRADOC (see below) installation located in the Mojave Desert, which pits U.S. forces against Soviet-style forces. Total MILES (see above) instrumentation with immediate feedback in the training vehicles.

OC—Observer Controller.

OER—Officers Evaluation Report. Periodically, officers are rated by their commander, using a standard form and methodology. "Good" OERs are needed for advancement, while "bad" OERs will get an officer thrown out of the service.

OPEC—Organization of Petroleum Exporting Countries.

OPERATIONAL ART. The employment of military forces to attain strategic goals in a theater of war or theater of operations through the design, organization, and conduct of campaigns and major operations. It involves fundamental decisions about when and where to fight and whether to accept or decline battle.

OPFOR—Opposing Force. The "enemy" in training exercises. Used to mean the Soviets. Now can mean all sorts of people.

OPLAN—Operational Plan. A plan for a single or series of connected operations to be carried out simultaneously or in succession.

OPLAN-1002. Central Command Contingency Plan to Counter Iraqi Attack of Kuwait and Saudi Arabia.

OPORD—Operational Order. A directive, usually formal, issued by a commander to subordinate commanders to effect the coordinated execution of an operation.

OPS—Operations.

OSD—Office of the Secretary of Defense.

OVERWATCH. The tactical role of one group of troops positioned to observe the movement of another group and to support it with firepower. Related to BOUND, which refers to movement from one covered and concealed position to another by dismounted troops or combat vehicles.

PGM—Precision-Guided Munition.

R&D—Research and Development.

RDF—Rapid Deployment Force. American forces organized, after the 1973 Arab-Israeli war, to intervene, if needed, in the Middle East (or other areas).

RECCE—Reconnaissance.

REDCOM—Readiness Command.

RETO—Review of Education and Training for Officers.

RIF—Reduction in Force. System that the military services have for rapidly reducing the size of their forces (term for military layoffs).

SAC—Strategic Air Command.

SAMS—School of Advanced Military Studies.

SDI—Strategic Defense Initiative.

SEAL—Sea, Air and Land. Navy officers and enlisted members specially trained and equipped for unconventional and paramilitary operations including surveillance and reconnaissance in and from restricted waters, rivers, and coastal areas. SEALS also are able to train allies in special operations (Navy).

SECDEF—Secretary of Defense.

SIMNET—Simulator Network.

SM—Smart Munitions. These munitions are part of the computer-chip revolution. They have the self-contained capability to search for, detect, acquire, and engage targets.

SOF—Special Operations Forces. These forces can perform a wide variety of missions. These include interdicting enemy lines of communications and destroying military and industrial facilities; organizing and training and advising resistance forces in guerrilla warfare, evasion and escape, and sabotage; personnel recovery; providing navigational guidance for strike aircraft and missile systems; intelligence collection; target acquisition (Iraqi missile systems); and psychological operations, which includes changing the attitudes and behavior of designated groups of people.

SPI—Simulation Publications, Inc.

TAC—Tactical Air Command.

TACTICS. Techniques by which corps and smaller unit commanders use their forces on the battlefield in the short term (days or weeks). A chess game is a good example of "tactical combat." A tactical commander uses his forces to create combat power (the ability to fight), which is a combination of maneuver, firepower, and effective leadership.

TARGET SERVICING. The capability of a force to acquire (spot), engage (fire at), and neutralize (prevent them from doing anything), or destroy enemy firepower systems (tanks, infantry fighting vehicles, etc.).

TCRP—Tactical Command Readiness Program.

TRADOC—Training and Doctrine Command (Army). Part of the Army's reform movement in 1973 to streamline its performance (Project Steadfast). It was given the responsibility for managing Army schooling, doctrinal and combat development programs, and primary responsibility for individual training for the Army. General DePuy was its first commander.

UAV—Unmanned Aerial Vehicle. Small aerial unmanned vehicles designed to fly into hostile territory and locate targets and perform surveillance, reconnaissance, and damage assessment.

USSBS—U.S. Strategic Bombing Survey.

VICTORY DISEASE. The affliction that is caught by most armies and nations after they have won a war. The disease is characterized by arrogance, a tendency to believe myths as to the underlying reasons for the victory, and a firm conviction that future conflicts should be fought the same way ("It worked so well before, why change?").

WARFIGHTING. An Army buzzword for what goes on during battle. "Warfighting skills," for example, means the ability of a soldier to do his job in combat.

WARGAME. This is a representation of certain selected aspects of conflict situations and processes using predetermined rules, data, and procedures.

Chess is a wargame, the oldest wargame still in use. Modern wargames tend to be larger and more complex than chess.

WIN THE FIRST BATTLE. Because the lethality of modern weapons continues to increase sharply, it is possible to lose a lot of troops in a very short time. The entire force could be destroyed quickly if they are improperly used. The outcome of the war could be determined in the initial battle. Therefore, it is critical to be trained and ready to win the first battle as well as all the other battles.

WPC—Warrior Preparation Center. Training facility set up in Europe during the 1980s to train commanders to handle their battlefield chores. Made extensive use of wargames.

1

Never Quite Got It Right

This chapter is both an introduction to and a summation of this book. If you are short on time, just reading this chapter will give you the key points we are making. You'll miss all the interesting details, but you can always come back later.

This book is about good news from an unexpected quarter. The good news is that some government employees with a longstanding reputation of haphazard performance finally demonstrated world-class abilities. The unexpected quarter is the U.S. armed forces. In particular, we are talking about the U.S. Army, although the Air Force, Navy, and Marines share in this achievement.

In February 1991 something unique in American history happened. For the first time in the American military record, U.S. troops won the first battle of a war and did so with minimal losses. America has a long tradition of not being ready for war. This habit goes back to before the American Revolution, and has continued until the 1980s. All of a sudden, between 1972 and the 1980s, this changed. There were several reasons for this newfound peacetime military effectiveness. The principal reasons were:

1. A well-trained officer corps with a pragmatic and professional attitude and a centralized system for selecting the most qualified officers for battalion and brigade commanders.
2. Volunteer, carefully selected, and well-paid troops.
3. Realistic, rigorous, and plentiful training accompanied by sound doctrine and tactics.
4. World-class weapons and equipment.

5. The bitter experience of a previous war (Vietnam) to spur everyone on to "do better next time."

None of these five items had been present before, much less all five. What caused all this fortuitous change is the basic theme of this book.

While the U.S. Army of the 1990s is a formidable professional organization, such was rarely the case in the past, particularly in peacetime. Compared to most other nations, America has never been very enthusiastic about its armed forces in the absence of war. Without nearby enemies threatening invasion, and with a population composed largely of migrants trying to escape wars in other parts of the world, it is understandable that Americans have been suspicious of large standing armies. Moreover, Americans had bad experiences with regular British troops before the American Revolution. Thus restrictions on the use of regular forces, and preference for a citizen militia, were written into the Constitution. Americans have never felt compelled to support the military when there wasn't a war going on. As a result, the U.S. armed forces have never been ready for war. When a war did appear, there were frantic and muddled efforts to get ready. Americans invariably lost the first battles and endured high casualties before eventually overcoming their opponents. The Gulf War in 1991 was different, and no one has quite realized what that means for America's future.

Americans still have an ambivalent attitude toward their armed forces. Most of the people, such as the Quakers, who migrated to the United States were not warlike. Indeed, most were fleeing wars and unrest in their own nations. This was particularly the case in the great nineteenth-century migrations. The 1848 revolutions and the constant military activity in late nineteenth-century Europe sent refugees and draft dodgers by the millions to North America. Many were also religious refugees, beginning with the first English migrants to America. The heresies these people had embraced were usually more pacifistic than the rulers in their homelands were willing to tolerate.

Once in the New World, the migrants discovered that the original inhabitants generally considered war a favorite outdoor sport. This fact was often glossed over in later attempts to portray the aboriginal inhabitants of North America as noble naturalists. While unfamiliar European diseases killed far more Indians than did colonists' bullets, the pre–American Revolution military experience was one of small-scale raids and paramilitary operations. Most of the formal fighting was done by British regulars imported for that purpose. The antiwar and pacifist attitudes of the American public have been a major element in national politics for over two centuries, despite the many wars America has gotten involved in.

In self-defense, a militia gradually developed. This was the forerunner of the current National Guard. For several centuries, the militia's primary opponents were Indians, bandits, and rioters in the urban areas. (This violence took many forms, none of it very serious.) When the militia saw large-scale use during the American Revolution, it quickly became obvious that the militia was no match for trained British regulars. Several years would pass before units of Americans could be drilled to the same standard of battlefield effectiveness as the British troops. And it took a number of "foreign advisers" (volunteer officers from various European nations, such as the Marquis de Lafayette from France) to speed this process along. The militia was not without value. For light-infantry tasks and patrolling the vast wilderness areas in the thirteen colonies, the militia was more than a match for the British. But the war was won, then as now, by controlling the populated areas. Ultimately, this had to be done with American troops trained to meet the British on their own terms.

Thus began the dependence on the ill-trained citizen soldier and all its attendant costs in terms of losing the first battles of future wars. The first taste of what problems this approach (as opposed to a large, European-style, professional army) could cause came in the War of 1812. This conflict involved more battles with British regulars, and generally disastrous results for the unprepared Americans. Thus began the custom of forgetting about the early defeats and concentrating on how well the troops did later in the war.

The Mexican-American war (1847) produced the same pattern, only this time Americans were up against Mexicans who were equally inept. Inspired leadership on the American side (by the likes of Zachary Taylor, Winfield Scott, and many future Civil War leaders) saved the day for the United States. But a lot of the U.S. success had to do with the even more ill-prepared Mexican troops. Thus the militia system was able to resist reform once more.

The American Civil War began with a tragicomic series of battles where victory did not so much go to the better side as it did to the force that was less inept. Generals like Burnside remain standards of ineptitude against which later incompetent commanders are still measured. The troops got better after four years of campaigning, competent leadership developed, and 1865 saw the state militias more revered than ever before.

The Spanish-American war saw so many organizational and battlefield disasters (even though the United States quickly won the war) that the military and civilian leadership was prompted to enact reforms. Logistical disasters saw troops stranded and many dead of disease. Sloppy battlefield leadership got reported promptly by the ever-present press. The aftereffects of this war were quite embarrassing to America's military leadership. Some of the reforms (staff colleges and better planning) were in place when the United States was dragged into World War I. But after World War I, whose scope and brutality caused many to proclaim it the "war to end all wars," everyone went back to sleep once more. World War II came along, more early battles were lost, and then, after 1945, a dramatically new era in U.S. military history unfolded.

The United States ended World War II as the world's most formidable military power without fully appreciating how it did it and how it might be able to maintain that power. In World War I, America helped its Allies win the war by sending to Europe masses of poorly trained troops, who soon acquired useful battlefield skills. But this cost a lot of American troops their lives, and many of these troops would not have died if there had been adequate training before battle. While many of the veterans who fought the war understood the techniques they had used to defeat their enemies, there was little institutional knowledge in the armed forces of exactly what went on. While individual soldiers and officers knew how ill prepared they were, and how costly it was to learn their jobs under fire, little of this knowledge was retained by the armed forces as an institution. This varied from service to service and even within the services. The Navy learned, and remembered, a lot about modern warfare, and the Marines absorbed many useful lessons. But the Army generally did not. Some branches of the Army (such as the artillery and air corps) came out of World War I with long-remembered experience, but other branches (like the infantry) gained little.

World War II saw, in many respects, a replay of World War I. At the end of World War II, there were millions of veterans and regulars who knew how to fight World War II over again. But the military as an institution did little but toy with future military development, nor was there rigorous analysis of exactly how World War II had been won. This led to lost battles and disillusionment in Korea and Vietnam. From this came the end of conscription and a Hollow Army in the 1970s. The stage was set for unexpected and unprecedented reform. This is a story that has not been told outside the military, and even many of the troops were not sure exactly what happened, except that it worked.

GETTING IT RIGHT, MADE SIMPLE

The story of the great reforms of the 1980s requires at least a book to explain in full detail. But for the impatient or short-of-time readers, we provide a chapter summary that gives the highlights. Each chapter in this book covers a different aspect of these problems—and their surprising solutions.

Chapter 1: Never Quite Got It Right (1700–1950). America's tradition of military unpreparedness starts before the Revolution and proceeds into the late twentieth century. The lessons of the previous wars were invariably lost and had to be relearned during the first battles of the next war. With the Cold War over, another bout of reform is unavoidable. Budgets are being cut and a new array of potential enemies has to be planned for.

Chapter 2: Lessons Learned—and Forgotten (1950–1955). False confidence from World War I caused a disastrous first battle in North Africa during World War II and later a similar experience in the Korean War with the ill-prepared Task Force Smith. Within the space of eight years, American forces were run off the battlefield during their initial battles. Nothing was really learned from this, and the mistakes were repeated through the 1950s and into Vietnam.

Chapter 3: The Army Gets Nuked (1955–1961). Introduction of strategic nuclear weapons took away any significant role for the Army in post–World War II military policy. For nearly a decade, the Army went nowhere. But by the early 1960s, the Army was able to overcome this somewhat, as many agreed that perhaps nukes alone could not keep the peace.

Chapter 4: The Central Front Fixation (1948–1980). Most of the Army "thinkers" concentrated on the potential war with the Soviet Union in Europe, to the exclusion of anything else. This has been a constant since the late 1940s and only began to fade with the collapse of the Soviet Union in 1991. Elements of this fixation will linger, even though the official line is to prepare for new wars against a vast array of new enemies in a variety of exotic locations.

Chapter 5: Vietnam: False Confidence (1962–1972). The lessons of Korea were forgotten and an illusion of competence and readiness met reality in Vietnam. Nothing seemed to work, despite various attempts to remedy the problems encountered. There was a long list of unique difficulties the Army had to face in Vietnam, and the sheer length of the list makes it easier to appreciate why there were so many obstacles to overcome in fighting the Vietnam war.

Chapter 6: The Hollow Army (1972–1980). The Army had been turned into a much less effective force by the Vietnam experience, as well as the Big RIF (Reduction in Force; 1970–1975). After Vietnam the Army had to greatly reduce its size and switch over to using only volunteers. Discipline had broken down during Vietnam, too many of the experienced NCOs left or retired, and quality volunteers were not forthcoming right away.

Chapter 7: Reform (1972–1975). The shock of the rapid and massive lethality of the 1973 Arab-Israeli War created the fear that the Warsaw Pact could conduct a surprise attack and overwhelm NATO in the First Battle. The realization that NATO might have to go quickly to using nuclear weapons or lose the war galvanized the American Army into a reform movement that was led by General Bill DePuy and his Training and Doctrine Command (TRADOC). This led to a host of new ideas, presented in the 1976 edition of FM 100-5 (the Army's manual on "how to fight"). This led to five years of debates over which of the new ideas were real and which were not. After the dust settled, the Army had a blueprint for battlefield success.

Chapter 8: Reeducation (1975–1985). Those who had commanded battalions and brigades in Vietnam were the future generals in the 1990s and these were the officers who led and implemented the reformation of the Army. The way officers were trained for combat was drastically changed. The emphasis was now on "how to fight" rather than "how to be a manager and a diplomat." It was quite a switch from all that these men had been taught as gospel since the 1950s.

Chapter 9: The Volunteers (1975–1990). The end of the draft and the increase in military pay rates enabled the Army to attract a very high caliber of personnel. This was not an easy, or quick, transition. It took over a decade before the Army saw tangible benefits from the volunteer force.

Chapter 10: New Ideas (1973–1991). The Vietnam experience forced the Army to take a hard look at how it functioned, creating a fundamental change in every aspect of operations. The big items were now training, mobility, C^3I (Command, Control, Communications, and Intelligence), and more effective selection of battalion and brigade commanders. This was a radical break with American military tradition, but it was the new direction that worked.

Chapter 11: Innovative Training (1970–1990). The new thinking, and new technology, created a revolution in training. Revolutionary training methods, stressing realism and brutal criticism of the participating officers, created "combat experienced" units who had never been in combat.

Chapter 12: The Fat 80s (1980–1988). The large military budgets of the 1980s did not loom as large as one would think in increasing Army capabilities. The reformers did not expect the Fat 80s and were ready to go forward with their programs no matter how much, or how little, money they had. The increased defense budgets of the 80s allowed the fielding of new equipment, and more time for training. This saved lives in the Gulf War, but didn't affect the outcome of that war, or the reforms.

Chapter 13: Proof of Performance (1990–1991). What really happened in the Gulf in terms of what the Army expected and what actually happened. The Vietnam experience clouded expectations. But the troops turned in a historically exceptional performance. The revolution succeeded.

Chapter 14: The Other Services (1945–1990s). The U.S. Navy (and Marines) had always been quite professional in peacetime, the Air Force somewhat less so. But the Vietnam experience, and subsequent developments, also had an enormous impact outside the Army.

Chapter 15: An Uncertain Future (1991–?). The end of the Cold War, and to a lesser extent the Gulf War, created another watershed in military affairs. This time it was victory that defined the era of change, not defeat. And therein lie the problems that historically have dogged victorious armies in the wake of their triumph.

WHAT HAPPENS NOW?

The Gulf War was unique in American military history. Never before had there been such a stunning American victory in the first battle of a war. One would hope that this would be the pattern for the future. One might hope in vain unless careful attention is paid to the "Victory Disease." Up until Vietnam, Americans had never felt that they had lost a war. But Vietnam was different. Although U.S. troops were generally victorious on the battlefield, the war ended with American goals abandoned and, in effect, an

American defeat. The feeling of defeat led to more peacetime reforms than the U.S. armed forces had ever experienced. The results were obvious in the Gulf War. What happens next will not be so obvious. What happens next is a long struggle against the insidious Victory Disease. This affliction has been caught by most armies after they have won a war. The American military has caught it after every war except Vietnam.

The Victory Disease throws the following curves at the conquering heroes:

1. It worked so well last time, let's do it again next time. When a nation is defeated, it generally looks for a different way to fight the next war. The old ways obviously didn't work and new techniques are not only sought out but practiced vigorously. The winners have a different attitude, best summed up as "Don't mess with something that works." Actually, this attitude was once sound advice. But in the last two centuries, new technologies have arrived at an ever-increasing rate and winners and losers have had to adapt and change quickly, or else. The Victory Disease tends to make winners blind to these needed changes. Worse yet, it does not concentrate the victors' efforts as much as it does the losers'. Already, one of the new buzzwords in Washington is "Desert Storm Equivalent." This is a false analogy; no future war will be a Desert Storm Equivalent, even another war with Iraq, or a new one with Iran. The reason there will not be another Desert Storm is that potential adversaries of the United States have learned the lesson not to give the United States six months to build up its forces. More foreboding is the comment of one Third World officer: "Don't go to war with America unless you have nuclear weapons."

2. Congratulations, you're fired. After a feeling of exhilaration, the victorious army's fellow citizens and political leaders then tend to think, "If these guys did so well, maybe we don't need as many of them." Nations, particularly democracies, do not willingly spend large amounts of money on troops in peacetime.

3. What exactly did we do in order to win? In defeat, everyone has some defects to work on. In victory, the defects are less visible and much more effort is spent on embellishing one's good points. This embellishment is often at the expense of a realistic assessment of what actually happened. Losers want to be winners again and are quick to dump old habits. Winners have nowhere to go but down and are reluctant to

fiddle with what is obviously a winning combination. This is further complicated when everyone tends to claim a larger share of the victory than a dispassionate analysis would confirm.

4. False expectations. The public, the politicians, and even some of the troops will form expectations about future wars that are unlikely to be realized. Senior officers fear facing Congress after a future conflict that gets more Americans killed than Desert Storm. The troops dread facing troops with more fire in their bellies than the Iraqis. And everyone fears surprise, yet surprise is one of the constants in warfare.

For the American armed forces, the Gulf War brought forth all four symptoms to one degree or another.

While no one seriously expects to fight a carbon copy of the Gulf War with Iraq or another adversary, the possibility of a similar war remains. Iran is the historical regional superpower and Iran was rebuilding its armed forces while the Gulf War was going on. This buildup continues, fueled by bargain prices for all those weapons the successor states to the Soviet Union no longer need. Although not mentioned in official pronouncements, there is also the possibility of civil war in the former Soviet Union. With over a hundred thousand armored vehicles in those countries, any peacemaking in such a conflict would require a lot of M-1 tanks. Meanwhile, the interest in "low intensity" operations continues. This is the Light Infantry program of the 1980s. Few senior officers in the Army were ever particularly keen on this, as use of light infantry in low-intensity warfare smacked too much of a return to Vietnam. After the spectacularly low casualties of the Gulf War, no commander is eager to face the media with the inevitably larger losses any light-infantry action entails. As many Army officers put it, "We do deserts, not jungles or mountains." Moreover, the mechanized warfare crowd has dominated Army thinking since the early 1940s. Old habits are hard to break.

The spectacular success of air power in the Gulf has also influenced thinking about future wars. Military professionals realize that the coalition Air Force operated in near-ideal conditions over the Persian Gulf deserts, thus providing near-ideal conditions for air attacks on ground targets. But this has not stopped many advocates of air power from privately and publicly calling for a far larger role for air power in any future war. If said war took place in forested, urban, or jungle terrain, reality would come down hard. Even in the desert you need to have a balanced force, and in anything but a desert, it takes a lot of infantry to poke around in those nooks and crannies that are nearly invisible from the air. With the new emphasis on a wide range of regional conflicts, the appropriate response might be just a team of special forces, a battalion of Marines, a brigade of paratroopers, or a B-2 bomber loaded with smart mines. A full mobilization, or even a partial one as in 1990, is only one of many likely futures. There might even be the equivalent of two Desert Storms at the same time (unlikely, but possible with Iran and North Korea still making angry noises). The key is that in this new world of uncertain threats, the president needs to have a mix of forces that can be tailored to the specific situation, and forces that can work together regardless of service. But since planning for a future war is not as full of surprises as actually fighting a war, much can be gotten away with in the meantime.

But first the services have to decide who will do what with the forces currently available. All the services are in agreement that future wars must be joint efforts, or at least more "joint" than in the past. The disputes continue to arise over how this "jointness" is defined. While the Marine Corps remains committed to putting a lot of infantry in harm's way on short notice, the Army is not about to cede all its infantry jobs to another service. Yet, expensive and specialist items like the Light Infantry Divisions are always under attack. The Navy, of course, feels that it can do it all, or at least most of it. But it would be politically impossible to legislate the Army and Air Force to the kind of minor roles the Navy feels the other services deserve.

The Goldwater-Nichols Department of Defense Reorganization Act of 1986 foresaw the problem of sorting out who would do what in a changing world. The act stipulated that the Chairman of the Joint Chiefs of Staff issue a report on the assignment of roles and missions at least once every three years. The Chairman must recommend modifications in roles and missions while considering changes in the threats being faced by the United States. After 1989, these reports had to deal with the collapse of the communist military threat and the public call for a reduction in American military spending. After 1991, there was a need to address the scope of the threats in the Persian Gulf, Somalia, Bosnia, and many other new hot spots. Congress also wanted to hear how the military was going to deal with unnecessary duplication of effort, and about changes in technology. The 1993 report, for example, refused to do much about the five separate air forces (Army, Navy, Marine, Air Force, and Coast Guard), or duplication of effort in general. Although the law is clear, tradition and service politics cloud and complicate any effort to change roles and missions, with a little Victory Disease thrown in.

Even before the Gulf War, most American officers and troops could see that the Cold War was coming to an end, along with their career prospects. Through the 1980s, information leaked out of the intelligence agencies indicating that political and economic matters were going downhill fast in the communist nations. Professional officers saw all this confirmed in 1989 and many began to investigate new careers. The Gulf War merely reinforced the feeling that America did not need such large armed forces. Moreover, it was a surprise to most Americans to find out how competent their armed forces were. So while the victory celebrations were staged, the cheering crowds could not help but think, "We don't need as many of these really dynamite troops now that peace has broken out." Even at the end of World War II, there were many who already saw the new enemy in the mighty Red Army. There is no such opponent now. The situation in the 1990s is similar to the one seventy years ago, at the end of World War I, although even then there was a growing and ever more expansionistic Japan to give one pause. And the communists who seized control of Russia in the wake of World War I were seen as at least a potential threat. But where is the threat today that can match those still on the horizon at the end of World Wars I and II? Getting ready to fight is a hard habit to break, but it's more difficult to justify the expense when there are no worthy opponents in the offing.

But there will be another war. Where, and under what circumstances, no one can say with much certainty. Bosnia, Somalia, Haiti, China, Cambodia, or sundry fragments of the former Soviet Union—take your pick. Preparations must be made for the next war and at the moment the only thing everyone can agree on is that it would be nice if the machines did most of the fighting and took most of the casualties. While most casual observers missed the overwhelming role of training in the Gulf victory, the public was suitably wowed by the array of high-tech hardware used. Politicians pay attention to what the voters notice, not to the reality of the situation. Besides, all that fancy hardware translates into jobs for voters. Thus the debate over how to get ready for the next war has become a search for ways to hang on to present, and future, high-technology equipment. While many of the troops and their families vote, they comprise only about ten million people compared to a much larger number of voters dependent on the economic zing defense spending gives to hundreds of congressional districts. Congress tends to pay attention to military *things,* not military *people.* Congress has never shown a lot of enthusiasm over the training and professionalism of the troops. Show Congress some neat new hardware or construction projects, and it will pay attention.

But as many Israeli commanders have pointed out in explaining their success, "We could switch weapons with the enemy and we would still win." The Israeli secret weapon was training. This was also the case in the Gulf War. But the Victory Disease is hard on something as low-key as training. Gadgets make better copy and training isn't noticed until the shooting starts. At that point it's too late. So you won't hear a lot of impassioned speeches about maintaining training levels. You *will* hear a lot of talk about how we must make sacrifices so we can pay $150 million each for the next generation of jet-fighter aircraft.

Another item you won't hear much about is the obvious fact that more money spent on defense means fewer dead American troops. If you think about it, this is obvious, but few soldiers, politicians, or journalists want to touch the subject. The reason no one will touch it is because, in general, no one wants to get a lot of troops killed in combat and, in a specifically American way, dead troops bring out a lot of kneejerk demagoguery on how awful it is that Americans are getting killed in combat and, by God, we should do something, anything, about it (even if it gets more troops killed). Americans have long been insulated from war to a greater extent than most other nations. It's not that other nations are callous about war losses, but the fact remains that if you use your troops, some of them, often a lot of them, are going to get killed or mutilated. American politicians have learned that there are some things that are best avoided. Dwelling on how many American troops will die for every billion dollars subtracted from the defense budget is one of them. It's much safer to talk about saving the spotted owl. This is not a pretty situation, but there it is. All this is beginning to change, as some journalists begin to compare troop losses with police and fire department losses, which is how a lot of other nations look at it. Some occupations are simply more dangerous than others, and the most dangerous of all is infantry in combat. Whether the American people, and the politicians who chase after them, will pick up on this angle, only time will tell.

The flip side of this issue is that the defense funds could save more lives if spent on nonmilitary items. But this opens yet another debate over how effective government spending is. A soldier has a tremendous incentive to be efficient, and the penalty for sloppiness in combat is death or injury.

Government officials, however, can be inefficient without much fear of bodily harm. The dollars and cents approach to defense also impinges on the touchy subject of American spending habits in general. As any Japanese will tell you, the American economy is in trouble largely because Americans spend too much on consumption and save too little for investment.

All of this is very much part of the Victory Disease. Whether the debate follows a victory or a defeat, you still have to decide how much to spend on defense and what you spend it on. Stop for a minute and consider how this debate would have gone if there had been no Gulf War. Assume Saddam had a fit of lucidness and withdrew from Kuwait after the first UN resolution came down on his head. It would have been a different debate on post–Cold War spending without the knowledge of just how effective the American military could be. The Gulf War victory also made the thought of sending U.S. troops into battle just a bit less frightening. The normally isolationist attitude of Americans would have come back stronger than it has if there had not been a Gulf War victory. Without the Gulf War, we would have come out of the Cold War with memories of nothing but the Vietnam War, a conflict that left most Americans with a decidedly mixed opinion on how competent U.S. troops could be under fire. Now Americans know they have effective armed forces, and this tempts government officials, and the voters who support them, to use the troops overseas. In the shadow of the Gulf War, using American troops appears as a diplomatic gambit more likely to succeed than fail.

The primary rationale for the large peacetime forces since World War II was to stop the Soviet Union. Over half the defense budget was specifically for this purpose. The Soviet Union began to crumble before the Gulf War and went down for the count a year after Iraq invaded Kuwait. Military leaders could see sharp cuts in the defense budget coming. In the two years before the breakup of the Soviet Union, a series of unprecedented disarmament treaties were signed between the Soviet Union and the U.S.-led Western coalition. Even as U.S. armored divisions were massing on the Kuwaiti border, American troops were being given pink slips as a result of these treaties and the perception that the Red Menace was fading. There is still a need for armed forces in the post–Cold War world. How many, and what they will be equipped with, is a debate that would have been much more low-key had it not been for the Gulf War victory. But that victory sows the seeds for another defeat, as the Victory Disease warps thinking and decision making on the nature of America's military future.

POST–COLD WAR REFORM

All branches of the armed forces have sought ways to reform and reorganize themselves for the post–Cold War world. In the early 1990s, the U.S. Air Force aggressively moved out front and made radical reorganization and integration of everyone's long-range weapons under Air Force control a goal. The Air Force wants to combine both tactical and strategic systems under a single command. In 1992 the Air Force issued a new doctrine manual that reflects the increased emphasis on power projection (delivering all sorts of firepower to distant parts of the world) and the national need for forces that can respond with speed, range, and versatility. It made major restructuring changes including the disbanding of the Strategic Air Command (SAC) and Tactical Air Command (TAC) and the forming of a number of new organizations. The new commands are the Air Combat Command, the Air Mobility Command, and the U.S. Strategic Command (USSTRATCOM). The first two were created to ensure that air power can be provided rapidly under every situation. USSTRATCOM controls weapons only in wartime, which could be a tricky switch. But at least the Air Force, as always, is trying new ideas. On the (potentially) downside, the Air Force has decided, especially after its performance in the Gulf War, that it is just too good for any potential opponent and has scaled back its Red Flag program. This means no more special aircraft and pilots trained to fly and fight like potential enemies. This aspect of Red Flag training was very expensive. After demolishing the Iraqi air force with the greatest of ease, the U.S. Air Force has decided that it can cut back on the training expense and put the money into more urgent programs. It may be right, it may be wrong. History will decide.

The Navy, for almost a century, has been primarily focused on controlling the open seas. Now it is changing its doctrine to place priority on the coastal areas of the world. This new approach will require the Navy to place more emphasis on cooperating with the Army and Air Force in joint operations as it "comes from the sea." The Soviet navy was the only force that could threaten the U.S. Navy on the high seas, and now the Soviet navy is gone. But there are many hot spots near the water. Somalia, Bosnia, and most other potential American battlefields are first entered over a beach. This "breaking and entering" (as the military now calls it) used to be a secondary job for the Navy. But now it's a primary mission and the Navy is changing to accommodate these new realities.

The Army has been undergoing major reforms for almost twenty years and is well postured to cope with the new realities of the 1990s. It had actually seen the handwriting on the wall and begun developing plans to reduce its size, reorganize itself, and remake its doctrine even before it went off to fight in the Persian Gulf. A major Army advantage is that it has the best officer-development program in the world. This can be seen in the fact that the Army has developed a better understanding of the operational level of war (which is simply the theory of larger unit operations such as an army or a corps), is better able to do "Joint" operations (operating with one or more of the other services), and far better at the details of coalition warfare (operating with the forces of other nations) than any of the other U.S. services. The Army is good at Joint because it has to be. The Navy could operate without the Army, and the Air Force would like to be able to. But the Air Force needs someone on the ground to, at the very least, go in and occupy what precision bombing has conquered (even if it is increasingly reluctant to admit this).

The Army and particularly the Air Force are trying their best to capitalize on the spectacular success of their post-Vietnam weapons and tactics during the Gulf War. Yet that victory was potentially an empty one. Most of the likely future foes will not be masses of armored vehicles parked in the desert, but thousands of irregular troops wandering around forests or urban areas. Army and Air Force generals do not relish explaining to Congress why mountains and forests make such a big difference in the speed and cost of an American victory.

A major problem in the post–Cold War military is getting used to a marked slowdown in research and development of new weapons and equipment. Budgets are being cut severely; many in the Pentagon expect budgets of the late 1990s to be half of those $300 billion ones of the late 1980s. Because so many R&D and weapons production programs were begun in the 1980s, all the services have to scramble to save as much of this work as they can. Most building programs are being sharply cut back, and research and development projects are being slowed down. The Army used the opportunity to drastically reorganize the way weapons are conceived and developed. The Training and Doctrine Command (TRADOC) set up a series of "Battle Labs" wherein officers who would use new equipment work with the scientists to develop new ideas and suggest how to best turn them into combat-ready items. This in itself is a novel (for the American military) concept, since previously the scientists tended to stay in an ivory tower while the troops wondered what new gadget they would end up with. Now with little money and plenty of time to tinker and brainstorm, the troops and the techies are expected to have new technology ready for production when the need arises.

The future reform efforts will first have to sort out who the enemy is, a rather dicey undertaking. Once a reasonably plausible enemy has been conjured up, the reformers must then figure out ways to reorganize the American armed forces to most effectively deal with the new problems posed by these new foes. This will require highly skilled operators for the increasingly complex weapons. All this can be done, as was demonstrated in the Gulf War. But better intelligence information on the enemy is also needed with these more complex and expensive weapons. Americans have not always been on top of the intel game. Americans are leery of secrets, and of those who collect, analyze, and use them. The CIA and the many other U.S. intelligence organizations compiled a very mixed record during the Cold War. A lack of adequate intelligence is often the weak link in the chain of capabilities required for victory.

CHAPTER

2

Lessons Learned—and Forgotten

Over the last two centuries, the American Army has gained ample experience on how to win the first battles in every war they fought. But Americans always managed to discard this hard-won experience by the time they entered the next war. What wasn't lost was a false confidence that the combat performance that finally won the previous war would somehow magically reappear as the troops marched off to the next conflict. False confidence and an inability to remember much about the early phases of the last war caused disastrous first battles in both World War II and Korea.

How to Lose the First Battle

After World Wars I and II, essentially the same mistakes were made in dealing with the combat experience obtained on the battlefield. These mistakes fell into the following categories:

Selection of Retained Officers and NCOs

As soon as the shooting stopped, most serving officers were evaluated on how well-behaved they would be for peacetime service. This put a lot of the natural warriors at a disadvantage. The warriors tended either to have bad manners or to be uninterested in peacetime politicking. Some warriors had good manners and a taste for politics, but this was not the norm. Commanders facing peacetime soldiering want troops who won't cause trouble. Another war may never come, but a commander's peacetime promotion prospects depend on avoiding the kind of bad press that rowdy warrior types are prone to produce. A lot of the warrior officers simply got out, realizing that their aggressive, no-nonsense attitude was more appreciated in the civilian economy. A lot of the warrior NCOs were involuntarily separated for their sometimes rowdy behavior, usually by not being allowed to reenlist. In peacetime, especially in an Army that cannot afford a lot of expensive time running around training areas with their equipment, warrior NCOs drift toward booze, brawling, and complicated love lives. It was noted that when the troops were in the desert for six months during the Persian Gulf War, cut off from alcohol and other temptations, discipline was a lot better. In that situation, the troops had their hands full being soldiers. Several incidents in the early 1990s, most notably the Navy's "Tailhook Scandal," are but the most recent examples of the kind of mischief warriors get into during peacetime. Some of the perpetrators get tossed out of the service because of this antisocial behavior. But these are usually the kinds of people who often make the best fighters in combat.

Recruitment Standards

The American Army in peacetime was never known for its competitive (with civilian jobs) wages. This changed only with the reintroduction of the all-volunteer military in the early 1970s. After World Wars I and II, the armed forces had to take whoever was willing to settle for minimal wages, poor food, and often marginal quarters. Many World War II vets vividly remember the often Neanderthal prewar NCOs they encountered early in their service. They were loyal and well-meaning soldiers, but often less capable and with less education than the flood of draftees they had to train in 1941 and 1942. These NCOs had enlisted in the 1920s, when the economy was booming and the Army had to take whomever they could get. Better NCOs would have produced better-trained soldiers faster in those early days of World War II. Poorly trained soldiers die faster in combat.

Training

This is costly. There's a lot of wear and tear on the equipment, and it's more expensive to supply the troops in the field, since to get the most out of the training, you should shoot off some high-priced ammunition. Traditionally, American peacetime officers did their training on the cheap, because the money simply wasn't there. So a lot of the prewar training consisted of marching around the parade ground and spending a lot of time trying to keep ancient equipment serviceable. The troops feel the effects of this only when they enter combat and discover they don't have a clue about how to survive.

Equipment Procurement

Just paying the troops is expensive, even if the wages are meager. After World Wars I and II it was felt that the troops could get by for many years with equipment left over from the previous conflict. This saved a lot of money, since developing and purchasing new equipment could be put off for a long time. It also ensures, however, that you will enter the first battle of the next war with obsolete and barely functioning weapons and equipment.

Maintenance

This is also expensive, but you can skip a lot of maintenance if you don't use your weapons and equipment. Modern military equipment is built to operate under severe conditions and take a lot of punishment, but as a trade-off, this gear goes through spare parts a lot faster than nonmilitary equipment. These spares are expensive, and it takes a lot of manpower to inspect and adjust military equipment that has been used. Simply not using the equipment much is yet another way to cope with shrinking military budgets.

Doctrine

Given the unreal attitudes outlined above, it should come as no surprise that these post–World War armies were unable to come up with effective tactics and procedures for fighting the next war. Experimenting and developing doctrine and tactics on the battlefield is costly—especially in lives of soldiers. The disasters for U.S. forces at Kasserine Pass (North Africa) in late 1942 and early 1943 and at defensive positions along the main highway between Suwon and Osan in Korea in 1950 are tragic examples of U.S. military unpreparedness to fight its first battles. A look at both of these debacles is very instructive.

THE ROAD TO KASSERINE PASS AND TASK FORCE SMITH

From the end of World War I in 1918, the military had been left to rapidly deteriorate because it was generally believed that war would not come to America anytime soon. Only after Germany had seized most of Europe was major funding authorized for the military. The Army then received more than $8 billion, which was more than it had received for the entire previous twenty years. It was felt that the money would make up for the time required to prepare the troops for a new and more complex form of warfare. This is yet another bad American habit (in war and peace): Throw enough money at the problem and it will be solved.

From 1918 to 1939, technology had increased the speed and tempo of combat and expanded the battlefield over the horizon and into the air to an extent never before thought possible. On December 7, 1941, the Japanese attacked Hawaii and the Philippines. These onslaughts caught the United States unprepared and American casualties were high. In early December 1941, the United States had only forty-five modern fighter planes ready to fly on the Pacific coast. Because of lack of supporting units, plus shortages of ammunition and equipment, only one division-size unit was sent to the far Pacific before April 1942. This lack of combat-ready troops resulted in the collapse of outnumbered U.S. defenders on the Pacific islands of Wake and Guam. Finally, on April 9, 1942, isolated and unreinforced U.S. forces surrendered in the Philippines.

The situation was not much better in the Atlantic. Because of Allied shortage of escort vessels, German U-boats succeeded in critically reducing shipments of Allied supplies and troops. America had only twenty surface vessels and approximately one hundred aircraft in late 1941 to protect the North Atlantic coastal area. It took a year of strenuous effort to clear the sea-lanes sufficiently to allow for the November 1942 Anglo-American invasion of North Africa (Operation Torch).

By February 1943, American and French forces had advanced into the Eastern Dorsal mountain range in Tunisia. In what is known as the battle of Kasserine Pass, German and Italian forces surprised and defeated larger American and French forces and drove them back fifty miles across the Sbeitla plain. The U.S. 1st Armored Division took most of the punishment. The Americans lost more than six thousand men while the Germans lost only about one thousand.

What exactly happened at Kasserine Pass? The American forces were just not ready to meet the highly trained and well-equipped German forces. The U.S. 1st Armored Division was spread out in uncoordinated detachments. The U.S. commander did not take advantage of terrain; the enemy did. Poor training of officers and troops was much in evidence. Many of the American officers were overly cautious, operating at a tempo that was more appropriate to operations in World War I. The Germans knew what they were doing; the Americans did not. The attack advanced straight through U.S. units, while Nazi bombers and fighters supported the attack. U.S. air and ground units were not able to coordinate their operations; the Germans were. Thus for over a week (February 14–22, 1943), American troops, no matter how hard some of them fought, were constantly outmaneuvered and defeated by their opponents.

The unprepared U.S. 1st Armored Division was not exceptional among American units in 1942. When World War II began in 1939, not a single U.S. division was ready for combat. Training programs were hurried because of the lack of time. Many of the regular NCOs and officers who were expected to train the new recruits were instead taken away to help form still more new units. A division might spend over a year in training but never really get anywhere because of the lack of experienced leaders. These units finally got their training on the battlefield, where "pass/fail" was replaced with "survive/die." The lack of modern weapons was also critical. The Americans' Stuart light tanks and their 37mm guns were no match for the German Mark VI Tiger tanks armed with the 88mm gun. Germany had modernized its forces before and during the war; America had not. American forces were underequipped and underarmed and could not counter the superior combat power of the German forces.

Battlefield leadership, which takes the longest time to develop, was also critically lacking at Kasserine Pass. The German forces in Tunisia were under the command of Field Marshal Erwin Rommel. Here was a soldier who had spent several decades studying war and had been commanding armored troops since 1940. He had thus developed the mental agility and aggressiveness to cope with the fast pace and spacious battlefield of modern warfare. Rommel's superior operational and tactical techniques for maneuver warfare gave him the freedom of action that overwhelmed Major General Lloyd R. Fredendall (the American II Corps commander). General Fredendall, like many U.S. commanders, was an excellent peacetime general, but did not understand the changes in warfare created by airplanes and motor vehicles. Fortunately for America, the overall strategic and logistical situation was much worse for the Germans and the Italians. The enemy had to get its supplies across the Mediterranean from Italy, and the Allies now controlled those waters most of the time. Few supplies or reinforcements were getting across.

Time and again, the Germans achieved battlefield victories, but they could not transform them into strategic victories. America and Britain were able to put much larger forces into North Africa and prevent the Axis from doing the same. Thus the Allied battlefield defeats, which always involved some Axis casualties, were gradually grinding the German and Italian forces down to nothing. America had the long-range strategic edge, but this was small comfort to those American troops so often defeated by better-trained, -equipped, and -led German troops. The American forces recovered from these early battles and learned quickly, and increasingly, large quantities of adequate (and at times even superior) weapons and equipment were in their hands. But it was a bloody way to learn. The battlefield is a costly place to grope around trying to find out how to fight effectively.

The cost in blood of unpreparedness that these early battles taught was soon forgotten after World War II. Americans took comfort in the fact that their losses (292,000 dead) in World War II were much fewer than any of their enemies' (2.9 million for Germany and 1.5 million for Japan). What was forgotten was the larger number of U.S. troops killed compared to German losses in similar situations. The ratio was over two to one early in the war, and never reached parity. It wasn't until the 1970s that U.S. officers noted that one could be more efficient on the battlefield and save American lives. But after 1945, the United States returned to the concept that security was maintained by mobilizing a civilian Army in the event of a war, not trying to prevent war by maintaining an adequate and ready force. The Army went from eight million men and eighty-nine divisions in 1945 to a million in 1946 (many awaiting discharge) and about half a million men and ten divisions in 1950. But it was not the smaller size of the Army that was the major problem. The historical unpreparedness of American forces was again caused by the lack of money for training and for modernization of equipment. The advent of the atomic bomb created the doctrine that the Army was no longer needed except for guard duty.

The secretary of defense at the time, Louis A. Johnson, was emphasizing that national security could be maintained primarily with strategic bombing. President Truman, also reflecting the current thinking, used a remainder concept to balance the budget. That is, he subtracted all other federal expenditures before recommending his military program to Congress. With this type of situation, the military itself became introspective, and military doctrine and vision looked backward to World War II rather than forward. There was little attempt to keep pace with the new battlefield realities. (For example, the 1949 Field Service Regulations, the basic doctrine for the

Army, did not even address tactics for an atomic battlefield.) This was a typically American approach to the rapid demobilization that has followed each major war. While it is true that other nations have gone through a period of intense experimentation and reform after a major war and demobilization, this was usually the result of that nation's being defeated. Germany after World War I is an excellent example. But victorious generals, stuck with a lot of the last war's leftover weapons and a much smaller budget, tend to make the best of the situation. American military and political leaders were betting the lives of their troops that the next war would be like the last one.

The American military leadership had short memories. What happened in the first weeks of the Korean War was a repeat of the first major American ground battles of World War II in North Africa during November 1942. The battle of Kasserine Pass was restaged in South Korea in the summer of 1950, less than eight years after "Bloody Kasserine."

The battle known as Task Force Smith was the first engagement fought by U.S. forces in the Korean War. In this case the opponents were North Koreans. Again, the U.S. troops did very poorly. Both Kasserine Pass and that first Korean battle epitomized the historical unpreparedness of U.S. military forces and the high cost in American lives. The American problems in both these battles ran the full gamut: training, equipment, planning, leadership, logistics, organization, doctrine, cooperation between branches, and so on. Underlying all this was also the preconceived idea that one Yankee could whip any ten foreigners.

The chain of events that led up to the Task Force Smith incident is worth recounting in some detail. It is similar to many situations we face in the 1990s. It's happened before, it could happen again.

When North Korea attacked South Korea on June 25, 1950, the U.S. Far East Command consisted of four understrength, underequipped, and undertrained divisions on occupation duty in Japan. Except for an advisory group, all U.S. forces had been withdrawn from Korea in 1949. The North Koreans attacked with approximately 90,000 men and 150 tanks.

The historical pattern of Kasserine Pass repeated itself. General MacArthur, the U.S. Far East commander, on June 30, 1950, ordered the Japan-based 24th Infantry Division to move to South Korea and engage the invading North Koreans. Using transport aircraft, he sent a task force (Task Force Smith, or TF Smith) from the division to be the delaying force. The task force was under the command of Lieutenant Colonel Charles B. Smith.

TF Smith landed in Korea on July 1 and 2, 1950. Like most "task forces," this one consisted of a mixture of different types of troops: approximately two understrength infantry companies supported by a battery of artillery. The task force's weapons would prove completely ineffective against the North Korean tanks. Most American task forces in World War II had some tanks, but these could not be flown to Korea. Early in the morning of July 5, 1950, TF Smith arrived at its defensive positions, and joined some South Korean troops who were already manning them. At around 8:00 A.M., TF Smith was attacked by an advancing North Korean column of tanks and infantry. The North Koreans were a Russian-trained army that, contrary to preconceived notions held by most contemporary American military experts, was well trained with solid doctrine and tactics and was well equipped. TF Smith was facing an overwhelming opposing force, and it didn't discover this until the fighting started.

The small U.S. unit was not holding a very wide front. The North Koreans quickly swarmed around, and through, the U.S. troops. TF Smith's equipment was substandard and its level of training low. The ability of the troops to meet the rigors of combat was woefully inadequate. Any help from the Air Force was precluded by poor weather conditions. In addition, American and Australian fighter aircraft had mistakenly attacked the American troops on July 3. Because of this friendly-fire incident, as well as poor communications, lack of practice, and the confused situation in the forward area, a restriction on forward air support was put into effect. After about six hours of fighting and sustaining heavy casualties, American forces were forced to withdraw, leaving their dead and wounded behind. The South Korean troops had also fled. TF Smith suffered 212 men killed, wounded, or missing. The North Koreans lost only about 42 dead and 85 wounded. The other 24th Division units, which were also understrength and underequipped and undertrained, soon arrived in Korea to be thrown into the battle, but they also suffered the same pattern of defeat as TF Smith. The lesson of unpreparedness was learned again in blood.

HOW TO WIN THE FIRST BATTLES, AND LOSE THEM LATER

What was so unique about the military operations in the 1980s (Libya, 1986; Grenada, 1983; Panama, 1989) and Desert Shield/Storm (Persian Gulf,

1991), as opposed to the military's previous practices, was that the lessons of the past were not forgotten. In describing how the military prepared for its vital role in ending the Cold War, freeing Panama, and reversing Iraqi aggression, General Gordon R. Sullivan, Chief of Staff of the U.S. Army, provided a summary of the preconditions for winning on the battlefield. "These accomplishments were not achieved by accident. They are the product of twenty years of dedication, planning, training, and just plain hard work. The warfighting edge of our military is the result of quality people, trained to razor sharpness, outfitted with modern equipment, led by tough competent leaders, structured into an effective mix of forces, and employed according to up-to-date doctrine."

While the U.S. armed forces of the 1990s have achieved an unprecedented state of peacetime capability, there is still the Victory Disease to worry about. While defeat spurs reform, victory stifles it or, worse yet, causes counterproductive changes. Vietnam was the only war America ever thought of as a defeat. The result was unprecedented reform. Ironically, the Desert One debacle (the failed Tehran rescue attempt in 1980), while it put many soldiers into a deep funk, also gave the reformers one more boost. There was no place to go but up after Desert One.

Reviewing the events of Desert One provides insights into many of the problems the reformers were trying to overcome. On November 4, 1979, Iranian radicals invaded the U.S. Embassy in Tehran, Iran, and once inside, seized the Americans as hostages. After months of planning, on the evening of April 24, 1980, eight U.S. helicopters took off from the aircraft carrier *Nimitz* in the Indian Ocean with the mission to fly to Tehran and rescue the U.S. hostages. Success of the mission depended to a great extent on maintaining secrecy to ensure that the ground rescue forces would have the element of surprise when they entered the U.S. Embassy. The rescue plan required the helicopters to fly at night at low altitudes and travel nearly six hundred nautical miles to a designated refueling site in the desert where they would link up with C-130 refueling aircraft and with the ground rescue forces that were carried in by other C-130 aircraft. The refueling site had been designated Desert One. On the way to Desert One, one of the helicopters had a mechanical problem and the crew had to land and abandon the helicopter. Also during the flight to the refueling site, the other seven helicopters flew into a dust cloud and one of the helicopters had to abort the mission and return to the carrier because of navigational problems. The dust cloud also slowed down the remaining six helicopters, causing them to arrive between fifty minutes and eighty-five minutes later than planned. This was a serious problem because of the limited time to fly at night and the need for secrecy. After landing, it was determined that a third helicopter was no longer usable because of a failure in its hydraulic system.

Now the rescue team did not have the required six helicopters that had been determined were essential for a successful mission. To make matters worse, when the rescue team arrived at Desert One, they encountered Iranian civilians traveling on a road next to the landing site. Most of the Iranians were taken prisoner, but at least one of them escaped. During the refueling phase, while one of the helicopters was being repositioned, it collided with one of the refueling C-130s. Both aircraft went up in flames, exploding the on-board ammunition. Eight crew members died and five others were injured. Shrapnel from the explosion of the aircraft and ammunition struck a number of the helicopters, making at least one of them nonflyable. With time and fuel running out for the C-130s, the rescue mission was canceled and the helicopter crews were loaded on the C-130s and departed the area. Desert One soon became the name that was given to one of the worst failures in the history of the U.S. military and a major embarrassment to the U.S. government. It was especially embarrassing when much smaller countries such as Israel were able to successfully carry out similar rescue efforts.

To the credit of the Joint Chiefs of Staff, they commissioned a Special Operations Review Group in May 1980 to conduct a professional critique of the entire operation. The purpose of the critique was not to present an after-action report or to place blame for the failures; rather it was to recommend reforms to improve the capability of the military to successfully carry out these types of operations in the future. The recommendations from this Review Group were a major force in supporting the military reform movement in the 1980s. The establishment of the U.S. Special Operations Command in 1987 (with the prime purpose of improving irregular warfare for the United States) can be traced directly to the recommendations of the Special Operations Review Group.

The military reforms that demonstrated themselves in Desert Storm had already been under way for several years before Desert One. But the problems in the Iranian desert pointed up that it wasn't enough for the individual services to improve themselves. There also had to be a greater degree of cooperation and coordination among the Army, Navy, and Air Force. Desert One, while a tragedy to the participants, served as a rallying cry for those in uniform who were calling for greater interservice cooperation. These officers got a hearing after Desert One, and in the 1980s they got results.

The Gulf War was a remarkable and striking victory, perhaps the most stunning victory in American military history. Coming on the heels of the Cold War victory, it added to the enormous pressure on the U.S. military to adapt to both the new conditions and its newfound self-confidence. At the same time, without the specter of Vietnam and Desert One hanging over everyone, a certain tension is missing when reform is proposed. This can lead to future first battles that are American defeats. It's happened before and, as we detailed the situation in the previous chapter, it can happen again.

CHAPTER

3

The Army Gets Nuked

In the 1950s, the Army went through a misguided, misfired, and mistaken reorganization. This was the "Pentomic Army," a force organized to fight on a nuclear battlefield, and nowhere else. While this period lasted less than ten years, it prevented the Army from doing any serious reform that would have prepared it for the ordeal in Vietnam that was to follow in the 1960s.

The performance of the American Army in Desert Storm, along with the exemplary teamwork among the services, is all the more remarkable when you remember that the Army was almost reorganized into insignificance during the 1950s. The introduction of the atomic bomb for battlefield use in that decade was, at the time, considered the most revolutionary development in the history of warfare. It turned out to be somewhat less revolutionary than everyone thought at the time. But the enormous destructive power of nuclear weapons and their capability to radically alter the time and space relationships of the battlefield did change the nature and strategy of warfare. For a time it was thought that the offense was now the master over the defense. Who could possibly defend themselves against the massive and overwhelming power of the atomic bomb? Or so the thinking went. With America having a monopoly on the bomb and the Air Force having one on the delivery system, the very need for an Army, except for minor roles, was questioned.

Underlying and fueling this questioning of the need for ground forces was the traditional American dislike of a large standing army and the insidious interservice rivalries. President Truman (1945–1953), like most Americans of his time, was a strong believer in a small standing army while depending on a well-prepared militia to mobilize in case of national emergencies. For most of his adult life, Truman had belonged to or associated with the National Guard, in which he served as an officer during World War I. With this dislike of a large peacetime military, Truman found himself at the end of World War II with armed forces comprising over nine million men and women with eighty-nine combat divisions and thousands of airplanes and ships. Now armed with the A-bomb, Truman set out to reduce the military quickly, but in an orderly manner.

The United States had learned a great deal about demobilization after World War I and had a well-prepared, detailed plan ready to implement once Japan surrendered. However, the pressure to bring the soldiers back into civilian life and return to "normal" was so great that the process went into free-fall and the detailed plan went out the window. The most powerful military in history disintegrated in a few years. During this post–World War II demobilization, the United States sent 75 percent of the troops back to civilian life in under two years (1945–1946, 9 million troops). Defense spending went from $453 billion (in 1990 dollars) in 1945 (38 percent of GNP) to $229 billion in 1946 (down 50 percent) and $59 billion in 1947 (an 84 percent reduction from 1945). Defense spending in 1940 was 1.5 percent of GNP, fairly typical of historical U.S. peacetime spending, but was still 5.6 percent in 1947 after this massive reduction. While the demobilization was vast and fast, the remaining armed forces were still the largest ever maintained by America in peacetime.

As arguments over the need for an Army and the headlong shrinking of the military were taking place, a major debate over the very structure of the armed forces itself was in full force. During World War II President Truman had headed an investigation into efficiency and effectiveness in the conduct of the war and became convinced that the United States needed a unified military command. When Truman attempted to bring the services together on command matters, he was supported by General Marshall and General Eisenhower. Marshall had been the principal military leader during World War II and Eisenhower would eventually become president. But the Navy, and the powerful House and Senate military and appropriations committees, joined forces to oppose the reorganization. The reform was opposed by the Navy and the traditionalists, both of whom wanted to maintain the early nineteenth-century arrangement of two separate Cabinet-level departments: the Navy Department (with a secretary of the navy) and the War (Army) Department (with a secretary of war).

This organization had proved very troublesome during World War II, particularly in the Pacific. The war against Japan had been constantly dogged by disagreements between the Army and Navy concerning how that campaign should be fought. Both services had their partisans, and disputes frequently had to be resolved by the president himself. Neither service was reluctant to go behind the president's back and lobby Congress, which further complicated decision making. President Roosevelt was able to prevent these disputes from becoming disasters, if only because he was seen as a "Navy man" while also having a strong working relationship with General Marshall. But Truman, as vice president, did not look forward to playing mediator between the Army and Navy. Moreover, Truman was seen as an "Army man," because he had served as an artillery officer during World War I.

In 1947, Truman was finally able to push through legislation that at least formed a single Department of Defense under a civilian head. This provided one Cabinet-level official the generals and admirals could harass, leaving the president out of it. In this same legislation, the Army Air Force was taken from the Army and set up as a separate organization (the Air Force). It is ironic that this legislation, intended to move the military toward a more unified organization, established an additional entity that would greatly add to the divisive infighting among the services.

Former secretary of the navy James Forrestal was appointed the first secretary of defense. Many people were convinced that Forrestal's subsequent suicide was caused by the pressures of dealing with the three squabbling services. After Forrestal's death in 1948, the secretary of the army, Louis Johnson, replaced him. There was great suspicion in the Navy over this appointment and these fears would soon prove well founded. Almost immediately after taking office, Johnson canceled the construction of a new Navy supercarrier. These new aircraft carriers were large enough to carry long-range bombers armed with nuclear weapons. The Navy had expected to be a major player in strategic nuclear warfare if it could get these large carriers. The Navy was convinced that cancellation of this carrier was in fact the opening shot in a campaign to shut the sailors out of the nuclear-warfare business and eventually to take the Navy's Air Force away.

A national debate ensued, which eventually turned into the "Revolt of the Admirals." Adding to the debate, and Navy fears, Johnson set forth a new military strategy that relied primarily on long-range land-based aircraft to deliver nuclear bombs. The Air Force responded to the new strategy by changing its aircraft building plans; it canceled outstanding orders for smaller aircraft and ordered seventy-five heavy, long-range B-36 bombers instead. Senior naval officers openly criticized this long-range bomber policy and warned against what they called "a short sighted and inflexible strategy of atomic blitz." The Navy felt that carriers equipped with short- and long-range bombers, as well as conventional and nuclear bombs, were a more prudent approach. The Navy and the Army also criticized the failure of the Air Force to provide both adequate numbers and types of aircraft to carry out its full range of missions. This was also the beginning of the Army's ongoing battle with the Air Force over the provision of aircraft to support ground forces.

This move to cut back on Navy carrier building was met by an anonymous charge that senior Air Force officials were involved in fraud and graft while purchasing the Air Force B-36 bombers. The charges were investigated by the House Armed Services Committee. Although everyone under investigation was cleared, severe political fallout and ill feelings were created when it was discovered that the anonymous charges were in fact made by a Navy civilian employee. Charges and countercharges continued with a number of high-ranking Navy leaders resigning in protest. Thus ended the Revolt of the Admirals. The Navy lost its supercarrier and the Air Force got its B-36s. The Soviet detonation of a nuclear weapon and the loss of China to the communists in 1949 changed the course of the debates, but the scars remained for a long time. In fact, they remain to this day. Ever since, the Air Force has been on bad terms with the Navy, and relations with the Army never improved much either. In the early 1990s, the Air Force again called for the use of long-range (B-2) bombers to replace Navy carriers while also trying to reshape its ground-support mission in ways the Army was not fond of.

As the 1950s approached, the services were all going in different directions. The Army was preoccupied with its paramilitary role as an occupation force while planning to refight World War II should war with the Soviets break out. This was, in fact, all the Army could do, as its budget allowed for little research and development on new weapons. In fact, the Army was having a hard time exploiting all the weapons technology (missiles, tanks, small arms, etc.) it had captured from the Germans at the end of the war. Much of this state-of-the-art German technology didn't show up in Army weapons until the 1960s. The Russians, with larger R&D budgets, were able to do it a decade earlier.

The Air Force was on a completely different course. The Air Force was big on strategic bombing. This was what the Army Air Force did a lot of during World War II, building 50,000 long-range bombers and sending them over a thousand miles into enemy territory to hit factories, ports, cities, and military bases. Even though the World War II U.S. Strategic Bombing Survey (USSBS) had concluded that the bombing could not have unilaterally won World War II, the Air Force was devoting most of its funds to building its bomber capability. The Air Force saw nuclear weapons as something that would make strategic bombing work. Many Air Force officers were only too aware of the USSBS findings. But they blamed the poor performance of World War II bombing on inaccuracy and small bombloads. Nuclear weapons were so powerful that even a near-miss still obliterated the target. However, the Air Force (and many civilian experts) took several decades to realize that nuclear weapons were too destructive for anyone to dare use, particularly since the Soviets now had them. Meanwhile, the more mundane tasks of supporting the Army ground forces had to be grudgingly relearned. And in the aftermath of the Air Force's triumph during the 1991 Gulf War, it was clear that the Air Force and the Army were still in the battle over who controls whom and who sets priorities and who supports whom.

The Navy was fixated almost completely on the carrier task force and control of the sea. World War II had demonstrated the superiority of the aircraft carrier, and the Navy had built itself up during the war to be the premier carrier force on the planet. The carrier task force consisted of one or two carriers (each with seventy to one hundred aircraft) and half a dozen or more escort ships. After World War II, the American fleet had more carriers than the rest of the world's navies combined. Thus the sailors found themselves in a stronger position than the Army or Air Force at the end of World War II, because most of the ships (and their crews) the Navy disposed of immediately after the war were things they didn't need, or want, anyway. These items included hundreds of convoy escorts and many amphibious and transport ships, as well as obsolete battleships that were useful only to fight the now-defeated German submarines or Japanese fleet. The most modern ships, and sufficient crews to keep everything functional, were retained. With no other major navy as a threat, the Navy could easily control the world's oceans. The Marine Corps (which was part of the Navy) was left with enough strength to make it a credible force in its traditional role of backing up the fleet, and the State Department, overseas. Carrier aviation gave the USN one of the world's largest, and most mobile, air forces.

The Korean War (1950–1953) would soon bring the services together, which is what wars tend to do, and the need for closely coordinated combat operations would be relearned once more. However, just as after every previous war, this costly education was soon forgotten. These were the same forces that had pulled the services apart after World War II.

- Fighting over a much-reduced defense budget.
- Traditional civilian suspicion of large standing armed forces.
- Belief in the virtues of relying on a civilian militia and mobilization.
- An organizational structure that fostered conflict, namely the traditional separate bureaucracies for the Army, Navy, and now Air Force. In the early 1950s Congress effectively made the Marines a "fourth service" by passing a law stipulating a minimum size for the Marine Corps. Thus, where there had been only two services (Army and Navy) in 1947, less than ten years later there were four. No nation has ever been able to avoid having separate organizations for the different services, since each has a very different job. There has been some progress elsewhere in getting the services to cooperate more effectively, but this cooperation is seen as something of an unnatural act. Progress will not come easily.

All these long-term problems were again driving wedges between the services.

By 1952 the American people were tired of the Korean War and its drain on their pocketbooks. The war had been a long and frustrating struggle with no clear end in sight. The military budget had grown to 70 percent of the total federal budget and was beginning to affect the very economic health of the nation. One of the major criticisms of the war was that America had failed to capitalize on its superior technological advantages over the North Koreans and Chinese. But the technology frequently mentioned was nuclear weapons, or long-range bombing into China. Both of these were political dynamite and no politician wanted any part of them. But this was technology that had cost the taxpayers dearly and the taxpayers were looking for some results.

The 1952 presidential race saw a World War II military hero, General Dwight Eisenhower, campaigning on a platform of ending the war in Korea and reviving the economy at home. Eisenhower was elected and delivered on his promises. Like Truman, Eisenhower was also a strong believer in a small standing military with reliance on the civilian militia that could quickly be mobilized in times of emergency, and he was even more adamant concerning a balanced budget. He believed that the economic threat to the American way of life was as important as the military threat. One of his first acts as president was to persuade the Chinese to sign an armistice. What finally persuaded the Chinese to settle the Korean War is still in question, but it was probably indications from Eisenhower that he was ready to use the "big bang" (nukes) to bring the war to an end.

Eisenhower also called for a New Look at defense policy. Springing from the apparent success of threatening the North Koreans and Chinese with the atomic bomb, this new doctrine was based on the threat of using nuclear weapons and little else. The United States still had a near monopoly on nuclear weapons. Although the Russians had detonated their first nuclear bomb in 1949, the United States had the edge in bombers that could deliver the weapons from bases close to the Soviet Union. The U.S. threat to use nuclear weapons in Korea was seen to have cowed the Russians also. It was no secret that the Russians were backing the Chinese intervention in Korea, and when the Chinese backed down, so the thinking went, the Russians also backed off. So all America needed was nuclear weapons. Everything else was, essentially, superfluous. All of this was taken quite seriously at the time.

This new policy of using nuclear weapons as a substitute for conventional forces resulted in the reduction of the defense budgets by approximately 25 percent in fiscal years 1954 and 1955. This was the flip side of the nuclear coin. While nuclear weapons were beginning to frighten a lot more people, especially now that the Russians had them, the concept that nukes would cut defense spending had obvious political appeal. An economic retrenchment in defense was initiated with major reductions in all aspects of the military. This led to a reduction in force, the military term for layoffs. The biggest loss with the RIF was the many warrior officers who had received battlefield promotions during World War II and Korea. While many of these officers were allowed to stay in the service as NCOs, the Army lost a lot of its battlefield leadership capability with the RIF. The military was using formal education, not battlefield performance, to set standards for officers. A college degree was seen as more valuable than combat experience. This is a concept that tends to wax in peacetime and wane in wartime.

While the post–Korean War defense-budget cutbacks hit the Army the hardest, the Air Force actually benefited (they had the nukes) and the Navy was hardly hurt at all (they also had long-range nukes). Moreover, the rules of the game (known as "military doctrine") changed almost overnight. This

New Look doctrine would be defined in a new defense strategy that would rely primarily on nuclear weapons and the Air Force. John Foster Dulles, in a January 12, 1954, speech to the Council on Foreign Relations in New York City outlined the new strategy, and called it "massive retaliation." Anyone who threatened the United States would have to face the prospect of massive nuclear bombardment. It seemed like a good idea at the time.

The Army was now faced not only with major reductions in its forces but with a debate over its very existence. What was the mission of an Army in a massive-retaliation strategy? Anti-Army partisans were calling for the reduction of the regular forces to a few divisions while the National Guard and reserves were expanded (an idea that has resurfaced in the early 1990s). This had great appeal to the states, since this meant more money for the National Guard forces which, in peacetime, were controlled by the state governors and other local politicians. This plan was not passed, but it came close enough to scare the regular Army into accepting a lot of silly new programs and doctrinal and organizational changes that were not in accord with available technology. The result was the "Pentomic Army."

THE PENTOMIC ATOMIC ARMY

The regular Army and its partisans rallied their political allies and fought back against drastic cuts in regular forces. The regulars avoided being cut back to practically nothing, but this was done only by jumping on the nuclear bandwagon. The ground forces took three steps that they felt would show them as very capable "nuclear warriors." Out of this came the Pentomic ("pent" for five, the new number of subdivisions of units, in contrast to the traditional three, and "omic" for the atomic connection) Army.

First, concerned that it would have no role on the battlefield with all this talk of massive retaliation, the Army rushed to develop a family of tactical nuclear weapons. Among these were nuclear shells for the heavy artillery, nuclear warheads for the Army's short-range rockets, and even nuclear mines. But at times this rush to develop battlefield nuclear weapons reached absurd proportions. The Army actually developed a nuclear warhead for the infantry in the form of a special recoilless rifle (the "Davy Crockett" system). It is a little difficult now visualizing a soldier running around the battlefield firing nuclear projectiles from this weapon, but that was the Department of Defense mentality in the 1950s. Fortunately, someone did his math, before too many Davy Crockett systems were handed over to the troops, and discovered that the range of this weapon was so short that the troops firing it were likely to be killed or injured by the nuclear weapon they were dropping on the nearby enemy. But the nuclear shells and rocket warheads survived until they were withdrawn in the early 1990s, another victim of the demise of the Cold War.

Second, in the name of restructuring for the nuclear battlefield, the Army made the most radical reorganization change in its history with the creation of the pentomic division. Instead of the traditional three regiments, the new division consisted of five battle groups (actually small regiments, or large battalions, take your pick). Each battle group was relatively self-contained and could operate independently; it was composed of five rifle companies, a combat support company, and a headquarters company. The division also had a tank battalion with five companies. This reorganization was much more than a structural change. It impacted on every part of the Army and throughout the military-school system that trained officers and troops. But the whole pentomic program fell apart when President Eisenhower further drastically cut the Army budget. The pentomic organization was used from 1958 until 1962, and was generally regarded as a bad joke by most of the troops in the pentomic units. The new organization was intended for a nuclear battlefield that was unlikely to occur, and was inefficient for conventional combat. In many respects, it was just too far ahead of its time. The technology was just not mature enough, there was not enough money to train intensively with the new organization, and the needed shift in thinking did not have sufficient time to take place.

The third step was leadership by management. The Air Force had achieved great press by getting in bed with the newly created "think tanks." The RAND corporation is the most well known of these and was, in fact, an Air Force creation. This was seen by the public and the politicians as a very progressive way to deal with military affairs. Not to be left behind in the public's eye, the Army began to tout their officers as "managers" rather than mere combat leaders. American industrial management techniques were then the envy of the world and the worship of these methods became a millstone around the Army's neck for several decades.

Many of the future problems of the Army would be rooted in this misdirected effort to search for a mission that would meet the national strategy. There were never a lot of uniformed managers developed, and in the process the ground forces lost a lot of needed combat leaders by having capable warriors pushed aside in favor of officers with executive potential. The legacies of massive retaliation would haunt the Army for decades, particularly because of the effort spent on nuclear research rather than conventional warfare. One of the more bizarre consequences was over a decade of nuclear warheads on Army antiaircraft missiles. These warheads were to be detonated over the cities they were defending. While this would have been painful for the approaching Soviet bombers, it would have been nearly as destructive to the citizens below. Yes, it was a dumb idea, but interservice rivalry dictated that the Army "do something" about the Soviet bomber threat. The only alternative was to cede the mission to Air Force interceptors. Later Army leaders shed a little cold sweat when they remembered these days of the Pentomic Army.

FLEXIBLE RESPONSE

On October 4, 1957, the Soviets launched their first sputnik satellite. This was perceived by many in the world as showing that the Soviets had emerged as a nuclear power with the potential of matching the United States. The thinking went that if the Soviets could put satellites into orbit, they could do the same with nuclear warheads. The rocket that delivered sputnik to orbit, so went the conventional wisdom, could also carry an atomic warhead to distant American cities. It also implied that the Soviets in the future could possibly even surpass the United States in technologically advanced weapons systems, particularly in the field of long-range missiles. One of the effects of this accomplishment by the Soviets was the initiation of a debate regarding the adequacy of the U.S. strategic concepts. All of a sudden many key people in Congress and the Defense Department realized that, while America could threaten the Soviets with its nuclear armed bombers, the Soviets could now shoot back with their own rockets. Senior government civilian and military leaders began to look for less potentially catastrophic strategies.

A solution to the American crisis over the nuclear standoff soon appeared but was not given much attention at the time. This was Army General Maxwell D. Taylor's book, *The Uncertain Trumpet*. Published in 1959, Taylor's book was critical of both massive-retaliation strategy and the way force levels were developed. He suggested that a concept of Flexible Response be adopted. This concept was based on the capability to react across the entire spectrum of possible threats—that is, to be able to respond any-where, anytime, with weapons and forces appropriate to the situation. This was a sharp break with the then current reliance on massive retaliation. Taylor pointed out that not all situations were solvable by a hail of nuclear warheads. One also needed conventional forces, particularly ground forces, to address many potential threats. John Kennedy (and many of his Harvard "best and brightest" cronies) read Taylor's book and liked it, and when he became president he adopted Flexible Response as a national military strat-egy. As a result, ever since the early 1960s, the national strategy was based on three basic concepts:

1. Deterrence. Persuading enemies by diplomatic and military means to refrain from starting anything damaging to American interests. The threat of nuclear retaliation was still there, but conventional military forces and economic pressure could also be put on the table during discussions with American adversaries.
2. Collective security. Getting all our allies to participate in the deter-rence. It was in this effort that America established its current status as "world leader." This was made easier by the establishment of organi-zations like NATO.
3. Flexibility of action. This was Taylor's Flexible Response. In other words, being ready for anything, from rescuing American citizens in danger overseas (usually with Marines), through small or large wars, and all the way to nuclear war.

The end of the Army's "atomic age" saw reorganization along more traditional lines—in effect, abandoning the Pentomic concepts and going back to a World War II style of warfare. There was now greater emphasis on "unconventional (guerrilla) warfare" and, as a consequence, increasing involvement in Vietnam. The communists had been supporting guerrilla movements since the 1930s, and the West was now catching on. Moreover, during the late 1950s and early 1960s the Soviets were also demobilizing a large chunk of their armed forces; thus the conventional-warfare threat in Europe was seen to be receding. All those new guerrilla wars were now viewed as the main threat to world peace.

But change was coming, change that the Army neither anticipated nor dealt with very well.

CHAPTER

4

The Central Front Fixation

From the end of World War II until 1990, the Army concentrated most of its thinking and resources on a possible war with communist forces in Central Europe. This was a war that was never fought, but it was the primary operation the Army was ready for all those years. No matter what else the Army was asked to do during this time, it was looked at from the perspective of the predicted Central Front battle.

Even before World War II ended, many senior U.S. military leaders saw the Soviet Union as the real enemy. Indeed, before the Nazis came along in the 1930s, the Soviets (the "Reds") were seen as the major threat. The communists were, from 1917 on, preaching (and often practicing) worldwide revolution and the destruction of the Western democracies. These threats did not go unnoticed. The Nazis turned Germany into a larger and more immediate threat during the 1930s. But by 1945 the Nazis were gone and the Reds were still there. As a result, General George Patton, one of the U.S. Army's greatest field commanders, suggested that the Allies plunge into Russia while Berlin was still smoldering. Patton was the most successful American general; even the Germans feared and respected him. Patton was your typical "warrior" general, and he saw military solutions where others preferred diplomacy. Correct in his appraisal of Soviet attitudes toward the West, he underestimated everyone's war weariness. To most Americans, the Soviets were still our Allies and few wanted to continue World War II by invading Russia. Everyone, including the Soviets, wanted peace in the spring of 1945.

The Soviets were not politically weary. While millions of their soldiers were sent home, the political police and paramilitary units continued their conquest of Eastern Europe. By agreement during the war, this region was considered a Soviet bailiwick and the communists made the most of it. By 1948, all the nations of Eastern Europe were political and military satellites of the Soviet Union. In 1947, Winston Churchill declared that an Iron Curtain had been erected between Eastern and Western Europe. The Cold War had begun.

The Cold War was a very strange conflict. Massive armies were soon concentrated in Central Europe, but all the fighting took place elsewhere (Korea, Vietnam, Africa, etc.) and rarely involved Soviet troops. By 1948 the Chinese civil war had concluded with a communist victory. Communist rebels were fighting the French in Vietnam. The "temporary" Soviet occupation zone in northern Korea became a communist "People's Republic." Communist-led or -inspired partisans fought in many other areas, but the closest any got to Europe was in Greece. While the situation in Europe was relatively quiet and nonviolent, it did manage to garner the bulk of the troops, money, and thinking that went into the Cold War. Thus, for the next forty years, most of the Army "thinkers" concentrated on the potential war with the Soviet Union in Europe, to the exclusion of anything else.

Immediately after World War II ended, the United States demobilized most of its armed forces. This was normal, but in a break with past tradition, substantial forces remained in being (over a million troops). Most of these troops were retained to occupy defeated Japan and Germany. This was another unique event in American history. The end of World War I saw some U.S. troops stationed overseas, but nothing like the post–World War II situation. For the first time in American history, there was a large, combat-ready (in theory) Army stationed overseas. The forces in Japan were actually larger than those in Europe for several years as a result of the North Korean invasion of South Korea and the subsequent Korean War (1950–1953). But the emphasis was always on the Central Front.

The U.S. Army became fixated on the Central Front because this was where America's most powerful allies were. France, Britain, and several other European nations were America's major trading partners going into the 1950s. These nations were also the most vulnerable to a Soviet ground offensive. While the Soviets had built their post–World War II empire without military action, it was always the threat of the Red Army marching west that was at the center of East–West relations throughout the Cold War. It became an article of faith in the U.S. Army that the Soviets were always striving to establish a large enough military superiority in Central Europe to enable them to make an overwhelming surprise attack on NATO.

THE CENTRAL FRONT FIXATION

It is paradoxical that America's most stunning military victory should occur in the desert of Southwest Asia and not in the forests of the Fulda Gap in Germany. Ever since America moved away from its traditional isolationist mentality after World War II, the energy, study, and orientation of the American military has been fixated on Europe. It is understandable why this focus was on Europe, for its most demanding mission has been the defense of Central Europe against the mass of Warsaw Pact forces facing NATO. After NATO was created in 1949, the U.S. military kept about a third of its active forces in Europe (including their families). In addition, most of the forces stationed in the United States were trained to rapidly move to Europe if needed. Greatly outnumbered, American forces in Europe had to face, for most of the period after World War II, more than fifty Warsaw Pact divisions ready for attack. In plain English, this meant that over half a million communist troops, equipped with over twenty thousand tanks and similar numbers of artillery and other weapons, were pointed at Western Europe. The American military structure, equipment, school systems, and doctrine have been focused to meet this challenge.

Another reason for this focus was that the American military tradition was inherited from Europe. Most of the key reformers throughout the history of the American military had obtained most of their ideas by visiting and studying the military systems of Europe. Therefore, a European orientation is embedded in the very heart of U.S. military thinking. For all these reasons, the defense of Europe became the central role of the American military from 1945 to 1991.

During the post–World War II period, most professional soldiers served at least one tour (three years) in Europe. These Cold Warriors had to face the thought of being the trip wire for World War III and most likely that war's first victims. Most line officers in the Army studied the Fulda Gap (a key pass on the East German border), the likely site of the first battle, in detail. This was done in field exercises, classroom lectures, terrain walks, and wargames. Many troops also learned how to speak German, as the West

Germans would be our primary allies in such a campaign and effective liaison with the many West German army units could be a matter of life or death.

After World War II, future fighting was visualized as a replay of that war with the basic model being the march of U.S. forces across Europe in a solid line supported by massive air and artillery support. Korea and Vietnam, as "limited wars," were seen by many in the military and civilian leadership as merely diversionary efforts by the Soviets to set up the United States for the main attack in Europe. The only variance from this was the Pentomic Army experiment in the late 1950s (which didn't last long).

The military professionals in the U.S. Army were always very much oriented to Europe. Although it had to be hidden during both World Wars, the statue of eighteenth-century Frederick the Great overlooks the parade field at the Army War College and it is the nineteenth-century German general and philosopher Carl von Clausewitz whose theories permeate most U.S. doctrine. But this is not new. Baron Frederick Wilhelm von Steuben, starting at Valley Forge in 1778, helped teach an understanding of war to the first U.S. soldiers. The American military looks at foreign nations for its land combat doctrine, never having experienced enough to develop its own. The influence of the European orientation can easily be seen in the U.S. Army basic manuals on doctrine which have used battles fought in Europe as the primary historical examples to illustrate combat techniques. All of these factors, most of them unknown to civilians, have contributed greatly to the U.S. military's fixation on Central Europe.

With such a major emphasis on Europe, it was a surprise to many that U.S. troops were able to perform in the alien environment of the desert with such effectiveness. However, one of the key reasons that U.S. forces were able to overcome their orientation to Europe, and adjust so well to desert warfare, was their return to the fundamentals of warfare during the 1980s. These are the ancient and reliable basics, things like hard training and careful planning. Moreover, in the last twenty years, American military professionals adopted realistic planning goals and established training centers and leadership development programs that fostered flexibility and agility. The most telling indication that the shift away from Europe has finally been made can be seen in the Army training manuals of the early 1990s. Currently, these same manuals are utilizing Just Cause in Panama and Desert Shield for examples. The early 1990s edition of FM 100-5 (the Army's "how to fight" manual) will also prominently feature examples from Just Cause and Desert Shield/Storm.

The evolution of doctrine and developments in training and planning techniques will be discussed in detail in later chapters.

THE BIG CHANGE

The shock of the oil-price increases following the 1973 Arab-Israeli War, and that war itself, caused the U.S. military leadership to begin rethinking its outlook on where it would fight and whom it would be fighting. The intensity of the fighting in the 1973 war exceeded the current estimates and it was generally agreed that American forces would have to change and adapt to these new realities. But it was the aftermath of the fall of the Shah of Iran in 1979, the taking of U.S. hostages in Iran, and the Soviet invasion of Afghanistan in December 1979 that really shocked the system into decisive change. These events forced the military to examine in detail Southwest Asia and the now more likely prospects that U.S. forces would be involved there in the future. The threat of a Soviet invasion into Iran became a major concern. The Soviet move into Afghanistan was physical proof that the Soviets were ready and able to move into neighboring areas. President Carter set forth the Carter Doctrine, which called for protecting free access to oil in the Persian Gulf. As part of this process, Carter authorized the creation of a new military organization, the Rapid Deployment Force (RDF), whose primary focus was this critical region of the world. As a result of Afghanistan, Carter now had no illusions about the imperialistic attitudes of the Soviets.

The failure of the Tehran rescue operation (Desert One) in April 1980 also pointed up the lack of options that the services, especially the Army, could provide the president for coping with crises in this area of the world. That abortive rescue mission was about all the Army could do on short notice. At the time, it was not possible to move large combat units into the area as was done in 1990. The Army didn't have the ships, aircraft, or plans for such an operation in 1980. What the Army did have was aimed at reinforcing units in Europe. As a result, General Meyer (the Chief of Staff of the Army) pushed a series of major reforms in planning, training, doctrine, etc. The purpose was to improve the readiness of U.S. Army forces to meet their global responsibilities not only in Europe but throughout the world, and especially in the Persian Gulf area. By late 1980, four Airborne Warning and Control Systems (AWACS) aircraft were operating in the Persian Gulf, providing surveillance and intelligence. The Reagan administration would expand on the Carter initiatives and make the RDF a unified command, the United States Central Command (CENTCOM). It was this organization that would run the operations in the 1991 Gulf War.

General Wickham would follow General Meyer as Chief of Staff of the U.S. Army in June 1983. Wickham had an extensive background with light forces. He created two new light infantry divisions, with an orientation toward the Persian Gulf. These divisions were meant to operate in the mountainous areas of Iran, not the desert. He directed that a whole series of mobility studies be conducted in support of planning for getting U.S. forces into the Persian Gulf quickly enough to be effective. By 1983, the U.S. military was on the road to moving out of the Fulda Gap fixation.

WARGAMES AND SIMULATIONS FOR BREAKING THE MOLD

To support the military and political leaders' traditional fixation on potential European conflicts, there were a number of simulations and wargames in the 1970s for assisting the military to examine contingencies in Europe. But there were few if any simulation tools available that were effective in assisting the military to examine alternative courses of action in crises in other regions of the world. The 1980s saw an intense effort to develop not only simulations appropriate for other regions of the world, but simulations that had the flexibility and versatility to be rapidly set up and that could rapidly evaluate a series of alternative courses of action. The major problem with most of the operational simulations in the 1970s was that by the time these ponderous, computer-driven systems were set up and modified for a crisis other than Europe, the crisis was over. Jim Dunnigan, Fred McClintic, Dave Hardison, and Mark Herman are some of the modeling experts who led the way in developing a new generation of models that could rapidly be set up for any region of the world so that alternative courses of action could rapidly be evaluated. When Iraq suddenly invaded Kuwait in the summer of 1990, CENTCOM (the Central Command Headquarters controlling all coalition forces in the Gulf) had the wargaming and simulation tools available to rapidly examine the crisis.

Complementing the wargaming of the Iraqi invasion being conducted by CENTCOM, the Joint Staff in Washington called upon Mark Herman to set up the wargame Gulf Strike for them. Mark Herman had designed this simulation of potential wars in the Persian Gulf during the mid-1980s. Gulf Strike had already been updated once a few years later and was still in print. Mark had, for several years, been working for one defense consulting firm or another, so the Pentagon knew who he was, what he could do, and where to find him. The Pentagon approached Mark at 10 A.M. on August 2, he was under contract at 2 P.M., and the game began at 3 P.M. (using various Pentagon Middle East experts as players). Before the day was over, Iraq had already conquered Kuwait, but the wargamers in Washington knew Iraq was doomed. The results of this manual game were the basis of much of the decision making in Washington during August. In Saudi Arabia, and elsewhere, other wargames were played intensely to refine the plans that led to Iraq's defeat. The key to the success of this new generation of wargames used by CENTCOM and the Joint Staff was that they could be rapidly set up and produce quick results, and that the models were relatively transparent and easy to use. Most of this new generation of models have been designed so that knowledge of the principles of war is more necessary than knowledge of the principles of computer programming.

Mark Herman was another member of the old SPI gang, the same crew that Colonel Ray Macedonia, chairman of the Department of War Gaming at the Army War College, had also called on to rebuild wargaming at the college in the mid-1970s. SPI (Simultaneous Publications, Inc.) was a commercial wargame publisher founded by Jim Dunnigan and some other New York wargamers in 1969. Dunnigan ran the company from 1969 to 1980. During that period SPI published over three hundred wargames. Most of them were historical, but several dozen were on contemporary subjects. These contemporary wargames demonstrated to many military commanders how easy it was to create their own wargames and models. SPI freely passed the technology of wargame design to any military organization that asked, and many did. Several of the numerous SPI "school of wargame design" graduates (former staff members trained by Dunnigan) were prominent as analysts on TV during the 1991 Persian Gulf War. One wargamer quipped, "Every time I turned on the TV news, it looked like an SPI reunion." For many years, SPI was the premier place to learn how to design wargames, particularly games on contemporary subjects. After leaving SPI, many of these designers went to work for the military or intelligence agencies.

CHAPTER

Vietnam: False Confidence

The defining military experience for most of the senior American military leaders in Desert Storm was the Vietnam War. Nearly all the senior leaders (colonels, generals, and senior NCOs) either went through a tour in Vietnam or were affected by the military and civilian reaction to the Vietnam experience. For these soldiers, it has been a long journey from Vietnam to the Persian Gulf. It was a dedicated and difficult effort for them to overcome the legacy of Vietnam.

One of the difficulties of assessing the Vietnam War is that it lasted such a long time: over fifteen years. So many circumstances changed over that long period—coups in the South Vietnam government, changes in presidents, strategies, and defense budgets—that it is possible to find any kind of failure that you are looking for. Because the nature and pressures of war evoke so much emotion, it is difficult for any of the participants or commentators not to be biased. What is striking is the fact that most of the failures of the Vietnam War, real or imagined, were avoided in Desert Shield and Desert Storm. The underlying reforms that have been instituted at all levels of the national security structure ensured that "Getting It Right" in the Persian Gulf also created the conditions that ended the Cold War.

Let's look at what has generally become accepted as the reasons and conditions for our lack of success in the Vietnam War. Our purpose is not to rehash the problems of that war; rather it is to place into perspective the Herculean efforts in reforming the military that were made over the last twenty years.

THE STRATEGIC LEADERSHIP FAILURE

The Vietnam "failure" had less to do with what happened on the battlefield and more to do with the problems found much farther up the chain of command. Many historians and military experts have indicated that our political objectives were not clearly linked with our military operations at the strategic, operational, and tactical levels. This meant that the orders the troops got, and often executed effectively, did not always produce results that the U.S. government expected, wanted, or anticipated. This lack of coordination resulted in apparent military successes on the battlefield that actually were counterproductive to our political objectives. The following examples give you a good overview of the problems the military had in Vietnam.

Hearts and Minds

Vietnamese civilians were alienated by the destruction of their lives and property caused by large-scale military operations. These American actions were attempting to win the "hearts and minds" of these very same Vietnamese. Some argued that more and smaller operations supported by quick-reaction reinforcements should have been employed, along with emphasis on Vietnamization (turning over more of the military responsibility to the South Vietnamese forces) and nation building. We'll never know if a different approach would have worked in Vietnam, and that is one more reason why the debate will rage on indefinitely.

Fear of Mobilization

Another problem was the failure of the president to mobilize the reserves, which could have been the principal means of gauging the support of the American people. In the past, when war was declared, reservists (civilians) were called to active duty. This upset a lot of the voters, and unless they were in favor of the war, the government had to back off. This issue pointed out the lack of decisiveness that many felt we exhibited during the Vietnam era. Calling up the reserves gets the people more involved, and more inclined to make it clear if the war has popular backing or not. Vietnam-era leaders remembered the uproar the mobilized reserve troops, and their families, raised as the Korean War dragged on.

Gradualism

The gradualism that characterized our piecemeal introduction of combat forces into Vietnam allowed time for the North Vietnamese to make adjustments in both their strategies and tactics. This advantage we essentially gave to the enemy and it was a leading cause of many of our problems. America had far greater military resources than North Vietnam. But by applying those forces piecemeal, we gave the North Vietnamese the time to adapt to, and defeat, each move America made.

Micromanagement

Another area criticized was the command and control structure. The lack of a single commander in Vietnam, with overall authority for running the war, was a major problem. One was never sure who was in charge. Sometimes the ambassador had the major role in making military decisions, sometimes the military had a greater role, but all the forces operating in the theater were not under a single commander for unity of effort. This lack of unified command was especially a major problem in the air campaign, where one day a general was calling the shots, another day it was the ambassador or someone in Washington. Korea taught us the indivisibility of combat power. Yet, less than a dozen years after Korea, we managed to forget hard-won lessons.

The division of responsibility led to mistrust between the military and civilian leaders and often the war was micromanaged from Washington by committees of civilians with little knowledge of how to conduct military operations. Also, the very nature of the authority and organization of the Joint Staff at the time interfered with the Chairman of the Joint Chiefs of Staff being able to provide the president with the necessary military advice that he often required (and didn't get). The president had too many military and civilian experts reporting to him. It was impossible to pick out the important information from all this babble. The president quickly got to the point where he trusted no one to have independent authority where the fighting was being done. It was President Johnson who was most afflicted by this malady. Eventually the president, or his aides, was picking up the phone and using the wonders of modern communications technology to take over the conduct of operations in the field. That was classic micromanagement.

Other People's Battles

A controversial area was America's relationship with the government we were assisting, South Vietnam. Some experts have argued that we did not control the Vietnamese government enough to force them to make necessary reforms. Others have indicated that we controlled them too much and created a situation that they could not deal with. A contributing factor was that the Vietnam War started as a typical Military Assistance Program with all the administrative and legal constraints that go with such aid. Most of these constraints were to prevent corrupt use of American aid, and to prevent the president from expanding the operation more than Congress was comfortable with. The president used gradualism not only to apply combat power in Vietnam but also to transform the Vietnam War from just another aid program for a small country to a cornerstone in American foreign policy and a major conflict that was never officially called a full-scale war.

We also approached the problems of Vietnam with our cultural constraints. These tended to make many Americans arrogant in dealing with the Asians, which was counterproductive to the political war with the communist nationalists. We had been so superior in World War II that it led us to confuse technological advantages with personal capabilities. The fact that we assigned captains to advise Vietnamese officers of much higher rank helped foster the feeling among the American military, "Just put us in charge and we will put a quick end to the war." It was not that simple. It took time to overcome cultural differences, to develop the understanding and teamwork required to achieve the outstanding coalition warfare fought in World War II. Unfortunately, this and many other key diplomatic lessons of World War II were forgotten in the Vietnam War. Not only were those lessons forgotten, but anyone who brought them up would likely be told, "That doesn't apply here." But through hard work, the lessons of past wars were relearned after Vietnam and were a major factor in bringing an end to the Cold War and were classically demonstrated in the Persian Gulf.

The Home Front

While it's vital to get the civilian and military leadership properly organized to fight a war, a democracy like the United States has additional problems. Many people in a democracy will criticize the very moral basis of any war and point out that a free society cannot long sustain a major conflict without a firm moral basis for involvement. In other words, if the people are not behind the war effort, they will vote out of office those officials who are. President Johnson lost his job because he was behind the war; Nixon became president because he promised to end the war. And he did.

A limited war by its very nature usually has many ambiguous objectives and goals which make them difficult to defend morally, especially using the traditional "just war" theory. Vietnam was just such a war of limited goals. Helping those Vietnamese who wanted an honest and democratic government was a laudable goal. But as the fighting escalated, it appeared that many of the Vietnamese we were trying to help were being destroyed in the process. Much has also been written claiming that President Johnson and President Nixon were too concerned about the Soviets and the Chinese with respect to escalating the war. The alternative strategy called for a more comprehensive involvement and this would possibly have been quicker and ultimately successful. Speed and success in the war would have made it easier to gain support from the American people. But the American population is traditionally isolationist and not eager to get involved in foreign affairs that do not have direct benefit for them. U.S. involvement in World Wars I and II was delayed several years until many Americans were killed by foreign armed forces. Korea and the Persian Gulf were able to drag Americans into combat somewhat reluctantly because these wars both involved U.S. allies being invaded by rapacious neighbors. But Vietnam was far away and the Vietnam conflict was for the most part a civil war. Many Americans had reservations about getting involved in a civil war, no matter how deeply sworn enemies of America (the communist nations) were involved.

The morality of the Vietnam War and the concerns over expanding the conflict outside the boundaries of Vietnam are open to debate, but it is not debatable that the divisiveness of these issues and the other problems discussed created major institutional problems both for the government and for the military. Congress was up in arms and church and academic groups were vocal in their protests. The ability of the U.S. government to wage war without the consent of the people was in doubt. The laws and Constitution of the United States vested this power in the people, or, to be more specific, the people's representatives in Congress. But customary practice had historically been different. The president was allowed by law and the Constitution to conduct affairs with foreign nations. This included treaties and the granting of aid. This aid had long been both economic and military. The president had increasingly pushed this military aid from assistance to direct involvement in military operations. In Vietnam, there was no declaration of war, but the direct military assistance had all the appearances of a major war. Half a million U.S. troops were in combat in Southeast Asia and to all outward appearances, this was a war. This ambiguous state of affairs created severe legal, political, and moral strains on the American people and their government.

These institutional problems could have resulted in a situation that threatened the very survival of a free America. The U.S. system of government is set up to prevent the Congress or, especially, the president from having too much unilateral control over the armed forces. But the American military was ever faithful to the Constitution. In the end, after watching its helicopters scoop Americans from the top of the U.S. Embassy in Saigon under the most humiliating circumstances, the military found itself the biggest loser for its efforts in Vietnam. The military was accused of "losing the war," and modernization programs for the previous decade had been stymied while the funds had been siphoned off to support the war in Vietnam, which had primarily been an infantry and air cavalry war. The military lost a decade of preparation for the confrontation with the Soviet Union, and was tagged a loser in the bargain.

Doctrine du Jour

For the troops doing the fighting, the most frustrating item was the continual zigzag of doctrine. A combination of military reality and political pressure produced a constant stream of directives on "how to fight." Some of these techniques were lethal to the enemy; some were more dangerous for our own troops. Nearly all were devastating for any Vietnamese civilians in the area and nearly all the bright ideas conjured up for the battlefield got savaged by the press and the growing chorus of critics back home. The military was eager to try new techniques, and it did. But unlike in previous wars, the details of how the troops went about their business in the combat zone became a matter of national debate. The military sometimes had to modify its methods to accommodate political pressures. It was no way to fight a war.

To make matters worse, the Army went into Vietnam while in the midst of reorganizing itself for conventional (nonnuclear) warfare. After its dead-end flirtation with the Pentomic Army in the late 1950s, Vietnam found the Army readying itself to fight a mechanized war against Soviet troops in

Central Europe. Several new weapons systems were coming on line when the Vietnam involvement began. There were new rifles, mines, machine guns, a new main battle tank, and most important of all, a new helicopter. This last item had the most profound effect on the infantryman's life and on combat operations in general. While the helicopter (the UH-1 "Huey") had originally been designed to support movement over radioactive battlefields, the Army quickly seized on the concept of airmobile (emphasizing helicopters) units operating with mechanized (lots of armored vehicles) ones. This emphasis on heliborne mobility was to define most of the tactical operations in Vietnam.

What Is Vietnam?

Before going into the details of military operations, we must consider what the U.S. military walked into. Vietnam is a region with a very checkered past. The "Great Indochina War" began in the 1930s and went on into the late 1970s. That's over four decades of mayhem involving French, British, Japanese, Korean, and American forces (plus minor contingents from other nations) as well as most of Vietnam's neighbors. Vietnam itself has never been a very peaceful or united region. Until about a thousand years ago, North Vietnam was actually part of China. The Vietnamese were originally migrants from China who developed a distinct language and culture because they were so far away from the center of Chinese culture to the north. In fact, many of the regions in southern China speak dialects of Chinese that cannot be understood by the Chinese up north.

Ancient Vietnam was a very rebellious part of China, and from the ninth century on the Chinese largely gave up and insisted only that (North) Vietnam say nice things about the Chinese emperor and pay tribute from time to time. This North Vietnam did, in between occasional Chinese invasions and raids. Once liberated from Chinese domination, North Vietnam proceeded to conquer its ethnic cousins in South Vietnam. The two parts of Vietnam were (and are) separated by mountainous highlands thinly populated by non-Chinese, with communication primarily by sea. Moreover, South Vietnam was more influenced by contact with nearby India, Indonesia, and Cambodia. More to the point, the Cambodians have long laid claim to nearby portions of South Vietnam. Until the North Vietnamese began moving south, the Cambodians were the major power in the area. This underlies the continuing animosity between Cambodians and Vietnamese.

After about five hundred years of effort, North and South Vietnam were more or less merged in the fifteenth century. At this time, modern Laos was largely a backwater anyone could claim. Burma and Thailand were not really part of all this strife, being separated from the Vietnam/China/Cambodia area by geography and a tendency to look westward toward India. Civil war and turmoil was a long-established way of life in Vietnam and the surrounding region when, in the late 1700s, French ships appeared, found yet another civil war under way, and offered assistance to whichever local warlord would present the best terms. Within a hundred years France had seized direct control of all Vietnam as well as Cambodia. China, meanwhile, was preoccupied by revolution and the transition from medieval to modern society and was unable to interfere. The French found the Vietnamese as troublesome as the Chinese had. By the 1930s, a half century after the French had taken full control of the region, French-educated Vietnamese students began yet another revolution. This one was based on a new ideology: communism.

Unlike previous civil wars, which pitted different factions of the nobility against one another, this revolution was led by the middle class. Actually, it was not the middle class as much as it was the educated class. Many of the first Vietnamese communists were the university-trained children of Vietnamese landowners. Wealth in Vietnam was still rather feudal, with a few percent of the population owning most of the land and using their economic power to control the bulk of the population. This was basically the same situation found in Russia and China before their revolutions, and the Vietnamese used the same pitch to the tenant farmers: lower land rents and the possibility of landownership. In a largely agricultural society, the possibility of landownership, not to mention lower rents, was an appealing prospect. The Vietnamese communists (Vietminh) eventually made it an offer that could not be refused by backing the offer up with the threat (and often use) of violence.

The revolution in Vietnam grew slowly before World War II. But once the Japanese took over in 1941, the struggle became heavily armed and supported by the Allies. Many of the resistance groups were not communist, a situation that continued until the communists suppressed all opposition in the 1970s. Once World War II was over, the armed Vietnamese resistance proclaimed its independence from France and the French had to fight their way back in. Thus ensued a more intense rebellion that ended with a compromise between the French and the communists in 1954. The United States had refused to become directly involved in the war, even though the Vietnamese revolutionaries were led by communists and received substantial assistance from Russia and China. The compromise that ended the war split the country in two. North Vietnam was controlled by the communists. South Vietnam was controlled by various groups that represented the ''old order.'' This made the South Vietnamese government a very shaky one, as it was led by the discredited nobility (who had collaborated with the French) and contained many of the Vietnamese who had worked for the French colonial government. Worst of all, few of the many factions in the south were willing to work together for any length of time. Vietnam was always full of factious groups and most of these ended up in South Vietnam after the partition. The North Vietnamese knew this, and felt they could foment another revolution in the south and thus unite all of Vietnam under communist control.

The North Vietnamese communist plan had a lot going for it. The landlords were relieved of their land in the north and the farmers given land of their own. The farmer's lot became considerably easier than it had ever been in the past (at least until the communists eventually collectivized the farms). As in most communist revolutions, the first-generation communists were still relatively honest in the 1950s and the North Vietnamese people were enjoying the rule of Vietnamese instead of foreigners and the absence of the rampant corruption that still prevailed in the south. The South Vietnamese communists (the Vietcong) were to build up their local organizations through the 1950s and then simply take over, using the same guerrilla-warfare methods the North Vietnamese Vietminh had used successfully against the French. But then the Americans entered the picture.

When the French departed in 1954, America stepped into the vacuum to provide support for the ''democratic'' and anticommunist South Vietnamese government. Before 1954, there had been some political pressure in the United States to support France's fight against the Vietnamese communists. However, there was less enthusiasm to help a colonial power (France) retake its colony (Vietnam). But once the French were gone and it was just the communist half of Vietnam versus the noncommunist half, it was a different story. At first, the American assistance was limited to training and money for the army and the government. U.S. advisers strongly suggested that the South Vietnamese government clean up the corruption and pay attention to the needs of the people. There were always some South Viet-namese who took this advice to heart, but increasingly most of them threw in their lot with the Vietcong or joined the government in plundering the nation. Most of the foreign aid went into the pockets of government offi-cials, as did much of the tax money collected. Unlike the Vietminh, the Vietcong were not a purely communist organization, even though they fought for unification with the north. Recognizing that many noncommunist elements existed in the South Vietnamese population, the Vietcong included many members from these groups. Moreover, the South Vietnamese still (after over a thousand years of separateness) considered themselves quite different from the North Vietnamese. This situation was to cause both the South Vietnamese government and the North Vietnamese communists a lot of problems until the Vietcong were virtually wiped out in the late 1960s.

Meanwhile, coup followed coup (often supported by the United States) in the late 1950s and early 1960s as the South Vietnamese ruling class searched for a stable government. Such a government was never found and by the early 1960s, the Vietcong guerrilla war was in full swing. This war did not proceed quite as it had when the French were the opponents. Because heavy U.S. involvement did not begin until 1964, the war before this was Viet-namese versus Vietnamese. The money and military assistance from the United States made the South Vietnamese administration a more formidable opponent than the communists anticipated. The Vietcong appeals for sup-port from the population eventually degenerated into an extortion racket. The people were asked by the Vietcong to support them—or else. The people mainly wanted peace at this point, and this was what American involvement initially tried to achieve by going after the Vietcong with massive firepower.

But the Vietcong did have time on their side. The increasingly corrupt South Vietnamese government became more unpopular each year. Any guerrilla war ends up with both sides using a fair amount of coercion, but the Vietcong coercion was becoming more tolerable than the official govern-ment kind. The government relied increasingly on brute force and firepower. The communists spent more time in the villages, generally behaving them-selves and running a political campaign for their version of the future. U.S. appeals to reduce corruption were ineffective. From 1960 on, it was pri-marily the South Vietnamese army that was running the country and it was increasingly running it for its own benefit. The South Vietnamese were not only stealing from their own countrymen, they were plundering U.S. military and economic aid also. By 1964 the United States chose to use American troops to go after the larger and more active Vietcong guerrilla units. It wasn't just the Vietcong anymore either, since the North Vietnamese had already been sending regular army units south for several years. The communists had decided that a little invasion activity would help the revolution along.

THE AMERICAN MILITARY EFFORT IN VIETNAM

At the peak of involvement, in 1969, the United States and its allies had 1.6 million troops in the field. Two thirds of these were South Vietnamese; another 72,000 were U.S. allies (mainly South Korean, who suffered 4,400 dead in the several years of action). For the entire war, the United States suffered 57,000 dead, the South Vietnamese 197,000, and other allies 5,200. The communists had nearly a million combat deaths (plus hundreds of thousands more from accidents and disease). Active communist guerrillas and regular troops totaled a million in the peak years, and never fewer than several hundred thousand. Civilian deaths were more difficult to keep track of; there were apparently between half a million and a million civilian fatalities. Many came from the aftereffects of fighting, principally disease. There was also a lesser amount of casualties from bombing and fighting in the neighboring nations of Cambodia and Laos, as well as in North Vietnam itself. In any event, nearly ten years of fighting left some two million people dead. This was not a little war.

This was not America's first experience in fighting guerrillas. The Indian wars of the eighteenth and nineteenth centuries, the Philippine insurrection at the turn of the century, and sundry Latin American conflicts in the first half of the twentieth century had all provided soldiers and Marines with a background for what they thought they were facing in Vietnam. But this war was different, and Americans were slow to appreciate the differences and react to them. There were several key differences with Vietnam and an examination of these differences says a lot about why the war turned out as it did.

Sanctuaries. None of the previous guerrilla wars the United States dealt with featured opponents who were supported by a major power. Nor did any of these conflicts involve nearby refuges for the guerrillas that were free from attack. Throughout history, external support and sanctuaries have been crucial to the eventual victory of successful guerrilla organizations. In Vietnam, the Vietcong and North Vietnamese were free from ground attack in North Vietnam and Laos, and only late in the war were they hit by ground units in Cambodia. This freedom from attack was the result of American fear of Chinese or Soviet retaliation. No one wanted to risk a nuclear war over Vietnam. Thus a tacit understanding arose that kept the Soviets from rattling the nuclear saber and the Chinese from sending in ground forces. In return, America kept its ground forces out of areas adjacent to South Vietnam. These sanctuaries enabled the communists to sustain their efforts against the formidable combat power of U.S. forces. In the past, guerrilla forces, no matter how determined, have been consistently beaten if they lacked such a haven while battling a much stronger opponent.

Nuclear Standoff. The principal reason the guerrillas had a sanctuary was that their sponsors, China and Russia, had nuclear weapons. At the time the United States was getting involved with Vietnam, American doctrine was developing into MAD (Mutually Assured Destruction). This meant that any use of nuclear weapons was to be met with all-out war. In theory, this would prevent anyone from using atomic weapons, as such use would result in the destruction of everyone and everything on the planet. Moreover, China was seen to be unstable and no one was sure what Russia would do if pressed on its support of North Vietnam. As a result, attacks on North Vietnam were always a contentious subject back in Washington. Over the years, attacks on North Vietnam gradually increased, but only from the air. No one had the nerve to order ground forces into North Vietnam lest the nuclear resolve of China or Russia be tested.

Cold War Politics. The nature of the Cold War drove nations to do things they shouldn't have done, and Vietnam was one of them. The epic struggle between communism and democracy was not always a "cold" war. The principal combatants, all armed with nuclear weapons, found that the principal way they could fight this war was through proxies. Each side would back a faction in some Third World nation and then struggle for a decision. In Korea, Malaysia, Afghanistan, and Greece the communists lost. In China, Cuba, and several other areas they won. In the United States these defeats were not taken lightly and the handling of the next round became a political hot potato in the United States. Woe to the president who gave any hint of being "soft on communism." Kennedy became president in 1960 and was immediately challenged to prove he could "deal with the communists." Kennedy failed with Cuba and then found Vietnam looming as the next round. Whatever Kennedy's eventual decision might have been, up to his assassination in November 1963, he had supported increased aid to South Vietnam. His vice president, Lyndon Johnson, nine months after succeeding Kennedy, landed the first U.S. ground units in Vietnam and presided over the massive involvement of U.S. troops. Only after five years of futile combat did increasingly sour public opinion force the government to begin withdrawing from Vietnam. As is always the case in politics, it was easier to do something than to undo it.

Maximum Oversight. In previous "Vietnams," the troops of other nations were sent to distant battlefields to do a job and they proceeded to do it without much supervision from the folks back home. This approach worked for thousands of years. Although telegraph and radio existed in the century before Vietnam, there was no way for anyone not in the combat zone to really get involved in the operations. Vietnam was different. Television put film of battle action in front of the American people within a day or so of the actual event. Military communications enabled the president to supervise operations in the field. In one of the more pointless battles of the war, Khe San, President Johnson had a model of the battlefield built in the White House and from there the president directed the colonels and their troops at the front. The battle was a major media event for weeks, and the commander in chief could not resist the temptation to micromanage. Throughout the war, the nation was watching in near real time. TV made the war subject to an ongoing referendum. The government had to continually respond to whatever the people thought they saw, courtesy of the media's editing and interpretation of the event. The government responded by making a lot of mistakes that were not all corrected by the time 1990 rolled around (where presidential aides still got on the satellite phone to "advise" commanders in the Persian Gulf). But micromanagement was recognized as a bad thing even during Vietnam and was purged from the system after the micromanaged debacle of Desert One in 1980. The officers who endured micromanagement in Southeast Asia simply refused to tolerate it as they rose through the ranks. A lot of the instant replay and second-guessing by the media also disappeared, if only because the military learned from its Vietnam experience and worked with the press more effectively.

U.S. Troops in Vietnam

Without recounting all the campaigns of the war, one good way to view Vietnam is simply to look at the number of Army combat battalions involved in the war at the end of each year and the total U.S. troops killed each year. The following chart shows only Army troops; U.S. Marines increased the number of battalions by about 20 to 25 percent for each year shown.

U.S. Army Combat Battalions in Vietnam

End of Year	U.S. Dead	Infantry Battalions	Aviation Companies	Armor/Cav Battalions	Artillery Battalions
1965	1,847	22	51	1	17
1966	6,053	54	73	9	37
1967	11,058	72	119	11	53
1968	16,511	81	134	12	62
1969	11,527	61	140	12	55
1970	6,065	41	113	7	35
1971	2,348	12	68	2	5
1972	561	0	0	0	0

Of the 57,000 Americans killed in Vietnam, the Army suffered 65 percent of these losses. Enemy action caused 83 percent of all losses; the rest were accidents, illness, and the like. The U.S. Marines, who put twenty-four infantry battalions into action at one time or another (usually for shorter periods than Army infantry units) took 25 percent of the fatal casualties. The Navy and Air Force suffered the remaining 10 percent of losses. The lowest four enlisted ranks (E-4, or corporal, and below), suffered two thirds of the fatalities. NCOs suffered most of the rest. Wounds, injuries, and serious illness (not all of them reported) were about four times the number of fatalities.

GETTING IT NOT QUITE RIGHT

The Army went into Vietnam while it was still fixated on the mechanized war it might have to fight against the Soviets in Europe. As a result, it didn't have a lot of infantry to spare for a major campaign in the jungles of Vietnam. But, as always, the Army was eager to give it all it had. What was available at this time was largely short-term (two-year) conscripts. Many of the key officers and NCOs were veterans of Korea or World War II (and sometimes both). Some of these leaders had fought in the jungles of the Pacific during World War II, but this experience wasn't terribly useful since those battles didn't involve antiguerrilla operations. The Army did have one new trick up its sleeve: helicopters. The UH-1 (Huey) came into use in 1960. It was originally intended to provide the Army with additional mobility on the nuclear battle-field. During the early 1960s a new type of division, the "airmobile" division, was developed to make maximum use of the helicopter's capabilities. This unit (the 1st Cavalry Division) was one of the first U.S. units sent to Vietnam in 1965, along with several hundred helicopters to provide the air-mobility. By 1968 there were seven Army infantry divisions, two Marine divisions, and four independent brigades in Vietnam. This was the largest field Army America had deployed since World War II. However, the Vietnam Army had some significant differences compared to its World War II counter-part. These can be summarized as follows:

Experience

Unlike those of World War II, the Vietnam troops were not in "for the duration," but only for a thirteen-month "tour." Worse yet, officers served only six months with their units. While World War II divisions went through a lot of manpower due to casualties and disease, they always had a battle-hardened cadre of experienced men. In World War II, officers didn't serve all that long with their units either. But again, the short tenure was due to the promotion of exceptional officers, the dismissal of incompetents, and the usual casualties and disease losses. The bulk of the World War II officers were battle-tested and experienced. This was more the case as the war went on. There were only about three years of continuous ground combat for U.S. soldiers in World War II, and those divisions that were in it for two or three years were far more effective during their last year of action than during their first. The only World War II combat veterans to be "rotated" back home were some aircraft crews. And this was only because these crews took such high casualties that without a rotation home after a certain number of missions, nearly all were sure to die and morale would be impossible to maintain.

In Vietnam, the sustained ground combat went on for nine years. But because of the rotation policies, there was much less improvement from year to year when compared to the World War II Army. Instead of gaining nine years' experience, the troops in Vietnam obtained one year of experience nine times. The enemy, by way of comparison, was in for the duration. Although the communist fighters took much higher casualties, their cadre of experienced soldiers and officers increased as the war went on. The enemy kept getting better compared to the U.S. units and their constantly rotating personnel. The difference in experience level of the communist and allied troops restricted how the allies could operate. The communists generally had much better knowledge of the area they were operating in and better relations with the local civilians. Add to this the language and cultural differences the allies had to put up with and you can see how crucial these differences were. Even if the U.S. forces had wanted to operate on a guerrilla level, they would have had to spend a lot of time in the bush acquiring sufficient familiarity with the local conditions.

New units in Vietnam had a particular problem since most of the troops had never operated in a "live fire" environment before. It wasn't until the 1980s that U.S. infantry training became realistic enough to condition soldiers to being under fire. As a result, a unit's first few months in Vietnam were marred by trigger-happy troops who often gave away their positions to more astute guerrillas and caused many friendly-fire injuries. Replacements coming into units already in Vietnam for some time had it a little better, as the veterans could clue them in. However, because of the thirteen-month rotation policy, it took several years before these replacements became spread out over the year. For the first year or so, large numbers of veterans in a unit would leave all at once, being replaced by an equally large number of rookies.

This type of replacement policy was itself another problem. Although the Army knew from World War II experience that the individual replacement policy was inefficient, it was not until the late 1970s that the official line changed and unit cohesion was respected. In plain language, this meant that units were replaced all together, so that the "institutional knowledge" of the troops who had worked together for a time was preserved. In Vietnam, U.S. troops always felt most of their comrades were strangers, and that was usually the case. Because a soldier is cautious to a fault when working with people he does not know well, this became a serious problem. Not so with the communists, who often operated for years in the same unit and at least knew their fellow troops well.

Tactics

The tactics of most nations in World War II were adapted from the successful German blitzkrieg techniques (coordinating air and ground forces in swift, offensive attacks). All the Germans had done was to successfully adapt to the conditions of mechanized warfare. The Germans were the first to realize the advantages of motorized armies and make them work. Their opponents quickly followed. In the Pacific, the United States also learned from the early successes of the Japanese in the use of amphibious warfare. In Vietnam, the United States did not recognize that the communists were also using a new form of warfare. The Vietminh, and later the Vietcong, used a form of high-tech guerrilla warfare. This meant highly organized and often quite well-equipped guerrilla units. Even the regular North Vietnamese units operating on the border areas adopted a lot of the guerrilla techniques. There was nothing mysterious about the communist doctrine; it had been practiced since the 1930s (and even earlier, in a more general sense). Put simply, guerrilla units attacked when they had the advantage and withdrew to their sanctuaries or remote areas when they didn't. The high-tech angle included a lot of radios, clever organization, and an impressive support system. Since many of the Vietcong were part-time guerrillas, they simply went back to their day jobs when not operating against U.S. or South Vietnamese units.

The American Army had learned in World War II and Korea that it could substitute firepower for manpower and, to a certain extent, for experience. Given the experience problems with U.S. troops in Vietnam, this seemed a logical technique to apply there. However, a major problem with guerrilla warfare is finding the little devils. U.S. commanders also realized that while the enemy itself might be difficult to find, even the Vietcong needed to stockpile supplies in order to sustain anything more than terrorist operations. By the time the United States sent troops to Vietnam, the Vietcong had indeed escalated the war to the point where there were large (platoon, company, and battalion, usually) guerrilla units operating in many areas. These units needed bases to operate from. The bases were well hidden out in the jungle and the Army proceeded to develop "search and destroy" tactics to find the bases and destroy them, and any Vietcong who happened to be in the way. Equipped with hundreds (later thousands) of helicopters, the U.S. Army felt it had the means to cut the enemy down to size and make it possible to give the South Vietnamese people a viable alternative to communism. American commanders eventually ran into a number of problems with this search and destroy technique:

Intelligence. Finding Vietcong bases, and large units, was very difficult. With today's sensors, it might have been a lot easier, but in the 1960s the jungle that covered most of South Vietnam was often impenetrable. Small patrols, electronic surveillance of Vietcong radio traffic, and interrogation of prisoners were all used to get a sense of what the Vietcong had and approximately where it was. An even larger problem was the difficulty in keeping U.S. search and destroy operations secret. Once the Vietcong found out U.S. troops were coming, the Vietcong units, and often the supplies, would move somewhere else. This lack of security was caused by a combination of U.S. sloppiness and the abundance of Vietcong sympathizers in the South Vietnamese army as well as among South Vietnamese employees of the U.S. Army. As a result, the Vietcong often knew more about the details of an upcoming U.S. operation than most of the U.S. troops participating. With this intel advantage, the communists "prepared the battlefield" with booby traps, mines, and ambushes. As the U.S. troops were advancing into territory the Vietcong were quite familiar with, the losses from these preparations were quite high and made the GIs cautious, sometimes to a fault.

North Vietnamese Escalation. As fast as U.S. units destroyed communist units, North Vietnam would send more into battle. At first, the communists up north thought they could take over through the use of South Vietnamese communists operating as guerrillas in the south. Once U.S. aid increased in the early 1960s, this became less likely and the North Vietnamese began sending troops in. These troops strengthened the South Vietnamese guerrilla units and soon there were purely North Vietnamese units operating as well. As America poured more troops into the south, so did the North Vietnamese. By the late 1960s, most of the fighting was between North Vietnamese and American troops. As long as the North Vietnamese were free to import weapons and supplies from China and the Soviet Union, and recruit troops in the north, it was strictly a war of attrition in the south; the communists were betting on U.S. public opinion getting tired of the carnage before the north ran out of troops. The communists were right.

Free-Fire Zones. The heavy use of firepower gave the U.S. forces a big advantage on the battlefield, but at the cost of angering the South Vietnamese civilians who often got caught in the crossfire. From the beginning of U.S. combat-unit involvement, the technique for using massive U.S. artillery and airborne firepower assumed that one would either move civilians out of a battle area or warn them in advance to leave or be considered the enemy. In practice, this didn't work very well and hundreds of thousands of Vietnamese civilians were killed or injured in the process. This made the Vietnamese angry at the Americans and made it much easier for the communists to recruit new troops and agents in the south. At the very least, it became difficult for the South Vietnamese government to keep the loyalty of its people. The South Vietnamese army was trained by U.S. advisers and used firepower as liberally as its mentors. The communists were more sparing in their use of firepower because they simply didn't have it.

Bait and Smash. Search and destroy tactics, originally developed to find Vietcong troops, supplies, and logistical bases, evolved to the point where American ground units were used simply as bait to locate communist forces. The artillery and bombers would then be called in to smash the enemy units. This did enormous damage to communists, but eventually did even more damage to the morale of U.S. troops. Often the "bait" was a very small U.S. unit that was sent off to encounter a very large communist unit. For example, a U.S. platoon (20 to 30 troops) would stumble across a communist regiment (1,500 to 2,000 troops). Before U.S. firepower could be applied, the U.S. unit was often severely mauled. Many U.S. commanders, however, preferred this for a number of reasons. First, it kept overall U.S. casualties down. Why send in a company (100 to 200 troops) to find the enemy regiment when a platoon could do it just as well? The troops felt that a company-sized (100 to 200 men) bait force had a better chance of getting away from the enemy regiment than a platoon, even if the company took more casualties than a platoon. They saw their chances were better in a company that took 50 percent casualties than in a platoon that took 90 percent casualties. But the grunts weren't running the war; officers who were assigned to units for only six months were. The officers had orders to keep overall casualties down, not listen to the grunts. By 1970, troop morale was down and dropping still further. A lot of communist casualties were being created, but at the expense of the will to fight among U.S. troops.

The Body Count. Keeping track of who was winning in a guerrilla war was a problem U.S. commanders eventually solved by counting enemy bodies. However, the theory didn't work out in practice. It quickly became customary for all commanders to calculate their success in the field according to how many enemy bodies they could count. In addition, these were evaluated on the ratio of American dead to enemy bodies counted. The average was 10:1 (communist:U.S. dead). But no commander wanted to be seen as "average," since it was understood that your career prospects depended on getting ratios of at least 15:1. A ratio of 25:1 or 50:1 was considered necessary to keep you in line for promotion. As a result, the body-count numbers became corrupted. There were many ways to do this. One was to simply lie. Another was to count any Vietnamese bodies, that is, civilians. Another was to use a multiplier, on the assumption that some of the dead or badly wounded would be dragged away by the communists or that you would miss a percentage of the dead because they were lost in the bush somewhere. Eventually, the U.S. headquarters in Vietnam applied a 1.5 multiplier to all body-count numbers before reporting back to the Pentagon. The assumption here was that since the troops in the field were being so scrupulously honest, someone had to take into account the bodies they could not actually find.

At the grunt level, the body count was seen as a perverse joke. U.S. troops often got killed or wounded by booby traps or enemy fire while sweeping the battlefield to count bodies. And the numbers that eventually reached the Pentagon became more fictitious through the late 1960s. Ironically, it was partially media pressure for more exact data (rather than the earlier use of "light, medium, and heavy casualties") that brought forth the body-count approach. Precision, or an attempt at precision, does not always increase accuracy.

Grab the Yankees by the Belt. The communists quickly developed ways to cope with the massive American firepower. The primary communist defense was the shovel. The communists would dig extensive protective works whenever possible and this gave them some protection. When confronted with U.S. "bait" units in the open, the communists quickly discovered that the safest thing to do was "grab the Yankees by the belt." That is, move as close as possible to the bait units. This would cause the U.S. artillery and air firepower to be applied in less generous amounts in order to avoid friendly-fire losses. Once the communists were seen as intermingled with U.S. troops, the lower amount of U.S. artillery and air strikes coming in would often allow many communist troops to sneak away unharmed. U.S. commanders would often put some priority on extracting their bait units before they were wiped out, particularly later in the war when an annihilated bait unit or two would send morale into the cellar. Another morale killer was friendly-fire casualties (U.S. troops hit by U.S. fire). Low morale would lead to refusals by troops to perform bait missions and would increase the incidence of fragging (attacks on officers and NCOs). The communists were also aware of these morale problems, and they knew that "grabbing the belt" would often create either friendly-fire losses or the rapid withdrawal of the U.S. unit. In that situation, the communists would avoid a hammering by superior U.S. firepower.

Lack of Offensive Opportunity and Experience. American troops fought a largely defensive war. This was just as well, because the thirteen-month (for troops) and six-month (for commanders) rotation policy ensured that U.S. units did not gain the combat experience needed to be consistently successful in offensive operations. The combat reports of U.S. units bear this out. Toward the end of the war, U.S. units were the attackers only 22 percent of the time. A third of these actions were meeting engagements where both sides were attacking, 40 percent were U.S. units ambushing the communists, and the rest were attacks on known enemy positions. Of all engagements, 30 percent were communist attacks on U.S. bases and 36 percent were communist attacks or ambushes of U.S. units in the field. About 12 percent were heliborne U.S. troops landing under enemy fire. Air superiority, helicopters, and massive firepower on call were never enough to make up for the superior tactical experience and skill most communist units had over their American counterparts. While the communists took far more casualties, they were willing and able to absorb these losses as long as they could keep the Americans from controlling any significant amount of real estate.

The Will to Fight. The search and destroy tactics did indeed search out communist bases and supplies. The enormous firepower the United States had available inflicted enormous casualties on the communist troops, and on any Vietnamese civilians who had the misfortune to be in the area. But because the communists ran a very tight ship, and were easily able to portray the Americans as just another bunch of foreign invaders, the Vietnamese population (north and south) was able to suffer horrendous casualties and still keep fighting—and supporting the communists. This should have come as no surprise to the Americans. As recently as the Korean War, U.S. intelligence analysts were able to confirm that communist Chinese troops were suffering over five times as many losses as American forces and yet the Chinese kept on fighting. Overall communist morale never broke, although individuals, and some units, did. The Vietnamese were fighting a patriotic war to "defend the motherland." While most U.S. troops saw their service as a patriotic duty, they were gradually dismayed by the corrupt South Vietnamese government they were defending. The corruption was everywhere, and so blatant that no one could miss it. By the late 1960s, there was one popular rock song that was heard where the troops were: "We've Got to Get Out of This Place." That said it all.

Hearts and Minds

The political aspect of guerrilla war was one that was never really wrestled to the ground in Vietnam. The major problem was the venal nature of many officials in the South Vietnamese government. By the mid-1960s, the South Vietnamese government was controlled by the South Vietnamese army. While there were many good officers and troops in this army, it was dominated by many who were corrupt and saw the war only as a means to get rich. Many South Vietnamese officers and troops proceeded to do just that. Since their own people were quite poor, the likely source of plunder was the enormous volume of U.S. aid being poured into the country. Corrupt U.S. troops contributed to this, creating a thriving black market in stolen U.S. equipment. As the war went on, U.S. troops began to notice that a lot of captured communist supplies were actually U.S. aid that had been stolen and found its way (for cash or as a gift) to communist supply dumps. Thus the communists were not only living off the land, they were also living off the very enemy they were fighting.

THE MEDIA AND MORALE

To most Americans of the Vietnam era, the war was what they saw on the TV and read about in the newspapers. This was not the same war the troops were fighting, although there were many similarities. The media, then and now, go for the extraordinary rather than the mundane. Yet wars consist largely of mundane events, not the exceptional items that make the headlines and the evening news broadcasts. It's the "man bites dog" story that will get noticed by the media, not the far more common "dog bites man." The war made much of American atrocities, which the communists were more likely to practice, and paid little attention to the real stories of poor U.S. training and the political infighting that South Vietnam was always (and still is) submerged in (particularly the bad blood between the Vietcong and North Vietnamese). Soldiers coming back from Vietnam and seeing the TV version of the war they had just fought in were often left wondering if it was the same war.

What the media concentration on the exceptional and bizarre did do was mobilize American public opinion against the war. This was not a bad thing, as the war was, in hindsight, not in America's national interest nor was it likely to be won the way it was being fought. But the public-opinion backlash was such that the troops were vilified and their often heroic efforts belittled. While most of the troops left the military and put it all behind them, the military professionals were left with a crippled and castigated organization. The military still had to defend the nation, and because of Vietnam it was less able to do it and was getting very little public support in the bargain.

While the fighting was still going on, the bad and misleading press the troops were getting was having its effect on the morale of troops in the field. Soon the attitude among the troops shifted to "If the folks back home don't care for what we are doing, why get killed while we're trying to do it?" Officers and NCOs made strenuous efforts to shore up morale and combat effectiveness, but this was a losing effort in the face of the media's increasingly strident message against the war.

What many did not notice at the time was that Vietnam created quite different relations between the media and the military than in any other American war in the twentieth century. Previous to Vietnam, the military and the media had a good working relationship, with the military calling the shots. Vietnam was different not so much because of TV (which was there from the beginning), but because it was not a declared war, had no "front line" that the military could control access to, and lasted so long. Because there was no formal declaration of war, the journalists were allowed to wander wherever they liked. But since the journalists did not see everything (particularly in communist-controlled areas), they formed their views of the war from the fragments they did see. Lacking knowledge of numerous communist atrocities or the rich internal politics of Vietnam, the media came to see the war as a misguided American crusade against Vietnamese freedom fighters. For most of the war, it was actually a civil war between the communist party and any Vietnamese who resisted communist power. Military attempts to correct this view were not successful and a mutual mistrust arose that persists to this day.

But the misinformed and misdirected power of the media was nowhere more apparent than in their reaction to the communist 1968 Tet offensive. This was a general offensive throughout South Vietnam that was supposed to mobilize popular support for the communists and bring the war to a sudden end on communist terms. That was what the Vietcong were told. In actuality, the North Vietnamese leaders who planned this offensive saw it differently. If the offensive worked—and it was seen as a long shot, given the increasing unpopularity of North Vietnamese communists in the south— that was fine. But if it failed, which was more likely, the bulk of the South Vietnamese Vietcong, who increasingly opposed northern domination, would be wiped out. Moreover, such a widespread offensive would play well for the communists in the Western (and especially American) media. For in the months before the Tet operation, American commanders had been loudly proclaiming their many victories in the field against the communists. This was true; the communists were taking heavy casualties in the field. But they weren't losing by their own calculations. For the communists to win, all they had to do was keep the fight going.

Although the Tet offensive was a military failure and a political victory for the communists, it could have done even more damage to U.S. forces. What the media were not aware of (for good reason) was the extent to which U.S. intelligence had penetrated communist communications. All communist units had to check in with Hanoi frequently by radio. As communist preparations for Tet increased, the amount of material being passed back and forth between communist units in the field and Hanoi increased. This alerted the U.S. intel folks that something was up. Many of these messages were intercepted and decoded. Many communist units were identified and their approximate locations plotted. U.S. commanders were alerted, but it seemed unlikely that the communists would attempt something so suicidal. However, there were enough local signs to alert U.S. troops. Tet did not come as a surprise to most American soldiers, who reacted quite effectively.

Militarily, Tet was a victory for U.S. forces, since the Vietcong forces were devastated. But because the United States could not publicly comment on what they were doing on the murky intel side of things (lest they let the communists know how much their communications had been compromised), the press saw the operation as a great embarrassment to U.S. efforts and soon came to regard Tet as a communist victory. Tet was a communist, not a Vietcong, victory. It was a victory of the North Vietnamese communists over the South Vietnamese communists (and the southerners' noncommunist allies).

AFTERMATH

In the early 1970s, the services were faced with rapidly declining budgets (one third less) and shrinking manpower strength (40 percent less). The atrocities in the Vietnam War were being highlighted in the press and some military members were even being spit upon as they returned home. Not only had the Watergate scandal created a loss of confidence in the government, the loss of Vietnam had created a loss of confidence in the military as a winning force as well as a loss of confidence in the professionalism of the military.

While the Vietnam War was going on, the rest of the armed forces were allowed to atrophy. As the undeclared war went into year after year of effort, the 70 percent of armed forces not in Southeast Asia was cannibalized to keep the Vietnam operation going. Experienced officers and NCOs were constantly being taken from their units to satisfy yet another levy (as the military called it) for leaders to fill slots in Vietnam. Units in Europe were particularly hard hit. Throughout the late 1960s, these units were chronically short of troops and particularly short of experienced officers and NCOs. There was little new equipment, or spare parts to keep what they had in operational condition. In the United States, most of the experienced officers and NCOs were busy training the hundreds of thousands of new draftees before they were sent to do their thirteen months in 'Nam. Research and development for new weapons, equipment, and doctrine came to a standstill for eight years (1965–1972). And when it became obvious in 1970 that there would be a decision to withdraw from Vietnam, much of the work on counterinsurgency (military, paramilitary, political, economic, psychological, and civil actions taken to counter enemy efforts to undermine the government) was cast aside.

There was one positive aspect for the Army, and that was the opportunity for the airmobility and SOF (Special Operations Forces, "Green Berets") advocates to strut their stuff. This they did, and quite successfully. The U.S. casualty list would have been a lot longer had it not been for the successful use of helicopters and SOF to put a little fear and uncertainty into the communist troops. Yet neither of these "unions" came out of Vietnam with a lot of support from the Army. The armor "union" was still top dog.

The next war was thought to be the Big One with the Soviet Union in Central Europe. This war was expected to be too full of antiaircraft weapons, and firepower in general, for helicopters to survive in, except in special and limited situations. The helicopter gunship was stressed as a replacement for the close air support the U.S. Air Force was increasingly reluctant to supply. The Huey transport helicopter was considered a fast and expensive flying truck for emergency missions behind the front lines. What drove this somber opinion of helicopter survival in a European war was the loss rate in Vietnam.

Overall Loss Rates

Year	Sorties (× 1000)	Loss Rate	Combat	Oper- ational
1966	2,993	38	22	16
1967	5,516	34	19	15
1968	7,418	29	14	15
1969	8,441	32	17	15
1970	7,564	37	19	18
1971	4,213	33	18	15
Total	36,145	33	18	16

The loss rates are per 1,000 sorties. The 4,300 helicopters lost also killed 5,000 crew and passengers. The overall loss rates were about twice what was considered acceptable for Air Force aircraft. Moreover, a far larger number of aircraft were shot up, often to the point where the Air Force would consider the aircraft "destroyed." But the Army helicopter mechanics and pilots were extremely resourceful. The maintenance troops would quickly patch up damaged choppers, and pilots would often fly machines that were barely flyable. There were commanders who ordered trashed helicopters to be listed as "damaged" rather than see their loss rate go up. But the pilots and repair crews knew that the infantry often needed air support in a desperate way and generally bent the rules themselves to get the birds flying.

These were the first generation of battlefield helicopters, and they often operated under particularly adverse operational and combat conditions. The high temperature and humidity of Vietnam reduced a helicopter's performance. The lack of a front line made them easy targets for enemy troops in the area. Helicopters were often literally a lifesaver in evacuating wounded or surrounded troops, or in quickly flying in reinforcements or supplies. But at the end of the Vietnam War, the debate began over the vulnerability of the helicopter. The helicopter pilots and aviation commanders believed that the Vietnam helicopter experience could be successfully played out in other battlefields. The people who operated the choppers in combat felt that they could rise to the challenge and develop tactics that would allow the helicopter to do its job without being massacred. This is one debate that has yet to be settled, despite spectacular success in the Gulf War and a new generation of more reliable and durable helicopters, as well as weapons designed specifically to capitalize on the helicopter's strengths. Since there is no battlefield as intense as that postulated for the NATO/Warsaw Pact in the offing, the issue may be moot for the moment.

The Special Operations Forces had other problems. The SOF were very successful in Vietnam, but senior commanders were rarely comfortable with them. These troops were a breed apart, accustomed to operating on their own and doing things their own way. This was what made senior commanders nervous. More conventional commanders saw SOF operations as "messy" and not conducive to a traditional, and relatively orderly, battle. One was never sure how the SOF would go about their business. From a regular officer's point of view, SOF people were too prone to get out of control. One thing a commander didn't want to lose was control of his troops, what they were doing and how they were doing it.

While American SOF troops continued to exist after Vietnam, their relationship with the Army high command did not improve much at all. At budget-cutting time, SOF commanders often complained that their programs were unfairly targeted for big cuts. Congress has tried to set up a system that will help ensure fairness for SOF units. The failed attempt in 1980 by Special Operations Forces to rescue the embassy staff held hostage in Iran (Desert One) and the problems that SOF encountered in 1983 during the invasion of Grenada by U.S. forces, created major concerns in Congress. To improve the capabilities of SOF, Congress passed the Cohen-Nunn Amendment to the fiscal 1987 Defense Authorization Act. This created an assistant secretary of defense for special operations and low-intensity conflict to increase the priority of SOF in the Defense Department. It also created the U.S. Special Operations Command (USSOCOM), which is a unified command that reports to the secretary of defense and the president. All SOF of the Air Force, Navy, and Army are assigned to USSOCOM. But even with these major initiatives by Congress and SOF successes in the Gulf War, attitudes by senior commanders are only slowly changing.

The Bottom

By 1972, the military was at a low point in its history. Low morale, low budgets, low personnel strength, and low prospects in general. However, although it wasn't noticed much of the time, Vietnam did not become a ball and chain for the military. It was seen more as a mistake, or rather a large collection of mistakes. And through the 1970s and 1980s, the troops concentrated their efforts on getting it right the next time. How the Congress, the administration, and the military responded to the aftermath of Vietnam was unexpected and unprecedented. There had been military reform in the wake of the embarrassing incidents in the Spanish-American War at the turn of the century. But those reforms were small change compared to what happened after Vietnam. The 1980s, which might have been the nadir in Army history, turned out to be the armed forces' finest hour. America was well served by military and public servants who understood their special responsibilities in a free society.

CHAPTER

6

The Hollow Army

The principal legacy of Vietnam for the Army was a breakdown in discipline, morale, and capability. The 1970s was a decade of negatives and low points. Few realize how bad things were in the Hollow Army of the 1970s. It was very bad, and the desire to get away from the Hollow Army was one of the principal issues driving the Army reforms of the 1980s.

In the 1970s, the Army had been turned into a much less effective force because of the Vietnam experience. American forces facing the Soviets in Europe were probably at their lowest level of readiness since the end of World War II. The Army's personnel-replacement program that gave the priority to units in Vietnam had drained those in Europe and created serious shortages of both officers and noncommissioned officers. But it was not only in Europe; personnel quality, readiness, and training throughout the armed forces were all at a post–World War II low. The aftereffects of conscription, draft dodging, and "ticket punching" brought troop morale and effectiveness to unheard-of depths. The ticket punching was particularly odious, as officers scrambled to get assignments that would enhance their careers, even if some of these tasks endangered the troops or simply made no sense. The too-short six-month combat tours for unit commanders were the prime example of ticket punching, as was the scramble to briefly get near the shooting in order to obtain some of the medals that were so freely given out during the Vietnam War. The effects of budget cuts in R&D, procurement, and maintenance during Vietnam and immediately after crippled equipment readiness and training.

Several things happened simultaneously in the early 1970s that brought the Army to this nadir. The killing of antiwar demonstrators by national

96

guardsmen at Kent State in 1970, racial conflicts, the 1971 My Lai investigation—which involved atrocities conducted by U.S. forces in Vietnam—and the withdrawal of U.S. ground forces from Vietnam in 1972 had not only eroded the public's confidence in the U.S. military. The military itself was facing a crisis of confidence. The principal events driving the reduction in readiness, however, were the Big RIF, anarchy in the ranks, and shrinking budgets.

THE BIG RIF (REDUCTION IN FORCE) 1970–1975

After Vietnam, the Army had to greatly reduce its size. This was called a reduction in force. As with previous RIFs, a lot of good people were let go and a lot of deadwood was retained. Moreover, the RIF caused a further decrease in combat effectiveness as the remaining troops took awhile to get used to the new crew they were now serving with.

In the early 1960s, Army strength had been 960,000 troops. This swelled to nearly 1.6 million in 1968. After President Nixon took office in 1969, on his promise to "settle the Vietnam issue," the cuts began. The changes in Army troop strength looked like this:

Army Troop Strength (in thousands)

1965	969
1966	1,200
1967	1,442
1968	1,570
1969	1,512
1970	1,323
1971	1,124
1972	811
1973	801
1974	783

The Army maintained a troop strength of 770,000 to 780,000 until the early 1990s, when yet another RIF took place.

To understand the impact of a RIF on a modern army, one must first appreciate the rank structure and normal turnover in the ranks. A modern army has about as many Indians as chiefs (one soldier for every NCO and officer). For example, in the late 1980s, the U.S. Army had the following rank structure:

Officers	14% (includes Warrant Officers)
NCOs	36%
Troops	50%

Warrant officers are a special case. They comprise about 14 percent of all officers (or about 2 percent of all Army personnel). They outrank all enlisted troops, but are in turn outranked by second lieutenants. Warrants are mainly technical specialists (often former NCOs) and helicopter pilots. As such, they do not command (in theory, anyway).

The high proportion of officers is a twentieth-century phenomenon. Before that, only about 5 percent of an army would be officers. The proportion of NCOs has also grown about as much as the officers. The increase in both these categories is largely a result of increased technology. More highly trained and educated troops are needed to operate and maintain all the increasingly complex weapons and equipment. NCOs today often have more responsibility, and deal with more complex situations, than many officers earlier in this century. Since pay is linked to rank, and more skilled people can be recruited only if you pay them what they want, the proportion of higher-ranking people in the armed forces has increased. This in itself is no big deal, as it's still the case that the highest-ranking 5 percent of the military generally run the show. A century ago, a major was considered an exalted rank; today you have to be a colonel to get the same effect. Rank inflation, so to speak.

A more meaningful difference has been the increased amount of training required to create an effective soldier. When conscription ended in 1972, many military professionals saw it as a very positive thing. When the draft was still in effect, half the Army was conscripts, or those who volunteered because of the draft. These troops were there for only two or three years. Including misfits (usually recruits) who were thrown out early, the lower-ranking half of the Army had to be replaced every two years. The half of the Army who are career professionals also lose 5 to 10 percent of their strength each year as a result of retirement, resignations, or medical reasons. Therefore, nearly 30 percent of the troops disappear annually. This is higher than wartime losses and is part of the reason why a wartime army is more competent than a peacetime one. In wartime, you stay "for the duration." While the losses in the combat units are high, the other 80 percent of the Army that does not get exposed to enemy fire gets better and better as a result of increased experience.

The Army got hurt worse by the RIF because it had expanded more than the other services. As the chart below shows, not all the services grew and contracted at the same rate during the Vietnam era.

Service	Increase 1964–1968	Decrease 1968–1975	Decrease 1964–1975
Army	61%	−50%	−19%
Navy	15%	−30%	−20%
Air Force	6%	−32%	−28%
Marines	62%	−36%	+3%
Overall	32%	−40%	−21%

In the Army of the early 1990s, some 100,000 officers and 250,000 NCOs (sergeants) are the long-term professionals who keep the military together and determine how effective the troops will be in combat. When the RIF began in 1970, there were over 200,000 officers in the Army, and over 400,000 NCOs. Note that not all officers are in the Army to make a career. Many stay for less than five years before returning to their civilian careers. This is particularly true when a war is going on and the number of officers must be rapidly expanded with qualified (and some unqualified) civilians. Thus only about 70 percent of the officers in Vietnam could be considered career officers, and some 80 percent of senior NCOs were career soldiers.

During Vietnam, as with most wars, a lot of additional officers and NCOs were needed in a hurry. In situations like this, the rapid addition of officers and NCOs causes a lowering in overall quality. Unlike earlier wars, the demands for junior officers and NCOs was much higher in Vietnam. There were several reasons for this lower quality of junior leadership in Vietnam:

1. The thirteen-month rotation policy meant that officers and NCOs had to be replaced every year. While many officers and NCOs did two or more tours in Vietnam, most were content to go once and leave it at that.

2. Since Vietnam was not a declared war, no one was in "for the duration," as was normal with other major wars. Thus conscripts (who made up an increasing proportion of the junior NCOs) would leave after their two-year term of service was up. Even troops who volunteered (and did three years) rarely did more than one tour in Vietnam.
3. While rotation and "undeclared war" were also present in Korea, Vietnam had the additional disadvantage of lasting longer (eight years of combat action versus three in Korea). Thus these factors caused problems in Vietnam that did not arise in Korea and few in the Army appreciated how big they would be.
4. Another new problem developed in Vietnam, as the senior NCOs who entered the Army in the early 1940s became eligible for their twenty-year retirement. Senior NCOs frequently stay for thirty years in order to get larger retirement benefits. But Vietnam changed a lot of minds, and going into the late 1960s, many of these experienced NCOs took their retirement as soon as they were eligible. Going into the early 1970s, the NCOs who had entered the Army during the Korean war also filed retirement papers in large numbers.

The end result of all this was the development of the Shake 'n Bake approach to obtaining junior NCOs. In this system, promising recruits were sent to an NCO course right after basic and advanced infantry training. Thus in less than a year these men went from civilian to junior NCO (usually "buck sergeant," or E-5 in the nine-level enlisted-rank structure). Many of these young NCOs did well in Vietnam, but too many did not. The Shake 'n Bakes did not have the experience of the traditional E-5, who generally had at least four or five years in the Army before becoming a sergeant. The new NCOs had the additional disadvantages of sullen troops, inexperienced officers, an unpopular war, and a formidable enemy.

The situation wasn't much better for the junior officers. Coming right out of West Point or college (via ROTC), they got a few months of additional training and then were sent to command platoons in Vietnam. As these ROTC lieutenants had only a three-year service obligation, they would do one Vietnam tour and, if they survived, leave the Army a year or so later. For morale purposes, the Army generally did not force troops to do back-to-back Vietnam tours, but allowed at least a year of service anywhere else between tours. Many officers and NCOs contrived to make that post-Vietnam tour longer, thus avoiding another tour in the bush.

Although there were many troops with combat experience, most of these left the service, and the quality of junior officers and NCOs steadily declined throughout the Vietnam War. Since the Army obtains its senior officers and NCOs from among the lower-ranking people, many of the Shake 'n Bake troops who stayed in began to move up in rank. When senior people retired or left, their positions had to be filled. Although many positions were left empty when no qualified candidates were available for promotion, most vacancies were eventually filled with whoever was available and met the minimum standards. In the past, many of these NCOs would not have been promoted, or at least would not have been promoted as quickly.

When the big RIF began in 1970, the Army knew it had an opportunity to rid itself of a lot of the deadwood that had accumulated during the Vietnam years. Junior officers were simply released from whatever remained of their three-year obligation, or were not allowed to sign on for another three or more years. Many officers with twenty years in were simply told they had to retire.

The Army has always been better prepared to deal with increasing and decreasing the number of officers it needs than the number of NCOs. Officers tend to remain officers as long as the Army will let them. Those who are not needed for active service can find a place in the reserves or National Guard. Retired officers are subject to recall, as their generous retirement pay has historically been considered something of a retainer. The junior officers, the lieutenants and captains, comprise two thirds of the officer strength and can be obtained quickly with the Shake 'n Bake method and by giving out promotions more quickly. Thus, when a wartime RIF comes, officer quality can be maintained in spite of the fewer number of officers in all ranks by:

1. Reducing higher-ranking officers to their lower, "permanent" rank. The most famous example of this was the Civil War–era general George Custer, who made that exalted "temporary" rank while still in his twenties. After the war his rank was reduced to its permanent level and in 1876 he died at Little Big Horn as a lieutenant colonel. This system was continued into the twentieth century, with notables like Douglas MacArthur going through the same process after World War I. MacArthur, unlike Custer, managed to stay alive and work his way back up to even higher rank. This was the incentive for officers to accept these postwar demotions.

2. Sending reserve officers back to the reserves or National Guard. That is, making them full-time civilians and part-time officers.
3. Forcing many officers, eligible for retirement, to retire. Sometimes special payments are offered to officers who do not have their twenty years in, to induce them to resign. In some cases, a lower-ranking officer is offered a job as an NCO, so he can complete his twenty years of active service and then retire as an officer. This was done with many officers during the Korean War and the late 1950s RIFs. Many of these officers had gotten battlefield promotion from NCO to officer rank and this was seen as a compassionate way to treat these veterans as well as a means to obtain some experienced NCOs.
4. Releasing junior officers in large quantities. All officers start out as lieutenants and there has to be a steady supply of new lieutenants to keep the system growing.

Despite the advantages, there were several downside aspects to this approach:

1. The wrong people were sometimes let go. Especially during the Vietnam RIF, a premium was placed on those who had their "ticket punched" correctly. A West Pointer with two tours in Vietnam was sure to stay, even at the expense of an officer who never graduated from college, received a battlefield commission, and was an ace in combat and a natural leader of men. A lot of these warrior types were not too pleased with the state of the Army anyway, and were not all that sorry to leave.
2. There was a lot of organizational confusion as officers were shuffled this way and that. Officers often receive training that makes them, on paper anyway, qualified to do several different jobs. In the wake of the RIF, many found themselves doing something they had received training for years ago but were no longer very good at. Moreover, most units lost whatever little cohesion they had as officers came and went with even greater than usual frequency. The officers in question didn't know their men or units very well and the many personnel and organizational problems in the post-Vietnam Army were thus made worse.
3. Promotions became very slow for five to ten years after the RIF, and many able officers realized that it would take much longer to advance in their chosen profession, despite their proven abilities. This, plus poor

troop quality, low defense budgets, and better prospects in the civilian sector, caused a constant brain drain from the Army during the 1970s.

4. Morale was hurt. The fear, uncertainty, and doubt caused by the RIF, and the future outlook for the Army in general, did little for troop or officer morale. Even without the RIF, things would have been bad. The RIF just made it worse.

5. There was senior-leader bloat. After the RIF, there tended to be, proportionately, a larger number of generals and admirals. The few hundred senior officers in the armed forces are all capable men, and know each other quite well. These guys (and a few women) stick together and look out for each other. This is especially true in times of crisis, like a major RIF. The result is that generals and admirals have better job security than other officers. There is some justification for this, as these officers are generally the best and the brightest, the result of a ruthless and demanding selection process. However, the natural urge of senior officers to look out for each other results in the creation of more permanent generals and admirals. In this century, this has proved to be a very difficult process to reverse.

Overall, the Army's officer corps came out of Vietnam in better shape than the NCO corps. Noncommissioned officers, while similar to commissioned officers in that they manage and lead troops, are different in several crucial ways.

NCOs specialize more. A sergeant is trained in one specialty and generally stays there for his entire career. This is one reason why senior NCOs are so valuable. Unlike the officers (or anyone else), the senior sergeant has seen it all, done it all, and knows what works and what doesn't. Junior officers with any sense at all pay close attention to their senior NCOs. Officers often are trained to do several jobs and frequently work in several different areas during their careers. Officers are meant to be specialists; NCOs *are* the specialists.

NCOs take longer to train. Only after Vietnam did the Army begin formal training programs for NCOs. Before that, you learned how to be an NCO on the job, and by watching senior sergeants do it. This took a long time, and because of its informal nature, gave uneven results. It took from ten to fifteen years of service to produce a ''seasoned'' NCO. Officers spend a lot more time in school, learning new jobs more quickly and thoroughly. Once more NCO schools opened in the 1970s and 1980s, the Army began to get more competent sergeants sooner. It still takes over ten years to produce a good first sergeant (the NCO who runs a company of one hundred to three hundred troops). There's often no substitute for long experience at something.

NCOs do not switch between the reserves and active forces as much as officers, nor do they use "temporary" ranks in wartime. This is a matter of custom, but the result is to make it more difficult to obtain additional effective sergeants on short notice.

Three events gutted the NCO corps after Vietnam, and we've already mentioned the more obvious one: the loss of World War II and Korea era sergeants during and shortly after Vietnam. Many of these people were going to get out at the twenty-year mark anyway. But the ugly atmosphere of Vietnam caused an even larger number to depart. These were the ones the Army could least afford to lose—those senior NCOs who would normally stay to the thirty-year mark or beyond.

A second blow was, ironically, the loss of conscripts. This event is often overlooked. But the fact is that many of the best NCOs would never have gone into the Army had they not been forced to by the draft. A number of draftees found the military life to their liking and remained to become career sergeants. This made a big difference, because prior to World War II and permanent peacetime conscription, the volunteers were often the dregs of society. In the past, Army pay was low and treatment worse. It was quite a shock to all concerned in the early 1940s when the better-educated civilian draftees met the peacetime-era sergeants. By the end of World War II, the NCO corps had been transformed into a more effective body. The golden age of NCO quality came to an end when the World War II and Korean War vets left by the early 1970s, and the draft was ended, cutting off the supply of new quality NCOs. This was felt throughout the Army, but particularly in the noncombat areas (over 80 percent of the Army that doesn't handle weapons for a living). Although the volunteer Army of the 1970s offered better pay, it took nearly ten years of effort before the quality of the troops recruited returned to what it was during the peacetime draft.

The third problem was the widespread use of Shake 'n Bake NCOs. These troops were selected in basic training, using test scores and apparent leadership ability. After a few months of additional training, they were sent off to the front as sergeants (E-5). Those who were not killed in action, or relieved for incompetence, did well enough to survive. Some were outstanding; many just got by. Most left the Army when their time was up and those who remained were the primary candidates for senior NCO positions in the 1970s and 1980s. By world standards, these young sergeants were quite good, but by previous U.S. Army standards, they were not. The Army tried to maintain the high standards and often did not promote junior NCOs, even when there were severe shortages of unfilled senior NCO positions. Thus, in the mid-1970s, combat units often had only about half the NCOs they needed.

Given the numerous problems the post-Vietnam Army had, the loss of the experienced World War II and Korea era sergeants was made worse by the considerably lower effectiveness of the NCO corps in the 1970s. It was worse for the sergeants themselves who had to go through the 1970s. Many of these soldiers had served under the previous generation of NCOs and knew well what their lack of experience was costing them.

The Shake 'n Bake problem was felt most keenly in the combat units, where most of these newly minted sergeants originally went. However, many combat NCOs customarily move on to noncombat jobs when injuries make them no longer fit enough for the rough-and-tumble of combat-unit work. Thus many of the Shake 'n Bakes moved on to noncombat units and were promoted there.

In many ways, quality NCOs are more important to an Army's effectiveness than good officers. Sergeants provide the stability and continuity in a unit, as they spend more time in a unit and in their particular job. This is particularly true at the platoon and company level, where the senior NCOs make about as much as the officers they work for. This is not at all odd when you realize that a lieutenant (O-1 or O-2 pay grade) commanding a platoon has usually been in the service less than three years and his platoon sergeant (an E-7) has ten or more years of service. Both of these ranks have about the same rate of pay. The Army adjusts pay for number of years in the service. Thus an E-7 with ten years of service makes about 16 percent more than an E-7 with under two years of service. An E-7 with two years of service is very rare, but that's the way the Army makes up its pay tables.

Paying an NCO more than an officer also makes sense when you realize that the thirty-year-old platoon sergeant knows a lot more about running a platoon than the twenty-two-year-old second lieutenant. In practice, the lieutenant is getting on-the-job training from the platoon sergeant. In combat, the sergeant often ends up running the platoon by himself when the lieutenant gets killed or injured. A major source of battlefield commissions is sergeants who demonstrate extraordinary ability to do an officer's job (and are turned into officers on the spot, thus a "battlefield" commission).

This situation extends up to the next level of command, the company. This unit is headed by a first lieutenant (an O-2 with two to five years of service) or captain (an O-3 with three to seven years of service), assisted by a first sergeant (an E-8 with ten to twenty years of service). Again, the first sergeant often makes more than the officer commanding and the NCO will often take over command of the company if all four or five officers in the unit are put out of action. But at company and higher levels, the NCOs serve mainly as supervisors and advisers to the officers on what's going on in the ranks.

The post-Vietnam Army, with its low troop quality, lower troop morale, and breakdown in discipline, needed highly experienced NCOs more than at any other time in the Army's history. Initially, the experienced NCOs were not there. By the 1980s, things had turned around, but it was a rough decade for all concerned.

ANARCHY IN THE RANKS

By the mid-1970s, the U.S. Army was not a pleasant place to be. Discipline had begun to unravel during the last years of Vietnam. Things got worse in the 1970s. Drug use, racial animosities, low-quality troops, and inexperienced NCOs resulted in a crime wave on Army bases. Officers, and anyone else handy, were mugged by their own troops. Some were even murdered. Theft, brawling, and insubordination were rampant. Officers in many units were reluctant to enter barracks alone, or without a pistol on their hip. Few of these incidents made it into the civilian press. But the military has the records of thousands of courts-martial and criminal investigations to document a very unpleasant period in American military history.

This chaos was made worse by the efforts of many senior officers to play down these incidents. Thus many perpetrators were not prosecuted and were often quietly let out of the service (and sometimes not). In some ways, this encouraged the bad actors. If they didn't like being in the Army (and they were all volunteers at this point), all they had to do was bad-mouth an officer (or worse) and then be rewarded with their walking papers.

All of this led to continued departures of qualified officers and NCOs. Moreover, the sometimes dangerous conditions in the ranks led good troops to decide not to reenlist.

There were several stark indicators of this sorry situation of the 1970s.

One was AWOL (absent without leave) rates. In 1971, they stood at 177 per thousand. That is, 17.7 percent of the troops left their units without permission that year. Many of these AWOLs turned into desertion (the soldier leaves with no intention of coming back). By 1980, the rate had gone down to 40 per thousand and kept falling through the 1980s. But in the 1970s, an NCO never knew how many faces would be missing at morning roll call.

Another telling statistic is the percentage of troops who do not finish their first three-year enlistment. This is called First Term Attrition. These soldiers either desert, or are released from their service obligation. The usual reason for letting these soldiers go is that they can't do their jobs or have discipline problems. The First Term Attrition rate was 26 percent in 1971, but thereafter began to rise sharply. This figure peaked at 38 percent in 1974, but stayed at 37 percent in 1975 and 1976. It began to decline thereafter and continued to do so into the 1980s. This situation was actually worse than it appeared in the 1970s. Throughout this decade, the Army was unable to meet its recruiting goals. The recruiters always came up a few percent short on their quotas. The Army commanders knew that if they could not keep their strength up to what they were authorized, Congress would be tempted to adjust manpower levels downward to a rate that could be maintained. Thus there was enormous pressure on unit commanders to not toss out any troublesome soldiers unless they absolutely had to. In effect, a lot of problem soldiers were allowed to stay in. This did not do unit effectiveness or troop morale much good.

One could see what was going on by looking at the reenlistment rates for first-term troops and for career NCOs. For first-term troops, the rate went up through the 1970s, while that for the career troops went down. A lot of soldiers the Army didn't want, did want to stay in. The career NCOs, who had to put up with the poor performance of these troops, increasingly voted with their feet and abandoned their military careers. You could tell when things had picked up in the 1980s because more sergeants reenlisted.

SHRINKING BUDGETS

While the Army got enough money to offer competitive (with civilian jobs) pay to new recruits, there wasn't much left over to buy new or replacement equipment. Worse, there wasn't much money to train with existing equipment or, in many cases, even maintain it properly. A time-honored solution for dealing with rambunctious troops is to take them out into the field and practice war. But this is expensive, and the 1970s Army couldn't afford much of it. So the troops spent a lot of time in their barracks, getting into trouble.

The Vietnam War had been a costly affair, but most of the money went into operations within Southeast Asia. This was all lost, either in the operations themselves or when the United States pulled out of Vietnam and abandoned billions of dollars worth of installations and equipment. During the war, every other part of the Army was put on short rations. When Vietnam was over, there wasn't even money to recover from that decade of neglect.

The Army budget was cut to levels below what it had been before going into Vietnam. Most soldiers who were there during the 1970s remember it as a decade of rundown bases, ancient and ill-maintained equipment, and dispirited troops.

THE ARMS RACE HEATS UP

While the United States was pouring so many resources into Vietnam, the Soviets decided to expand their military. And expand it a lot. This went largely unnoticed for a while, partly because the Soviets are good at keeping secrets and partly because Americans were so distracted by Vietnam. In the early 1960s, the Soviet Union was still demobilizing troops and cutting defense expenditures. But a change of Soviet leaders in 1963 brought with it a Soviet decision to seek military superiority over the West. By the late 1960s, the Soviets were spending more on defense than the United States. We'll never know for sure just how much the Soviets were spending, as one aftereffect of the collapse of the Soviet Union was their acknowledgment that even they were not sure how much they were spending. One thing we did know, from satellite photos, was that there was suddenly a lot more Soviet military equipment sitting there, and every few years there was a new generation of weapons. The Soviets were not only building a lot more, they were spending enormous sums on developing new items. After 1965, the Soviets had increased their offensive capabilities against NATO by adding five tank divisions to their forces in Central Europe and significantly increasing the number of tanks in all units. The Soviets were outproducing the United States in all areas and were introducing new models much more frequently than anyone else. But of major concern, the Soviets were moving their forces to bases closer to the border with NATO, thus vastly increasing the danger of a surprise attack. After Germany was reunited in 1991, an inspection of the former East German army and its facilities revealed that the Warsaw Pact was even more ready to launch a surprise attack than the CIA had estimated.

By the early 1970s, even the slow learners realized that we had a full-blown arms race on our hands. No one knew quite what to make of it. The Soviets said little about their intentions, so most people in the West feared the worst. It was felt that the Soviets were seriously planning military operations against Western Europe. This meant that sufficient Western military forces had to be raised and their readiness improved to counter such a move. As the Soviets were rapidly expanding their ground, air, and naval forces, this meant that the West had to do likewise. By the end of the 1970s, most leaders in the West agreed to this and were taking action. Despite the credit President Reagan gets for "building up defense," the first U.S. "arms race" defense budgets were President Carter's doing. President Carter understood the military situation better than the conventional wisdom gives him credit for. A lot of this is partisan politics; the Republicans went out of their way to paint Carter and the Democrats as "antimilitary" during the 1980 presidential election. Some of this muck stuck permanently. In any event, the 1980s saw a return of the Cold War in the form of a very expensive arms race.

The increased U.S. defense spending, however, was not the primary solution to the Army's problems. It did provide funds to replace equipment and maintain what was already on hand. The additional money also went for increased training. But the Army had already come up with solutions to its most pressing problems: personnel quality and effectiveness. This is important to remember, because it is not always the case that money solves problems. More generally, it is people getting out there and doing something with whatever they've got.

THE SOLUTIONS

To solve the many personnel problems of the 1970s Army, a number of solutions had to be implemented simultaneously, and quickly. Fortunately, there were senior officers in charge who knew what had to be done and were able to do it. Moreover, enough quality officers, NCOs, and troops stuck it out to make the solutions work.

Officer Training

Through the 1970s and into the 1980s, the Army reformed its officer training program. The results were obvious in the 1990–1991 Persian Gulf operations (especially to foreign military officers and those who had seen American officers in action during past wars). The officer's formal education is a process that begins after the officer is commissioned (either from a service academy, ROTC, or Officers Candidate School). Between World War II and Vietnam there developed a system whereby the new officer immediately received two to five months of training in his specialty (Infantry, Armor, Quartermaster, etc.) and then went to work as a second lieutenant (O-1). Once an officer became a captain (O-3), there was a six-month-long (or more) advanced course, which taught staff work and the details of commanding a company-size unit.

Officers who get promoted to major may be (and usually are) sent to Command and General Staff School. This one-year course prepares officers for work on higher (brigade and above) staffs and introduces them to the situations they will encounter later in their careers. Beyond that there are more selective schools, like the Army War College and the National Defense University. Officers are also encouraged to attend civilian schools to obtain advanced academic degrees. Selected officers are sent to these schools at government expense, but many obtain degrees in their spare time and pay their own way. Officers can also apply for specialized military training (airborne, ranger, flight school, etc.), as well as technical courses with manufacturers of Army equipment (these courses are sometimes mandatory). Officers, since World War II, have spent a lot of time in the classroom. In many cases, officers will spend 20 to 30 percent of their military service in training courses of one kind or another.

During the 1970s and 1980s, there were many changes in the content of these traditional courses. But several new items were added. One of the most important was the CASSS (Combined Arms and Services Staff School, or CAS^3). All officers attend this course before their ninth year of service. While somewhat similar to the Command and General Staff School course, the nine-week CASSS course prepares officers for staff work (especially at battalion and brigade level) and handling weapons and equipment outside their area of specialization. In addition to getting the infantry officer more familiar with what armor, artillery, and engineer officers do, CASSS basically prepared officers to do staff work: write papers, do briefings, prepare complex battlefield messages in a standard (easily understood) format, write OPORDS (operational orders, telling troops what to do during battle), and calculate logistics requirements.

A key innovation was the addition of a second year to the Command and General Staff course. This second year took only the top graduates of the first-year course. This second year emphasized how to fight at the operational level (division and corps). In other words, this course began training in fighting with the combined arms team (all weapons available in the Army). This is the only way to fight and win and something that was given much greater emphasis after Vietnam. Officers were also taught to deal with the increasing use of computer technology and technology in general. Computers are now a common item on the battlefield and American officers are probably the most proficient soldiers in the world in this area.

Because this "Operational Art" (training how to actually fight a battle) was new for the Army, and enthusiastically accepted, the graduates were called "Jedi Knights" for their expected battlefield prowess. This prowess turned out to be real, as the 1991 Gulf War demonstrated. It was the graduates of the Jedi Knight course who did much of the planning, and a lot of the execution, for the ground fighting in the 1991 Gulf War. It was, so to speak, their final exam. They passed.

Electronic Field Training

First the Navy in the 1960s, then the Air Force in the 1970s, and finally the Army in the early 1980s began extensive use of electronic aids to provide less expensive and more realistic training. This is discussed more extensively elsewhere when we cover the National Training Center (NTC). While the NTC and electronic training aids were costly, they were still an inexpensive way of obtaining a vast improvement in battlefield capability.

Ruthless Culling of the Ranks

The horrendous personnel problems of the 1970s Army were dealt with in a draconian fashion. Soldiers were increasingly released early if they proved more trouble than they were worth. Drugs, a major problem since Vietnam, were the cause of many of these early discharges. Drug testing began in the early 1980s and any officer or senior NCO who tested positive was immediately thrown out. Other ranks got one warning and a mandatory rehab program. By 1983, discipline and troop quality were noticeably improved. The recruits who came in during the 1980s had a much better time of it and many of them passed the word on to their civilian friends. The Army began to attract a better-quality recruit and by the late 1980s overall troop quality was the best it had ever been in peacetime. This was partially due to a weak economy, but the good word of mouth was far more important.

NCO Training

One item most senior officers (and sergeants in general) are most proud of was the much improved NCO selection and training introduced throughout the 1970s and 1980s. Senior sergeant promotions were now selected centrally (at the Pentagon), like those of officers. NCOs got more training courses. During the "culling out" of the 1980s, promotion standards were maintained, even if it meant shortages of NCOs. The Army believed, rightly, that it was better to be short a lot (often half or more) of the qualified sergeants in a unit rather than promote just anyone. Before long, officers and troops all realized that an NCO was a highly qualified individual, not just someone who was moved up because there was an opening. The morale among sergeants, which had taken a big hit during and immediately after Vietnam, improved. The special schools for training NCOs not only created more capable sergeants but added a bit of prestige to the profession. The officers had always had their professional schools; now the NCOs had theirs too. With better sergeants, the capabilities of the troops and units grew. Desert Storm was no fluke or walkover. The victory was won on the backs of a world-class NCO corps.

After the RIF

It took the Army over ten years to recover from the post-Vietnam RIF. It was a recovery not everyone, in or out of uniform, expected the Army to make. History was against the recovery, as peacetime is usually an occasion for armies to develop a lot of bad habits. But the Army went straight from its 1970s "RIF Recovery Program" to a decade of reform in the 1980s.

But now, in the 1990s, another RIF looms. More budget cuts. More changes in doctrine and a new cast of potential enemies. Whether the Army can repeat its success remains to be seen.

CHAPTER

Reform

The shock of the rapid operations and massive lethality of the 1973 Arab-Israeli War galvanized the Army into a reform movement led by General William DePuy. In some respects, it was a false start because of the constraints of the national policy of détente. The major players were a small number of senior generals and the younger officers who worked for them. The principal document this crew produced was the 1976 edition of Field Manual 100-5 (the Army's "how to fight" manual). Following its appearance, there was nearly a decade of debate and intense thinking about what the modern battlefield was and how an army could best prevail on it. The new emphasis was on "coming as you are" to war.

The decade of the 1970s was truly a paradoxical period for the American military, especially the Army. During a period that was one of the low points in its history, it would emerge as the greatest fighting machine in the history of warfare. America was, against all historical experience, exceptionally well served by the peacetime military leaders of this period. As bad as the 1970s were for the American military, it could have been even worse. The military could have fallen victim to the "Defeat Disease" of searching for scapegoats and finger pointing at the civilian leadership over the outcome of events in Vietnam. The television images of American helicopters evacuating people from Saigon at the end of the war will be long remembered with chagrin and sorrow by the military. However, instead of self-defeating searches for scapegoats, American military leaders pulled together to develop a plan of reform that would be tested in the Persian Gulf. They would seize on the 1973 Mideast War to serve as the catalyst to refocus the military on Europe. That war's lessons were used to develop new doctrine, organizations, equipment, training techniques, and ways of viewing the battlefield to meet the challenges of the future, not the past. These reforms, along with new leadership and personnel programs in the 1970s, would become the foundation for the even more vigorous reforms of the 1980s. These two decades of effort gave us the quality military that made it possible, within twenty-four months, for the Cold War to end, Panama to be liberated from a dictatorship, and Iraqi troops to be overwhelmed and expelled from Kuwait.

The contrast between the American Army of August 1973 and the American Army of August 1990 is mind-boggling. The Army of 1973 was in the throes of coping with the fallout from the Vietnam War. Although the American soldier had done well during the early phases of that war, this changed in the later periods. By 1969 the emphasis was on keeping friendly casualties to a minimum by deemphasizing maneuver and concentrating massive firepower on the enemy. The troops sensed this, and some units began to have major morale problems that resulted in drug abuse, attempts on officers' lives, and racial problems. This did not go unnoticed back home.

The Vietnam experience had created pressure to bring the soldiers home not only from Southeast Asia but also from Europe. In 1971, Senate Majority Leader Mike Mansfield introduced an amendment to reduce by about half the U.S. forces permanently stationed in Europe. The amendment was narrowly defeated, but a majority of the Senate indicated a desire for some reductions. In an environment of low morale, with a dismal budget future, and calls from Congress to bring American soldiers home, the Army was searching for ways to attract quality young people for its new volunteer Army.

With the drain of resources to support primarily an infantry and airmobile confrontation in Vietnam, the Army had lost over a decade of effort in the Soviet-inspired arms race. There was little hope for any significant improvements for the foreseeable future. The services were locked in competition for the declining budgets. It was one of the low points in the history of the United States Army.

What saved the Army was someone else's war, and the unexpected way that war was fought. In October 1973, the Arabs attacked Israel. Israel and its Arab neighbors had been at loggerheads ever since Israel was founded (with the support of America and some of its European allies) in 1948. The Western support of Israel gave the Soviets an opportunity to increase their presence in the Mideast. Arab nations were eager to accept generous offers of Soviet weapons and military advisers. This aid increased enormously after the mortifying defeat the Arabs suffered in their 1967 War with Israel. By 1973, most Arab armies were armed with Soviet weapons and, to a large extent, trained to fight in the Soviet style. The 1973 War was the first major confrontation where two forces were ready to fight each other with weapons similar (and often identical) to those of NATO and the Warsaw Pact. It was a sobering experience. In just over two weeks, the Israelis lost nearly five hundred tanks while the Arabs lost over two thousand. It was more than the high lethality and intensity of the battles; history is replete with battles that had massive casualties. What was most alarming to the U.S. military was the realization that the Israeli forces, which had previously been considered invincible by many American officers, had almost collapsed under the massive surprise attack of the Arabs. The Arabs had used Russian weapons, equipment, and, to a large extent, doctrine and tactics. If this was what the Arabs could do, what were the Russians now capable of in Central Europe? Equally troubling was the specter of the 1967 Arab-Israeli War, where the Israelis had less capable weapons than NATO had at the time, and handily smashed the Soviet-equipped Arab armies. But in 1973, new generations of Soviet weapons were in Arab hands, as well as new Soviet tactics. In 1973, the massive modernization program the Soviets had begun in the 1960s was being noticed in the West. The 1973 War made this arms race a vivid danger to the West, and America in particular.

A host of researchers rushed to the Middle East following the cease-fire to gather lessons. Some of the key lessons were as follows:

1. The importance of balanced teams of combined arms. Israeli tank forces without infantry support had been decimated by Egyptian antitank forces. Despite repeated battlefield lessons in this century, units consisting wholly of tanks or infantry still tended to attack without the assistance of other arms (especially artillery). This often happens at the beginning of a war, when the lessons of the last war are at their dimmest. Ideally, attacks are made with tanks, infantry, artillery, and aircraft cooperating closely.

2. Modern weapons had increased in lethality by more than ten times since World War II. This had been suspected for some time, but now it was proved. Paper and computer calculations indicated that the more powerful modern weapons would be more lethal. More powerful weapons

do not always create more casualties, as the defending troops have strong incentives to find ways to avoid the increased chance of destruction. It takes a war to do that. But the new weapons were also faster, and the fighting proceeded at a more furious pace. There wasn't time for the troops to figure out how to cope with many of the new weapons before the war was almost over. The lessons learned in the 1973 War had to be passed on to American and NATO troops before the Soviets could take advantage of a similar situation in Central Europe. This situation gave Western generals the cold sweats, as they tended to fear that the Soviets had developed some new approach to offensive warfare and the results of the 1973 War tended to confirm this.

3. Training was critical to surviving and winning on the modern battlefield. This was an old lesson that traditionally gets forgotten during peacetime. There was no mistaking the superior effectiveness of the more successful units on both sides during the 1973 War. The Egyptians had trained hard and long. The Israelis had ignored this.

4. Modern air-defense weapons created severe problems for close air-support aircraft. The Soviets had given the Arabs a new generation of battlefield antiaircraft missiles and radar-controlled guns. The U.S. Air Force was convinced that this would happen; the Israelis were not. The U.S. Air Force was right. The Israelis had declined to purchase the expensive U.S. electronic countermeasure equipment. These devices had been designed to negate the effect of the new Soviet weapons, but the Israelis thought this was too expensive for them and that pilot skill could accomplish the same thing. The Israelis were wrong and they lost scores of aircraft as a result.

5. Electronics had added a new dimension to warfare, allowing communications to be jammed or more easily overheard by the enemy. The 1973 War was the first time post–World War II electronic-warfare devices had been used on a large scale between two mechanized armies, and the results were yet another surprise to the Israelis, who found the Soviet-supplied jamming gear quite capable of disrupting communications. Actually, electronic warfare had been used quite a lot in Vietnam, but an atmosphere of secrecy, and a public attitude of "so what," kept this story in the shadows.

6. The complexity and intensity of combat had expanded at an alarming rate. Ground and air units were able to move faster, for a longer period

of time, and generate more firepower than in any past war. This made it more difficult to command during these fast-moving battles.

7. The Israeli intelligence service, one of the best in the world, had failed to foresee the extent and potential effectiveness of the Arab attack. If Israel could be tactically surprised, why not NATO? This was possibly the most serious issue. NATO had invested heavily in creating intelligence organizations that would provide a timely warning of an impending Soviet attack. It was well known that the Soviets were masters at the art of military deception. They had provided instructors for the same Egyptians who got by the much-respected Israeli intelligence establishment. It didn't take too much imagination to conjure up what the Egyptians' teachers could do to NATO intelligence efforts. The fear was that with a successful surprise attack, the Soviets might very well be able to seize most of Western Europe before NATO could mobilize and reinforce its troops.

The 1973 Mideast War was not the only factor that motivated the American armed forces to change their thinking. In that same year, General William E. DePuy became the first commander of the newly formed Training and Doctrine Command (TRADOC). The mission of TRADOC was to develop ways to fight and to train the troops in the new methods (whatever they might be). This in itself was a revolutionary approach to the uniquely twentieth-century problem of keeping up with military change, and making sure all the troops kept up also. The 1973 War gave General DePuy a unifying force to make a fundamental change in how the United States Army approached its job. Bill DePuy was typical of the post-Vietnam generals. Most of them saw a need for drastic change, and DePuy found himself in a position to do something about it.

While the national strategy was putting forth the concept of sufficiency and détente, General DePuy and his staff and commanders were emphasizing development of new tactics. This had always been the weak link in the American Army. We could produce weapons and put civilians into uniform, but we generally failed to make the weapons and troops work effectively together. This was especially true when compared to our opponents. The Germans demonstrated this time and again during World War II. The price paid was dead American soldiers and a very expensive way of fighting. DePuy sought to provide ways for Americans to fight and win outnumbered in the crucial battles of a future war. By concentrating on the organizing and employment of weapons rather than on units and formations, TRADOC began creating the Army that finished a war with only a three-day ground battle in 1991.

DePuy had more to worry about than simply reforming the Army. The ground forces did not, and could not, operate alone. DePuy was supported by most of the senior Army generals. This was crucial, otherwise TRADOC wouldn't have been created and DePuy wouldn't have gotten the job of running it. But these generals also made it possible for DePuy to gain the cooperation of other commands in the Army, other services, and key foreign armies (especially West Germany and Israel). Thus DePuy was able to gain the assistance of General Robert J. Dixon, commander of the Tactical Air Command. This was a key alliance, as the Air Force was still responsible for providing tactical air support for ground troops. This Air Force support was crucial, not just because it was a separate service but because many senior Air Force leaders were decidedly lukewarm about close cooperation with the Army. A major DePuy accomplishment, and one often overlooked, was the forging of new links with the Air Force.

Within the U.S. Army, DePuy also received the strong support of General Creighton Abrams, the Army's Chief of Staff, and eager cooperation from General Walter T. Kerwin, the commander of Forces Command (FOR-SCOM). Cooperation from FORSCOM was crucial, as TRADOC proposes and FORSCOM disposes. It is FORSCOM that actually supervises the training of units and sends them overseas to the field commanders. DePuy was supported by an exceptionally able staff and also had the cooperation of the majority of the senior officers in the various branches (Infantry, Armor, Artillery, etc.). While DePuy was the sparkplug and point man for the reform, it was very much a group effort. Someone had to get out front and DePuy was not shy about taking that role. But there was a widespread desire for reform within the Army, and without this, DePuy's efforts would have been futile.

DePuy even sought assistance overseas. He and his staff constantly exchanged views and ideas with the leaders and troops of the Israeli and West German armies. DePuy's interest in the German Army was based on a number of factors. First, if there was to be a major war in Central Europe, the Germans would be America's principal ally on the battlefield. General Abrams wanted to make certain that there was close cooperation with them.

Second, DePuy recognized the superior experience and traditions of the Germans in tactics and unit organization. The Germans might have lost their last two wars, but they were more often successful on the battlefield than anyone else. DePuy had firsthand experience against the Germans during World War II. Even the Russians adopted many German doctrinal and organizational techniques after that war. So did the Israelis, which is something Israel doesn't discuss officially. Israeli officers and troops are less circumspect on the matter, being quite willing to admit the German origins of many of their fighting techniques.

Thus prepared, General DePuy led the effort to utilize the lessons from the 1973 War, and to develop a doctrine that would emphasize fighting outnumbered and winning. General DePuy worked closely with key commanders and their staffs. One of these crucial commanders was General Donn Starry, who at the time was a major general and commander of the Armor Center and commandant of the Armor School at Fort Knox. Because a future war was seen as one dominated by armored vehicles, it was essential to get the Armor Center involved in the new ideas. General Starry continued to push reforms throughout the 1970s, and his intellectual force would be a major factor in developing additional innovations in the 1980s. Starry would also eventually became commander of TRADOC and father of the concept of AirLand Battle doctrine. This new doctrine was applied successfully in the 1990 war with Iraq.

DePuy got his ideas into print as official doctrine in July 1976, with Army Field Manual FM 100-5 (Operations). He used many historical examples (from World War II and the Arab-Israeli wars) and compared these to contemporary situations. The manual was full of these examples and profusely illustrated "tricks of the trade." The use of realistic graphics to show how the new tactics worked was also a striking departure from past Army manuals. Even if you only glanced at it, you could tell that this manual was "new." The intense and exhausting 1973 Mideast War had convinced the authors of FM 100-5 that it was critical to win the first battles and then be capable of winning the second, third, and final battles. The nature of war had changed to the extent that the first battle could be the last battle if American forces lost. This was an unprecedented situation for the American military, which has historically been unprepared for its first battles but managed to win in the end. America has traditionally depended on winning by building up and bringing to bear the weight of its material and population after hostilities have been initiated. But the then current Central Europe situation was such that losing the first battle could mean losing Europe. While Europe had been lost before only to be retaken later, that was before nuclear weapons entered the picture. In the nuclear age it was considered essential to win the first battle for the defense of Europe to avoid one or both sides resorting to nuclear weapons. Thus there was more at stake than simply winning the first battle.

Successfully implementing the doctrine required a major shift in how the U.S. Army dealt with readiness, mobilization, and the traditional ways of operating on the battlefield. General DePuy also became convinced that a new approach to command and control must be implemented to cope with the increasing complexity, intensity, and lethality of modern warfare. It was almost an impossible task for a commander to coordinate the concentration of combat power at the right time and place in modern combat. In the early nineteenth century Napoleon had to be concerned with approximately ten major functions. Today, a commander has over three times as many things to keep track of and coordinate. Napoleon, for example, didn't have to worry about electronic warfare, air power, or many other items. The battlefield has expanded into the dimensions of space and undersea operations while weapons have multiplied in range, lethality, and mobility many times over anything pre-twentieth-century commanders had to work with. Missiles, helicopters, air strikes, airborne troops, and chemical weapons made a big difference.

Part of the command and control problem was the issue of where a commander best positions himself on the battlefield. In early twentieth-century warfare, with its larger and more far-flung armies, most generals in charge of a battle rarely went near the fighting and usually made their decisions many miles behind the lines. The Germans in World War II developed a system that put the commander up front and a qualified Chief of Staff in the rear with the headquarters. The system enabled the Germans to fight on against heavy odds. With the commander up where the action was, and making decisions on the spot, the Germans were able to take better advantage of opportunities. A highly trained officer stayed at the unit headquarters as Chief of Staff and made all the key decisions one expected to come out of a headquarters. Although this technique wasn't enough of an advantage to win the war for Germany, it did win a lot of battles and prolong the fighting. These German techniques also caused more Allied than German troops to be killed or injured. Russian and American generals practiced the German technique at times during World War II, and the Soviets adopted a form of it after the war. General DePuy was aware of this and knew that "commanding up front," along with a good staff backing you up, was one way to overcome the overload twentieth-century commanders were getting buried with.

Army doctrine writers began emphasizing using mission orders (a key element in AirLand Battle doctrine) and the commander's "concept of operations" (general plan for the battle) as tools for integrating the thousands of tasks that modern-day commanders are required to coordinate. The "mission order" was simply telling subordinates what their general objective was and leaving it to them to figure out the best way to get the job done. The "commander's concept of operations" was the use of a concise statement by the senior commander as to what he wanted done. The staffs and subordinate commanders would then work out their own plans without requiring the senior commander to lay out everything in excruciating detail. These were concepts that the Germans had used successfully on the battlefield in World War II. To make sure these concepts worked, all the subordinate commanders had to memorize and practice the same set of "correct solutions" for various tasks. For example, when different types of units were ordered to move to a certain position and attack and defend, they would do it "by the book" (FM 100-5, and a collection of even more detailed manuals). These manuals don't tell you exactly how to do it every time, but they do lay down procedures and timetables that allow any other commander you are working with to easily figure out how you are going to get there, in what formation, and approximately how long it will take. This approach allowed the commander to give his intent by giving general (and succinct) orders to a number of subordinates without worrying overly much about the subordinate units lapsing into confusion with the commander and each other.

DePuy's approach required all officers and troops to be retrained. The new methods were unlike all that had been used before and quite unfamiliar to most American troops. These new techniques provided the guidelines for the development and purchase of an array of computers, software, and communications equipment that is available today to unify the efforts of thousands of men and women performing thousands of essential tasks on the modern battlefield. Even with everyone operating the same way, the complexities of modern warfare required enormous communications capabilities so that the dozens of different units could keep in touch to resolve small problems before they became large ones.

THE FM 100-5 DEBATES

DePuy's FM 100-5 was a controversial document on several levels. Although the doctrine in the 1976 edition of FM 100-5 addressed both offensive and defensive operations, it was DePuy's new (for the U.S. Army) concept of "active defense" that received the most attention and resulted in a debate over the viability of FM 100-5 itself. One of the purposes for the active defense, as defined and described in FM 100-5, was to force the enemy to mass his forces together so that he would be more vulnerable to the concentrated firepower of the defending force. It was a defensive tactic, but it required the friendly forces to be mobile and able to maneuver on the battlefield to keep the enemy off balance and unable to launch a set-piece attack against a static defender (a favored Soviet technique). Active defense is an ancient technique in warfare, which consists of deceiving or maneuvering the enemy into gathering a lot of his forces in such a way that you can hit him with your maximum amount of firepower. Today it is done with mines, bombs, and artillery. Thousands of years ago it was done with bows and arrows. In some cases, such as Hannibal's massacre of the Romans at Cannae, the victor simply tricked the enemy into massing together so that the defender could not effectively use his troops. All of this was a novel concept for the U.S Army and it was not received enthusiastically by everyone. After all, with the possible exception of Vietnam, the U.S. Army had never lost a war. But DePuy didn't dispute that point. What DePuy was trying to do was prevent America from losing a future war. Thus DePuy had to put untried (by Americans) ideas up against bureaucratic inertia and the weight of various interpretations of history.

Active defense was attacked by numerous civilian and military critics. One of the more bizarre assertions was that it was too radical for American sensibilities. This implied that the U.S. units engaged in rapid maneuvers would likely move into part of Eastern Europe in order to defend Western Europe. This certainly made the Soviets nervous, and made some Western critics nervous because it was making it difficult to get the Soviets to talk about arms reductions. On the other end of the spectrum there were those who dismissed the active defense as typically static, defensive American thinking spruced up with a few new buzzwords. Both criticisms were the result of not doing a little homework and appreciating the rich historical lineage of the new approach. The active defense was an offensive doctrine that pushed mobility and flexibility. By American standards, it was different, and this was the source of most of the criticism.

The tragedy of the 1976 edition of FM 100-5 was that DePuy didn't get his point across. The essence of the active defense doctrine was understanding and exploiting the advantages of the defender. The fundamentals that it set forth were:

Understanding the Enemy. This was something the United States rarely tried to do in peacetime, or even, at times, during a war. In the early 1960s, there was a lot of good work on Soviet and Chinese armed forces published by the military. This gave the officers and troops some knowledge of whom they might be fighting. But in the mid-1960s it was decided that such information was too sensitive for just anybody to see and it was classified and withdrawn. This was plain silly, but few were willing to openly challenge such "security considerations." When DePuy took over TRADOC, he again began publishing useful data about potential enemies. A major contribution in the effort to provide the entire Army with a better understanding of Soviet forces was the outstanding *Threat Manual on Soviet Forces* compiled by the BDM Corporation. Ironically, one of the people BDM had gone to for analysis of Soviet capabilities in the 1970s was Jim Dunnigan. The policy of publishing unclassified information on Soviet capabilities continued until the Soviet Union itself disappeared.

Seeing the Battlefield. This involves more than just having good maps and adequate air reconnaissance. It's most important to know what to look for and when to look for it. DePuy taught the troops what different types of terrain mean to different friendly and enemy units and how this would change with the weather and time of day. DePuy pushed for better maps, better reconnaissance, and especially, quicker transmission of recon information to the troops who would need it. This approach to looking at the battlefield was one of the most profound changes U.S. troops had undergone since Vietnam.

Concentrating at the Critical Times and Places. Or, as one American Civil War general put it, "Getting there first with the most." This concept is the most ancient of military techniques, and the most difficult to pull off in combat. Everything works against you: the weather, the enemy, and your own organization and equipment (or lack of it). This was where FM 100-5's emphasis on speed and coordination came in. If you were faster and better coordinated than the enemy, you would get there "first with the most." This was what happened in the 1991 Gulf War. The Iraqis were not slow by historical standards, but the U.S. Army units were much faster. The American troops were faster because they were trained to move faster (in faster vehicles), think independently, and use a communications, command, and logistical system that could support that kind of speed and decision making. There was also no micromanagement as in Vietnam. The commanders in the Gulf got a lot of anxiety calls from Washington, but many only had to give progress reports, not receive detailed instructions about what to do.

Fighting as a Combined Arms Team. This is the most difficult task for a peacetime army, as it is impossible for training exercises to re-create all possible (and unforeseen) conditions of actual combat. DePuy and his commanders and staffs came up with a program of historical study and a wide range of wargames to solve these problems. The history made the troops more aware of how their jobs involved timeless problems, and that ancient solutions often worked again and again through the ages. The wargames were not the actual battlefield, but they were time better spent than sitting around just worrying about one's chances in combat. DePuy's solution was not perfect, but it was better than anything anyone else had ever come up with in the past.

Exploiting the Advantages of the Defender. All things being equal (which is not always the case), the defender has an advantage in combat. The more successful commanders in the past, and these are usually noted for their mobility and aggressiveness, have used the defense as a powerful weapon. In the defense you can use a small portion of your force to preoccupy a larger number of the enemy. This was what DePuy was advocating. With the bulk of the enemy force hammering away at your excellent defenses, you have sufficient forces remaining to get a good offense going. This was the "active" part of "active defense." DePuy was telling the troops to keep thinking, keep fighting, and always stay one step ahead of the enemy. This is the lesson of history and DePuy was trying to pass it on.

DePuy's basic concept was for the commander to organize his forces so that the following type of action would unfold:

First, a covering force would compel the adversary into revealing his strength, his location, and the general direction of his main attack. The covering force was basically 5 to 10 percent of the entire friendly force and especially trained to operate independently and in very vague situations. The covering force should have one of the better commanders, and his troops should have a lot of training in reconnaissance and moving fast.

Second, the commander would concentrate the mass of his combat power against the enemy by taking risks on the flank with economy-of-force operations. This means leaving most of the front (as represented by the presence of enemy units) empty, to be covered by small patrols, backed up by aircraft (particularly helicopters) and artillery. The commander is thus able to put a larger (than the enemy opposite them) force against the portion of the enemy front he decides to attack. This technique is also ancient, but few armies have been able to consistently make use of it. The most recent successful practitioners have been the Germans in World War II, where they used this concentration technique as a crucial component of their blitzkrieg doctrine. The Israelis and Russians adopted this blitzkrieg as their doctrine after World War II, and the Israelis successfully practiced it in all of their wars.

Third, the friendly forces then would fight a succession of advantageous actions exploiting the terrain and the concentration of combat power. It's not enough simply to mass more troops in an area than the enemy has. This third phase requires troops and commanders who have trained in similar terrain and situations and know how to take advantage of both. Here we can see why DePuy was not only trying to change the way American troops thought about combat, but also how they trained for it. The American ground forces that blitzed through Iraqi positions in 1991 followed the drill just described. It does work.

The key lessons from the 1973 War emphasized the importance of fighting as combined-arms teams and the use of tactics that would obtain the maximum effectiveness from superior new weapons. Both the Egyptians and Israelis had used new weapons successfully in the 1973 War, but only by virtue of hard training in peacetime. A major Israeli mistake before the war was to underestimate the extent and effectiveness of the training Egyptian troops were getting. Both nations also had to rapidly learn how to correctly use some of their new weapons under unforeseen battlefield conditions. The Israelis were more adept at this and thus were able to win the war. The 1973 conflict was a wake-up call for all the world's major armed forces. The message was that the era of World War II weapons and doctrine was now officially over. Those who did not adapt would be vanquished if they fought anyone who had acclimated.

THE CRITICISMS

As with any new doctrine, the critics weighed in from all sides. The criticism centered on several issues, the general ones being:

1. The emphasis on winning the first battle. This had never been crucial in the past, and accepting the loss of the first few battles was a hard habit for many military commanders to break. Of course, DePuy's point was that in Central Europe we couldn't afford to lose the first battle. Our European allies, particularly the Germans, were quite receptive to the idea of focusing on winning the first battle. If that battle were lost, Germany would be lost with it. West Germany was too small, physically, to survive two lost battles.

2. Lack of a large reserve. Given the differences in the number of troops available to the Warsaw Pact and NATO forces, it made no sense to keep a lot of the NATO troops in reserve while the rest got smashed by a more numerous Warsaw Pact host. But the American tradition was to maintain large reserves. This made sense when the reserve was being kept an ocean away from the larger enemy army. With an ocean to slow a victorious enemy down, the reserve could be used as a base upon which to build a larger army and go another round with the foe. In World War II, the Soviets were able to make similar use of reserves because Russia had empty land areas nearly as vast as the Atlantic Ocean. Although the country was battered for two years, Soviet reserves were safe in the heart of Asia, and were eventually built up and brought forward to smash the weakened Germans.

3. The requirement to concentrate forces by moving units laterally even in dense urban areas. Moving large Army units (brigades, divisions) quickly through urban areas in Europe was thought to be a particularly tricky undertaking. DePuy was aware that the Germans had formed large second-line army units to keep order in the urban areas and to assist the movement of ground units through these areas. While DePuy believed the Germans could keep the traffic moving, many other American generals did not.

4. The dependence on early detection of and timely communication about the enemy main thrust. We'll never know if NATO intelligence resources were up to the task of keeping an accurate eye on those elusive Russians. Much was made of the Russian ability to hide their movements. DePuy believed NATO would be able to maintain an accurate and up-to-date picture of what the Russians were doing. So he made this part of his new doctrine. At least he was willing to make a stand.

5. The vulnerability of concentrated forces to massive artillery attacks. The Russians were eager believers in the massive use of artillery against enemy troop concentrations. Moreover, the Russians now had long-range rockets with chemical and nuclear warheads. The Russians also had (in the 1970s) a new generation of more capable fighter-bombers (the MiG-27, etc.). Again, DePuy was willing to bet the farm that NATO could do it better. Post–Soviet-collapse discussion with Russian generals indicated that the Russians tended to agree with DePuy. But in the late 1970s, no one on our side knew that.

6. Highlighting only one scenario for the Warsaw Pact, the penetration scenario. This scenario had the Warsaw Pact concentrating most of its forces to penetrate NATO lines so they could romp around in the NATO rear area and get to NATO reserves before these reserves were ready to fight. There are certain risks in using the penetration scenario. This was a risk the Germans were willing to take in World War II with their blitzkrieg doctrine. More often than not, it worked. And blitzkrieg worked for most World War II armies that tried it. However, American and British forces had mixed success with these tactics. There were good reasons why it sometimes failed, but American generals tended to remember the failures, not the reasons why these failures could have been turned into victories. Thus many senior leaders were concerned that the Warsaw Pact might use another tactic, such as infiltrating all across the front.

7. Overemphasis on attrition at the expense of maneuver. This is one area where the jury is still out. The Russian army planned to travel light in the first week or so of a Central European campaign. This meant that the combat units could survive a week or so after NATO units got into the Russian rear area. For this reason, FM 100-5 still put emphasis on destroying a lot of Russian units. But critics felt that if FM 100-5 was going to be the "Book of Blitzkrieg," it ought to be blitz all the way.

Much of the criticism could be argued to be unfair when the national and international political context in which it was written is taken into consideration. In the late 1970s, America's major military commitment was in Central Europe, where NATO troops faced more numerous Warsaw Pact forces. The doctrine FM 100-5 had set out was a clear solution to how American land forces could fight outnumbered and win even against the massive armor forces of the Warsaw Pact. It would be difficult to develop a clearer and more readable doctrinal manual. However, the criticisms had to be read in the context of the time that it was written. When the 1976 FM 100-5 came out, the following issues (some of them contradicting each other) were being debated among the political leadership, the media, and the public:

1. Détente. In the 1970s, the last thing the American public wanted was another war, or threat of war. The official, and actual, policy toward Russia was détente. This allowed for defense, but not for anything that smacked of aggressive adventurism.
2. Sufficiency. But Russia still maintained the largest peacetime army in history and most of it was aimed at Western Europe. To have a chance at playing power politics with the Russians, there had to be effective NATO forces in Europe. If not in numbers, then in quality and fancy footwork.
3. Bring the American soldiers home. No more increases in the forces in Europe, and growing pressure to bring home many of those already there. Because of this attitude, the units overseas would have to make the most of what they already had. It was, however, permissible to ship over new doctrine and training methods. FM 100-5 was the only reinforcement the troops could receive, so DePuy tried to make it count.
4. Constrained defense budgets. The aftereffects of Vietnam cut defense budgets through the 1970s. The troops had to go with what they had, and sometimes not even that if what they had was falling apart from old age.

THE FM 100-5 REVOLUTION

Despite the debates and criticisms, the doctrine in the 1976 edition of FM 100-5 would set the framework for developing the winning team that would help end the Cold War and win Desert Storm. It moved the Army to concentrate on how to win outnumbered. It revolutionized military thought with the emphasis on the firepower of weapons systems and the practical use of technology.

As opposed to previous doctrine, FM 100-5 emphasized the importance of air power in the combined arms battle. The fact that an A-10 ground-attack aircraft could carry thirty times as much ordnance (bombs and bullets) as its World War II equivalent (a P-47) was part of the air-power revolution. The other lesson came from the closing days of Vietnam, where one guided bomb destroyed a bridge, after massive attempts with conventional bombs and the loss of many aircraft had failed. These two aspects of modern aircraft were not lost on the doctrine writers. The traditional methods for employing aircraft on the battlefield had been fundamentally changed. The challenge would be in finding how to capitalize on these advancements.

FM 100-5 provided the underlying structure for revitalizing the importance of the commander's concept of operation as a tool of command and control for integrating and coordinating the thousands of individual tasks that must be performed at the right time and place on the battlefield. It also set in motion the reform of the training programs that would help develop the professional Army. But just as important, the active defense doctrine would serve to foster a debate by both military and civilian experts that would stimulate the intellectual development of military strategic and tactical thinking to new levels. Just as the 1973 Mideast War was used as a catalyst for the reforms of the 1970s, the debate over the doctrine in the Army's 1976 edition of FM 100-5 would be used to help foster the development of AirLand Battle doctrine (published in the 1982 edition of FM 100-5) and provide the bases of many of the military reforms in the 1980s.

CHAPTER

8

Reeducation

While the senior leaders of the Army agreed on what had to be done, these new ideas had to be transmitted to the officers and troops. This was done via a wide-ranging reform of how the Army trained everyone.

Winning the first battle decisively and doing it with a minimum of casualties were not the only precedents achieved in Desert Storm. The American military also broke the mold in having its senior officers prepared and ready to win the first battles. The outcome of Desert Storm was no fluke. Going all the way back to the War of 1812, when war came, most American senior officers had to go through a major reeducation process of adapting to a new enemy, new weapons systems, and unforeseen circumstances and learning new tactics and doctrine. All this had to be done under fire. Historically, America has paid a high cost in lives for this learning process. Studies of initial battles fought by U.S. forces since the War of 1812 have concluded that one of the primary reasons for the lack of success by American forces in these battles has been the inadequate training and readiness of commanders and staff above the battalion level. In Desert Storm, the senior officers were superbly prepared to fight and win. The 1990 U.S. commanders knew and understood their enemy, the terrain, their equipment, tactics, and doctrine, and they had the confidence that comes from having the edge. This was an officer corps that had shed its past history of traditionally not being ready to fight and win its first battles. But it was a transformation that was the product of exceptional vision and hard work by many dedicated and committed people in and out of uniform. It was a process that was twenty years in the making.

When American investigation teams were sent to Israel after the 1973 Mideast War, it became clear to many of them, still steeped in the lessons of World War II fighting, that warfare had fundamentally changed in a number of ways. Modern conflict with conventional weapons was now approaching the destructiveness that was thought to be typical only of nuclear weapons. Also, the world had entered a new age, where combat in developing countries was no longer between ill-trained mobs using simple, low-tech warfare requiring unsophisticated weapons. The study teams were also amazed at the sheer intensity of modern combat and its fatiguing impact on commanders. After receiving the reports from the study teams, many senior leaders in the American military became convinced that new educational and training programs were needed to help improve the readiness of senior commanders to adapt to the new changes.

The massive lethality of modern weapons, the high mobility that modern tanks and helicopters provide, the long, vulnerable supply lines involved for U.S. forces, the relatively limited distance between opposing forces (especially in Europe), and the high probability of short-warning attacks could make the next war very brief in duration. The implication of a brief war was that America could not rely on having the time to mobilize its vast resources and overwhelm the enemy. It also meant that there would be little time available to adapt to new tactics and doctrine.

It was imperative, with the changes in modern warfare, that American forces be prepared to come as they are and be ready to fight outnumbered and win immediately. The doctrine and tactics of U.S. forces had to be up-to-date, as there would be little or no opportunity to experiment on the battlefield. It meant that equipment and weapons had to be modern and designed to be effective, efficient, and deployable. This was necessary not only to overcome being outnumbered, but also to help compensate for the unavoidably long U.S. supply lines. It meant that the volunteer Army had to be of high quality and trained to have the fighting edge. You cannot weed out the deadwood on the eve of battle. This meant that officers must also be superbly prepared to perform their battlefield tasks at the unpredictable moment when war broke out. This was a radical departure from the past practices of the American military.

Ever since 1915, the Army educational and training system had been designed to support mobilization for war. Until 1973, it was assumed that forward deployed forces along with allied forces could contain any attack from an aggressor and thereby give ample time to mobilize and train new forces. These new forces would be committed to battle as soon as they were ready and eventually enough forces and equipment would overwhelm the enemy. The senior positions in these new units would be filled by officers and NCOs of the peacetime Army. To support this mobilization plan, officers in the active forces were educated and trained to assume positions in wartime that called for a higher rank than their present grade.

After the 1973 War, there were two major changes to the way the Army trained its troops. First, instruction materials and methods were reexamined and revised throughout the TRADOC school system. Second, the entire training system was reoriented to prepare the Army to be ready to fight and win from the first battle to the last battle. In practical terms, this resulted in the following changes:

- New "How to Fight" manuals were written that clearly described techniques for fighting outnumbered and winning. Many of these were in comic book form. These were often edited so that key points could be made in the average reading time a soldier had while waiting in line for something, or sitting in the latrine.
- Training was designed to be performance-oriented with realistic and quantifiable standards. This meant testing everything from how well a soldier could handle his weapon to an officer's ability to lead. Units and individuals were regularly tested on their military skills. Previously, the training for both individuals and units was time-oriented. Individuals and units would spend a designated period of time on a subject or task, then advance to the next level. With performance-level training, neither individuals nor units advanced to the next subject or task until a specific level of performance had been achieved. Also doing well on these tests determined who got promoted and who got invited to leave the military.
- Training centers were created that provided for tough and realistic battlefield conditions.
- Training centers added opposing forces that were expertly trained in the doctrine, tactics, and organizations of Warsaw Pact forces.
- The new training centers were instrumented to provide performance feedback so the trainees and instructors could realistically grade the training effort.
- Whole families of simulation and other training devices were created to

give commanders the opportunity to "fight their first battle" and experiment with new concepts, doctrine, and tactics without getting their troops
killed in the process.
* Organizational studies were completed that provided a clear road map for
restructuring the organization of the Army based on future war requirements and not just on trying to refight the last war better.

ACHIEVING JOINTNESS

The 1973 Mideast War also highlighted the indivisibility of combat power
and the need for effective coordination between the services. The troops
called this approach "jointness," and it was something that was rarely
achieved in peacetime, and not always in wartime. In other words, the
infantry, armor, aviation, and artillery units had to learn how to work
together under battlefield conditions. Most important, the Army and Air
Force began to work and train together as they had never done before.
Jointness in training and education at all levels became a priority.

When the Goldwater-Nichols Department of Defense Reorganization Act
of 1986 was passed by Congress, jointness became even more of a driving
force in the Army's training and educational system. Goldwater-Nichols
turned the Joint Chiefs of Staff from a debating society into a disciplined
military organization. The Chairman of the Joint Chiefs is no longer a peer
of the other service chiefs of staff, although he still does not have command
authority in the classical sense. But the Chairman is now the principal
military adviser to the Commander in Chief (president). Previously, the
only tool available to the Chairman for controlling the other chiefs of staff
was persuasion. This often did not work. Now the Chairman returns from
his meetings with the president and passes on the president's orders to the
other chiefs of staff.

The primary purpose of Goldwater-Nichols was to encourage jointness,
and that it did. Not perfectly, but it was a big improvement over past
practices. But probably its greatest contribution to Desert Shield/Storm was
increasing the authority of the combatant commanders in chief (CINC),
such as General Norman Schwarzkopf.

The shock of the 1973 War and increased jointness were desperately
needed, because most of the Army training system had essentially remained

unaltered since World War II. The results of the 1973 War gave the Army a reason to change, and increased jointness gave it the means to make the changes work.

TEACHING THE OFFICERS HOW TO FIGHT

Of all these efforts to reshape the Army's educational and training systems to respond to the lessons of the 1973 Mideast War, perhaps the most challenging task was the retraining and reeducation of the senior officers. As stated before, studies of American first battles had indicated that poor preparation by senior commanders above the battalion level was often the major reason for both the defeat and high casualties. For over a decade, American officers had been concentrating on a counterinsurgency in Southeast Asia against a Third World country utilizing infantry tactics. Those officers who had not been swept up in the counterinsurgency mania were still preparing to refight World War II in Central Europe.

To place this problem into perspective, a little background on the education and training programs for senior officers might be helpful. The Army had closed its senior war college from 1940 to 1950. From 1940 to 1945, it had been closed in order to meet the Army's mobilization requirements; all officers were needed to fight the war. From 1945 to 1950, the War College had remained closed primarily because General Marshal and General Eisenhower were committed to the creation of a uniform military education program. Their experiences during World War II had convinced them that a uniform military educational system was the most effective approach to preparing senior military commanders. Unfortunately, not only did the uniform military educational system fail to materialize, but all the facilities of the Army War College (shut down) along with much of its institutional memories (the records and staff dispersed) were lost. The opposition by the Navy and its supporters in Congress was just too strong for creating a joint military educational system.

It was not until the Korean War that the Army was able to reopen its own senior war college. This was done when it became clear that there was a major deficiency in the educational preparation of many senior officers for battlefield command. A decade's worth of fast-track lieutenant colonels had not been given academic preparation for the promotion (of some of them) to general's rank. The peacetime Army was much larger than it had ever been before and it seemed unlikely that the service would shrink back to its pre–World War II size anytime soon. This had been realized since 1945, and now, in 1950, it was urgent to remedy the situation. Damage had already been done; many generals of the 1950s and 1960s would assume their positions without adequate preparation. Many of the problems encountered in Vietnam can be traced to this ten-year lack of an Army War College.

It was a major task starting up a War College in the middle of a war. And just as the college was defining its future, President Eisenhower changed the national strategy to one that emphasized massive (nuclear) retaliation. Just as the Army would find it difficult to define a role for itself on a nuclear battlefield, the War College would also struggle to define its role for preparing senior Army officers in such an environment. More problems appeared in the 1960s, when the Defense Department pressured the college to place more emphasis on counterinsurgency and scientific management at the expense of operational instruction on corps and higher levels of command. By the mid-1960s, even wargaming was discontinued, the key tool that had been used since the founding of the War College in 1903 to prepare senior officers for their duties on the battlefield.

In 1976, Major General DeWitt Smith, the commandant of the Army War College and one of the most brilliant and articulate officers in the Army, instituted a series of reforms that would have a major impact on the future readiness of the Army. He ordered the reintroduction of wargaming into the War College curriculum along with increased instruction on the operational art of war. Many noted simulation experts, including civilians such as Jim Dunnigan and Seth Bonder, volunteered their expertise and services to assist the War College to reintroduce theater-level wargaming. As the War College increased its capabilities in war planning and wargaming, General Smith requested and received approval from General Rogers, the Army's Chief of Staff, to offer this capability in supporting senior commanders in the field. This new effort was a return to pre–World War II years when the War College assisted commanders in reviewing their war plans. Army study teams for improving the professionalism of senior officers also recommended that the War College begin providing more support to the senior field commanders. The model that the Army War College adopted for this new program was based on the Fleet Readiness Program long used at the Naval War College.

The Navy's Fleet Readiness Program consisted of fleet commanders bringing their subordinate commanders and staffs to the Naval War College to test their operational plans on realistic wargamings and to update their doctrinal knowledge as well as to increase their warfighting edge. The interaction of selected students and faculty members with fleet commanders and their staffs, using current real-world military problems, benefited the professional development of all involved. The program at the Army War College became operational in 1979 and was named the Army's Tactical Command Readiness Program. The two initial tests for the Tactical Command Readiness Program were a strategic deployment exercise for the 1st Infantry Division (Mech) and a transition from peace to war for the VII Corps in Germany. General Gordon Sullivan (Chief of Staff of the Army in the mid-1990s), was the operations officer for both these units when the tests were carried out. He would have a major influence on shaping the senior officers' development programs.

The Army received two major shocks in 1979. The Soviet invasion of Afghanistan (December 27) came only a month after the Iranians took hostage the American Embassy staff (November 3). The subsequent failure of the rescue attempt in 1980 highlighted the problems with U.S. military planning. But it was the Soviet actions that created the most concern about the viability of U.S. contingency plans, as it appeared that the Soviets might also invade Iran. As a result, the Chief of Staff of the Army, General Meyer, directed that the War College and the Command Readiness Program place more emphasis on contingency planning instruction for senior officers. Contingency planning is not "spur-of-the moment" planning. It is what the military calls deliberate planning for a situation that can be reasonably expected to take place. For an ongoing crisis, the military uses another type of planning, which is called "crisis action" planning.

General Meyer ordered that special emphasis be placed on finding a more systematic way of developing concepts of operations. The term "concept of operations" is nothing more than the military's way of saying, "How do we go about getting a specific job done?" Normally, when a commander and his staff are examining a potential situation, they need to formulate and test alternative courses of action. The measures used to test each course of action are its suitability, feasibility, and acceptability. (Will it do the job? Can it be accomplished? What are its costs and benefits?)

The key to a systematic process for developing, evaluating, and selecting alternative courses of action was the availability of a combat model that would allow senior officers to rapidly test their alternative operational concepts as well as to evaluate likely enemy concepts. In other words, a simple, but realistic, wargame was needed to allow commanders to play around with a situation before making decisions. The Germans, who developed many of the techniques for formulating and evaluating courses of action, had effectively used wargames. But the American Army, with a few exceptions, didn't regain access to wargames until the late 1970s. It was the concern of General Meyer that too often, vast numbers of very bright staff officers and subordinate commanders were working hard and developing excellent plans for implementing "dumb" concepts that had not really been put to the test until it was too late. Unfortunately, around this time, most available combat models ("wargames") of theater operations were incredibly complex computer-based systems that required months to get ready. These combat models were not wargames in the classic sense, but planning tools determining logistics and combat support needs in a future war. These models were not normally used by commanders for planning combat operations, but they were all that was available in the late 1970s. A true wargame allows the commander to move and fight his combat units on a map, and uses a realistic set of rules and probabilities. This type of wargame had largely disappeared from the American inventory after the late 1940s.

To meet General Meyer's directive, the War College developed a new approach to combat modeling. It used a top-down programming approach and a systems architecture for conceptualizing the battlefield that was based on writings by General DePuy, General Starry, and General Richardson. In effect, it was a simple wargame that commanders could quickly understand and use. Before being released for use by the Army at large, the new procedures for formulating and testing alternative courses of action were personally tested by General Meyer and all his division commanders in a contingency planning exercise at the War College in November 1980. With these new wargames, commanders could practice creating a "concept of operations" for their subordinates and then watch them work out the battle plans, and the battle itself, in a realistic wargame. It all seemed very convincing at the time, but was not proved in practice until 1991 in the Persian Gulf.

In many respects, it was history repeating itself. In 1810, Prussia established a War Academy in Berlin for training officers for high command and general staff work. This training included a systematic planning process, a major innovation in military affairs. This was a revolutionary event in that the Prussians were declaring that military command and planning could actually be taught. They were rejecting the prevailing eighteenth-century view that skill at military strategy, tactics, and planning were the sole domain of charismatic leaders who had been born to perform those roles. The Prussians were also rejecting the idea that war could best be fought by amateurs. The dramatic victories by the Prussians over Austria in 1866 and France in 1870 showed what an educated Army could do, and the Prussian war college became the model for military education in most of the nations in the West. What was particularly useful to the other nations of Europe was the vast body of writings that the Prussians had developed in structuring their military planning process. The Prussians called their approach "the System" or "the Estimate of the Situation." This was a logical and systematic approach at developing plans and selecting courses of action. It required commanders to state their mission in terms of purpose as well as task and to systematically consider the situation, including enemy capabilities, before arriving at a course of action. In other words, an "estimate of the situation."

The Estimate of the Situation approach was not new for the U.S. Army. Back in the nineteenth century, an American officer, General Emory Upton, went to Europe and studied the Prussian system, including the Estimate of the Situation, and he was largely responsible for bringing the Prussian educational system to the United States. His observations were included in his book, *The Armies of Asia and Europe*. The Prussian educational model that General Upton brought back had a major impact on both the Naval War College when it was started in 1884 and the Army War College when it was started in 1903. But tradition dies hard; teaching a systematic approach to war to professional warriors does not appear to fit normal American values. That is, the belief that any American can rise to the occasion in time of crisis and overcome any enemy has been a part of the American folklore and it still prevails to this day. This is all part of the American image of the macho frontiersman and embattled farmer. Whether all this played a role in General Upton's eventually going mad and committing suicide is hard to say. Yet it is not surprising that debates have continued in the United States over teaching such concepts at the war colleges. When the revised system for contingency planning was integrated into the curriculum of the Army War College and into the Army's Tactical Command Readiness Program in 1981, the Estimate of the Situation was again central in the military planning process. The military reformers had prevailed. No one has gone mad over it yet.

To further assist corps commanders and division commanders and their staffs to maintain their warfighting competence and maintain the edge, the Army created at Fort Leavenworth, Kansas, a Battle Command Training Program (BCTP) in the 1980s. The BCTP staff provided special support to deploying divisions to Saudi Arabia for Desert Storm and Desert Shield. They also sent a team to Saudi Arabia and assisted each corps in its battle plans.

But of all the educational efforts for senior officers, it was the emphasis on the operational level of war that was the most intellectually challenging. AirLand Battle doctrine and the 1982 edition of FM 100-5 added the operational level of war to Army doctrine. This is the intermediate level of war between strategy and tactics. It is primarily the planning and conduct of campaigns (which are series of battles and oftentimes include simultaneous battles). For example, most of the military actions of General Schwarzkopf during the 1991 Persian Gulf War were at the operational level. Senior commanders have traditionally learned their skills and how to perform at the operational level on the battlefield rather than at training centers or in academic classrooms. One of the most difficult problems at the operational level is the required shift in thinking with respect to time and distance. It is a process that involves the coordination of thousands of military personnel performing massive numbers of functions over vast areas and time in order to concentrate combat power at the right time and place.

The Army has instituted a number of programs to assist officers in this shift of thinking. After being excluded from the curriculum of the Army school systems for over forty years, campaign planning is again being emphasized. A School for Advanced Military Studies (SAMS) was created at Fort Leavenworth in the 1980s. After taking the regular Command and General Staff Officers Course, a selected number of officers are assigned an additional year at SAMS to study the theory and application of operational art. The purpose is to teach "how to think about military operations, not necessarily what to think." At the Army War College, the Army's most senior school, emphasis is on the higher operational and strategic functions.

Training at the operational level of war is as important as education on the subject. To be effective, officers must actually practice functioning at that level. This usually requires realistic wargames that put the commander under the same limitations and pressures he would encounter in wartime. In this way the officer forms the habit of correctly appreciating the new time and distance relationship demanded at the operational levels. An example of the type of training that has been established to give senior commanders and their staff hands-on experience is the computer-driven exercises run at the War Preparation Center (WPC) at Ramstein Air Base in Germany. The WPC is a joint effort by the U.S. Army Europe and U.S. Air Forces in Europe. At WPC, vast numbers of senior officers have been trained in the operational level of war and in rapidly making decisions under realistic (albeit simulated in wargames) battlefield conditions. This paid off in the Gulf War where most officers led their units at breakneck speed, while remaining ready for combat, suffering minimal casualties, not getting lost, and not running out of supplies. This was not a result of Iraqi incompetence, as many Iraqi units did stand and fight. But the American troops were competently led at the operational level; otherwise the defending Iraqis would have caused much damage to uncoordinated and poorly led U.S. units. This was what would have happened to an American force from the 1970s. Over a decade of hard training and clear thinking about the modern battlefield paid off.

A Middle Eastern History Lesson

One of General Meyer's concerns in 1978, while chief of Army operations, was for improving contingency planning and the Army's readiness to fight in any environment. To this end, he sent a study team of officers to the Middle East to analyze what would be the major problems U.S. forces would face as well as what type of leadership problems senior officers were likely to encounter if U.S. forces were employed in the Middle East. Selected from faculty members and students from the Army War College, the team visited Egypt to brief the ambassador on its task. They also asked the military attaché, an American Air Force general, for his thoughts on problems that senior officers are likely to encounter in the Middle East. Without hesitation, the general reached into his desk drawer, pulled out a book and gave it to the group. It was Russell Braddon's *The Siege,* an account of the British experience in World War I when they sent a division of troops to Mesopotamia (Iraq) to protect British oil interests. The specific objective of the British expedition was to protect the oil refinery in Abadan (which is not far from Kuwait City) and the pipeline from Abadan to the coast (only about thirty miles). The attaché said that most of the problems American senior officers would face in the Middle East were the same as those the British officers encountered in 1915: heat, sand, disease, lack of water, navigation, and the most dangerous problems that the Middle East fosters—ignorance, overambition, and sheer stupidity. He told the group to take the book and learn from it. They did and he was right, but the pitfalls that the British fell into in 1915 are still very real today.

The power of Braddon's book lies in the fact that he based it on eyewitness accounts of survivors who were with the British division. Braddon described how the British in 1915 landed in Basra with only about a thirty-mile march to Abadan. The British government had given the force commander orders to protect the oil refinery and the pipeline at Abadan. So the British commander seized a number of surrounding towns. These places were defended by local Arabs. The British forces kept winning their battles so easily that the commander kept advancing, disregarding his objective and exceeding his orders.

As the British kept penetrating into enemy territory, the problems for the British forces began to increase exponentially as the lines of communication became stretched. Also, as the British kept advancing north toward Baghdad, the terrain became increasingly difficult to traverse as it turned into sandbanks and marshes. But the British kept winning and the thought of capturing Baghdad, with all the glory that would be involved, began to overwhelm the British commanders. The British were in desperate need of some good war news because of the bloody stalemate in Europe, and these easy victories over Arab reservists seemed to be a godsend. So regardless of the political objective, which was the protection of the oil refinery and pipeline at Abadan, the British commander headed for Baghdad.

The British advanced without adequate artillery, supplies, transport, or combat forces. At Kut, which is just south of Baghdad, the Turks (not just Arab reservists) sprang their ambush. Kut was 250 miles away from the original objective given to the British commander by his civilian leaders in England. Here the British Army suffered one of its most humiliating defeats. When the military in the field lost sight of their political aims, it cost the British some 38,000 casualties. Over 7,000 casualties were incurred in reaching Kut, about 6,000 casualties during the siege, over 23,000 casualties by the British forces sent to try to relieve the forces trapped in Kut, and over 7,000 deaths of the troops who were captured. All for nothing—not for any political objective or for any territory. A vain attempt by a glory-hunting commander turned to disaster, as such things usually do. It is a lesson that should not be forgotten.

After members of the study team visited Egypt, they went on to Israel to visit Colonel Moshe Leshme, the head of Combat Doctrine for the Israel Defence Forces. They asked him a question similar to the one they had asked the American military attaché in Egypt: In his opinion, what would be the major problems that U.S. senior officers would face if they were leading forces into combat in the Middle East? To the amazement of the study team, Colonel Leshem went to his bookcase and came back with Norman F. Dixon's book, *On the Psychology of Military Incompetence.* He gave the book to the study team and said that it contained a summary of Russell Braddon's book, *The Siege,* which provided all the answers to the study team's questions. He stated that he hoped and prayed that it might help someday save a lot of American lives. When the team returned to the United States and had reported to General Meyer, the lessons of the Siege of Kut were integrated into the curriculum of the War College. The commandant of the War College also assigned some of the leading military historians in the Army to the War Gaming Department to ensure that the lessons of Kut and similar historical examples were being integrated into the combat simulation exercises for the students.

It is interesting to note that *The Siege* was one of the books that was distributed to many of the incoming officers who participated in preparing the plans at CENTCOM during the initial stages of Desert Shield. Like Napoleon, and many earlier soldiers of note, they studied earlier campaigns, and learned from them. The military that went into the Gulf was prepared, not by accident but by tremendous effort in the preceding twenty years. The American taxpayers got their money's worth, and a lot of American soldiers owe their lives to these two decades of effort.

The Volunteers

How the post-Vietnam Army came to grips with the largest, and eventually highest-quality, force of volunteer peacetime troops America has ever known. There were several false starts before the military learned how to best use the new Volunteer Force. At first, the end of the draft in 1972 was a disaster for the Army. It took nearly a decade to set things right.

The crucial element in the transformation of the U.S. armed forces between Vietnam and the Gulf War was the fact that after Vietnam all the troops were volunteers. For most of its history, America relied largely on volunteers to fight its wars and man the ranks in peacetime. There was some conscription in the Civil War, but the first large-scale draft came during America's brief participation in World War I. Between 1917 and 1918, the United States put over four million troops into uniform, most of them conscripts. World War II also used the draft, and on a much larger scale. Between 1941 and 1946, over sixteen million Americans served. Conscription, in practical terms, lapsed for a few years after World War II, but picked up again for the Korean War and kept up right through Vietnam. Yet in 1972 the U.S. military ended the longest period of conscription in its history. From 1941 to 1972 America drafted over thirty million men to fill the ranks of the largest armed forces it had ever fielded in war or peace. With the end of conscription, the American military was forced to come up with ways to induce two million citizens to serve in the armed forces during peacetime.

The volunteer program got off to a rocky start. Over thirty years of conscripts, plus the recent trauma of Vietnam, had caused a number of troublesome habits:

- The draft allowed the military to grab a lot of highly educated, or simply quite bright, young men who would have otherwise not enlisted. Not everyone who was eligible for conscription was taken. The armed forces took only the best. Up until Vietnam, the military was well populated by the graduates of the best colleges. Many of these troops even volunteered for combat jobs, simply for the "experience." More common was the assignment of these troops to complex or technical jobs that could best be handled by some bright and well-educated young soldier. The military had grown accustomed to this, and was not prepared to deal with losing a lot of these people.

- Because of changes in the laws during the Korean War, students were now able to defer the draft until they finished school. At that point many of these college-educated men were conscripted. This gave the armed forces a large number of older and well-educated recruits, many with freshly learned skills the military could put to use right away. These troops were easier to train and generally made better soldiers than younger and less well-educated men. The military lost most of these when the draft ended and it was not realized how important these older and better-educated troops were until they were gone.

- The existence of the draft had always induced many young men to enlist. In these cases they had to serve one or more years beyond the two years required of conscripts if they wanted some choice of assignments. Qualified enlistees could be guaranteed technical training while in uniform, which often was useful after they left the armed forces. At the very least, many young men asked to be taken by the draft as soon as they were eighteen, just to get it out of the way and not have to worry about being called sometime in the next few years. These draft-induced enlistments favored the Air Force and Navy (including the Marines) at the expense of the Army. Air Force and Navy service was seen as less unpleasant than being in the Army. This was the case even before Vietnam. The Marines were a more prestigious service and needed fewer conscripts anyway. Thus the threat of the draft gave the Air Force the lion's share of the most qualified recruits because the Air Force promised easier conditions of service and more mentally challenging work. The Navy was next best off, as it had the offer of travel to distant parts of the world and better living conditions than the Army. The Marines didn't need that many rocket scientists, but because of their elite attitude, they did want volunteers and they generally got them. The Army had to make do with what was left over and, in many cases, suffered for it.

But it got worse. Although the military could now pay more to its volunteer troops, there were several other problems it encountered when it switched over to the volunteer force.

Vietnam Era NCOs

The NCOs (sergeants, petty officers, etc.) are the backbone of the military. NCOs train the troops and are their immediate supervisors. Thus NCO quality has a direct impact on how well the troops do. The quality of the Vietnam era NCOs that the volunteer Army inherited was the lowest it had been since early in World War II.

There were three reasons for this:

First, the military had been benefiting from the NCOs of the World War II and Korean War era. These were experienced men, but nearly all were dead or retired by the early 1970s. Many of the World War II era NCOs were eligible for retirement just before Vietnam. Typically, a lot of the NCOs will not retire when they become eligible after twenty years of service, but will continue to the thirty-year mark in order to receive a larger pension.

Second, Vietnam had a negative effect on many of these NCOs and they retired with between twenty and thirty years' service during the Vietnam War. The Korean War era NCOs first became eligible during the early 1970s and an above-average number took retirement as soon as they were eligible. This early attrition was particularly noticeable in the Army (because of the greater exposure to combat in Vietnam). Since the NCOs were promoted from the lower-ranking enlisted men, and the NCO positions had to be filled, the standards of the past were lowered.

Third, all this was compounded by the Vietnam War practice of sending promising new recruits straight to an NCO school and making them junior NCOs with less than a year of service. This was necessary because so many junior NCOs were being killed or wounded in the combat units. Some of these Shake 'n Bake NCOs were good, but many were not, and many of the less capable ones stayed in the military and were thus promoted when openings appeared and there were no candidates. This was an obvious problem within the military and the only solution was to raise the standards as much as possible and wait for time to solve the difficulty. Unfortunately, it took most of the 1970s for the military, and particularly the Army, to raise the standards of its NCOs. In the meantime, troop quality and performance suffered.

Errors in Screening

The military had a series of screening tests (known then as the AFQT, or Armed Forces Qualification Test) dating from the World War II era. This test performed well in selecting candidates for service according to their potential for doing well in military jobs. The higher the score, the easier the recruit will be to train (and vice versa). The quality of the armed forces depended on how high the cutoff was for new recruits. The lower the cutoff, the lower the average AFQT score was for all troops. But in 1976 a new version of the AFQT tests was introduced that gave erroneous results. The flawed test made the scores of candidates appear higher than they were. Thus for several years, a large portion of the recruits accepted were not really capable of being effective soldiers. Moreover, at the same time, the military had put a lot of pressure on its expanded number of recruiters to produce.

Typically, recruiters were evaluated on how well, or how quickly, they could fill their quota of recruits. Each recruiter had to obtain a certain number of recruits each month. To be accepted for service, these recruits had to pass the AFQT. Since the new, flawed AFQT was accepting recruits who were really not qualified, a few recruiters immediately suspected there was something wrong with the new AFQT. But they also knew they had a quota to fill and in the mid-1970s that was not an easy thing to do. As a result, about one quarter (over 350,000) of the recruits accepted by the Army between 1976 and 1980 (when the test was corrected) would not normally have been allowed to enlist. The first people to notice the reduced quality of the recruits were the NCOs running the basic training centers. Many of these unqualified recruits could not even complete basic training successfully. Many of those who did later flunked other Army schools or got into trouble and were thrown out of the service. The military also knew from past experience that most recruits who scored below a certain AFQT level would not be able to complete Army training or would become disciplinary problems. Not everyone can handle the demands of the highly regimented and disciplined military life, and the AFQT was used as a screening device to keep out those who had the least chance of coping. The lower-quality NCOs available during this period simply made the problem worse. As a result, morale and effectiveness reached a post–World War II low during this period.

Antimilitary Attitudes

The peacetime military had never been all that popular among Americans, and the antimilitary attitudes that developed during the Vietnam War guaranteed that the popularity of the military after Vietnam would reach a record low level. It did, and this made it all the more difficult to recruit. At the highest levels, in Congress, this resulted in lower military budgets. At the other extreme, it made the recruiters' job very difficult. Officer recruiting was also more strenuous; the bad feelings of the Vietnam era made a military career less appealing to the many college graduates who normally supply the military's officer needs. Standards for officer candidates were lowered, although not as far as with NCOs.

CARRYOVER OF VIETNAM ERA PROBLEMS

The Vietnam era brought to the military a number of social problems from the civilian sector. The major ones were drugs, racial animosities, less discipline, unit instability, and soldiers' families. In addition, the military had long had problems with alcohol and, especially in the ranks, sexual promiscuity. While these latter two problems had been part of the military life for centuries, the Vietnam era difficulties were rather new. As a result, the military had a more difficult time adapting to them. The Vietnam War had also exacerbated all of these problems, and to further complicate matters, the end of conscription came along before they could be brought under control. Thus, the military had to simultaneously deal with the end of the draft and a lot of leftover social issues from the Vietnam era. Before the military, and particularly the Army, was able to reach its Golden Age of the 1980s, solutions were found for at least the worst manifestations of each of these difficulties.

The problems, and their solutions, were:

Drugs. This was pretty straightforward. The military adopted a screening program. There were scheduled tests and random tests. The troops were warned, and if found still using drugs after a second test, they were often separated from the service. Since the military was now a voluntary force, the threat of being thrown out was tantamount to getting fired from a civilian job. This was a sanction that the military had not been able to use as much when many of the troops were draftees or volunteers forced into the service by the threat of the draft. By the early 1980s, the tide had turned and the drug problem was on its way out. Alcohol abuse did increase, but the military had centuries of experience in dealing with that and it was relatively easier to handle than drugs. As the quality of the military leadership increased, it was easier to keep the alcoholism under control. Heavy drinkers were easier to cure or get into treatment than drug users. But this required strong leadership throughout the armed forces. Moreover, a certain amount of heavy drinking was always tolerated in the military. Only when discipline broke down did this get out of hand.

Racial Animosities. The Vietnam War period saw a lot of progress in racial integration within the military undone. While blacks had fought in all of America's wars, from the Civil War on they fought in segregated units. In the late 1940s, the military was ordered to integrate. Some services had an easier time of it than others. The Navy, which had used blacks as sailors extensively during the Civil War and for some time after, had the hardest time. Early in this century, the Navy had adopted the policy of using blacks only as shipboard waiters and servants for officers. During combat, these black sailors had battle stations and many won awards for valor under fire. But the Navy had never allowed blacks to train for the many technical jobs available, or to advance very far in rank. Thus it took the Navy several decades to fully accept blacks as competent sailors. Until that time arrived (in the 1980s) there was always a lot of tension among racially mixed crews.

The Army and Air Force were one service until 1947, when the Air Force was separated out. During World War II, the Army air corps (or, later, the Army Air Forces, as it was officially known) operated semi-independently in a fashion similar to the way the Navy and Marines do to this day. During World War II most black troops served with the Army ground forces. This was because the air corps needed better-educated troops and the generally less well-educated blacks usually operated in nontechnical support units. By 1950, most black soldiers were still in segregated organizations, although some of these were combat units. One of the few black combat regiments had been sent to Korea in the first months of the war and had outperformed most of the all-white regiments. The Army already had some World War II experience with small black combat units and with integrating infantry units under emergency conditions. But in 1948, President Truman ordered the military to begin ending segregation and in 1950 ordered it to expedite this process. It's easier to do some things during a war, so the Army quickly began integrating its units in late 1950. By the end of the Korean War in 1953, the Army was integrated.

The Air Force and Navy did not feel the same battlefield pressure as the Army and moved more slowly, not completing integration until the late 1950s. Although the Air Force commanders of the early 1950s could still remember a time when they were Army officers, the Air Force had a higher proportion of technical jobs that most blacks did not have the educational preparations for. And since the Air Force got more volunteers than the other services, they had fewer black conscripts. Nor did the Air Force have many black pilots, and pilots are the elite of the Air Force.

The Army also got the most black officers. Moreover, the word got around that the Army was "a place where blacks could make it." By the early 1960s this had proved to be the case. Blacks held many senior NCO ranks, and an increasing number of junior and senior officers were black. Most traces of overt prejudice were eliminated during basic training as recruits quickly learned how to obey black drill sergeants (quickly and unquestioningly). Black and white troops lived in the same barracks and, in a custom that was largely lost during Vietnam, often socialized together.

Vietnam brought to the military the side effects of the growing civil rights movement. Ironically, the Army was the most integrated and discrimination-free segment of American society at this point. But the steady influx of young black recruits brought into the ranks the calls for "Black Power" and "Fight the Oppressor" that were all the rage outside the military. This caused racial separatism in the ranks and additional headaches to already overburdened NCOs. However, the drug use and breakdown in discipline that characterized the last years of the Vietnam War gave the military bigger problems to solve than those related to race relations in the ranks. It wasn't until the early 1980s that race relations returned to a semblance of their pre-Vietnam condition. But from the end of Vietnam to the early 1980s, poor race relations were yet another problem to overcome in trying to reform the Army, and the other services as well.

Less Discipline. U.S. troops were never the most disciplined in the world, but neither were they the most unruly. Lacking the professional military tradition of many older nations, and being a democracy of individualists, it's a wonder that American troops were able to buckle down to the kind of discipline needed to win wars. But this is what Americans have traditionally done. Except in Vietnam. For the first time in American history, the discipline of the troops actually declined as the war went on, especially in the Army. The causes of this go back to the Korean War. In that conflict, trained and experienced troops were needed in Korea within months of the war's outbreak. The only source of such troops was the veterans of World War II who were kept on the rolls as "inactive reserves" after being discharged. When infantry was needed quickly in 1950, these inactive reserves were promptly mobilized and sent into battle along with regular Army units from the United States. Meanwhile, organized National Guard units were sent to active duty to replace the departed regular Army units. This was all happening at the beginning of the Cold War.

It was known that the Soviets had a hand in starting the Korean war (via their support of North Korea) and many feared it was a ploy to get America bogged down in the Far East while Soviet armies marched into Western Europe. So the National Guard divisions were mobilized to be available to take care of any threat in Europe. The threat never came, and the erstwhile civilians who happened to be World War II combat veterans found themselves fighting once more in Korea. These troops didn't feel it was quite fair for them to be fighting while the National Guard troops, who had been paid for their peacetime soldiering, were sitting around the barracks back in the States. The public didn't think it was fair either, so the decision was made to bring the troops back from Korea after thirteen months of service. Draftees were sent as replacements. This worked in Korea because most of the worst fighting took place in the first year. Barely trained draftees were then able to man the trench lines for the last two years of the Korean War.

The same system was immediately used in Vietnam. This time the thirteen-month "tour of duty" was justified because most of the troops were draftees who were in for only two years anyway. Normally, when a war is declared (and such was never the case in Vietnam), troops are in "for the duration." The downside was that the Vietnam War fighting went on from 1964 to 1972. There was no "one year of hard fighting and two years in the trenches." Vietnam was eight years of hard, difficult-to-master fighting. It was bad enough that the troops, most of them right out of civilian life, spent only a year in the field. The officers usually spent only six months with a combat unit. This was so more officers could "gain combat experience." This system ensured that very little experience was gained. The officers were never in the field long enough to learn their jobs, nor were they with their units long enough to gain the trust of their troops. The troops were never in the field together sufficiently to develop a unit spirit or a high degree of combat skill. The result of all this was a breakdown of discipline, not to mention effectiveness, in the field. This process was speeded up by the increasing retirement of experienced and Korea era NCOs and the increasing turmoil back home over the war in general. Thus discipline decreased as the war went on, and these low discipline levels continued after the last U.S. troops withdrew from Vietnam in 1973.

Unit Instability. Going into, and especially coming out of, Vietnam, the U.S. Army had a very poor sense of unit cohesion. That is, the troops in units felt more like isolated individuals than members of a cohesive combat unit. Until the 1950s, the U.S. Army had maintained the ancient "regimental" system. This meant that troops stayed with their units for long periods of time and often for their entire careers. The officers were more prone to move on to other assignments, but they always thought of themselves as belonging to their "old regiment." The bonds were particularly strong for troops who had been in combat with their regiment. But even during World War II the regimental system was being weakened by the practice of sending individual soldiers as replacements to battle-depleted units. The Army was also quick to break up regiments to obtain cadres for new units and to generally ignore the importance of unit cohesion. The Germans, and most other World War II combatants, were less likely to tamper with unit cohesion. But America did win the war after all, and even though American scholars had investigated and described the highly effective German methods of maintaining unit cohesion and effectiveness, this was not given much attention by the U.S. military.

In the late 1950s the regiments were broken up to form "pentomic battle groups." This lasted until the early 1960s when the current "brigade" system was adopted. The regiments were brought back, sort of, but unit cohesion was not. While the regimental designations for battalions were now used, the regiments as units with three battalions permanently attached were gone. By comparison, the Marine Corps maintained its regiments throughout this time and had far fewer problems with cohesion. Few people in the Army noticed this. As U.S. Army combat units were sent to Vietnam, and had their officers and troops rotated through the units frequently, any semblance of unit cohesion was lost. In terms of cohesion and effectiveness, Army combat units came out of Vietnam in worse shape than when they went in. The introduction of the volunteer Army thus began with units that had nowhere to go but up in terms of unit cohesion and effectiveness.

Soldiers' Families. Before the volunteer Army, most military dependents were the families of career NCOs and officers. The bulk of the troops were draftees and short-term volunteers who were mostly unmarried. The military families always had unique problems. These were largely the result of the stress of frequent moves to new military assignments and long absences of the uniformed husband from his family. The result was most obviously expressed by a higher than average divorce rate. The volunteer Army changed all this, for the worse. Since all the troops were volunteers, and an increasing number were women, there were now more dependents as these younger troops were more likely to marry and start families. Since the younger married troops were making less money, there were more financial strains on their marriages and the result was a higher divorce rate. This led to a higher number of single parents. All of this was something the military wasn't really prepared for. Of all the problems that the post-Vietnam Army inherited, this was one of the most intractable. Going into the 1990s there is still no solution for the single-parent situation. The Gulf War highlighted another aspect of this problem: the failure of many single parents to plan on a place to leave their children if the parent is ordered overseas on short notice. Children are the parent's responsibility in the military, and single parents aren't always up to the task when there's a national emergency and troops have to be moved quickly overseas. Expect to see more headlines on this problem during future emergencies.

LEARNING HOW TO RECRUIT

The military had always assigned experienced officers and NCOs to recruiting duty. It had operated this way for generations, but recruiting duty was not very popular. Recruiting was not an easy task and there were always demands for more, and better-quality, recruits. Failure to perform as expected when recruiting could hurt a soldier's career, but a high degree of success at recruiting didn't give a commensurate boost. In light of this, it's no mystery why recruiting duty was so unpopular. But it had to be done, and when conscription ended, recruiting became more important than ever.

Even during the period of post–World War II conscription, recruiting served a vital role. Draftees were in uniform for only two years. As good as many draftees were, career NCOs and longer-term enlisted specialists were always needed. As warfare became more technical, the recruiters were urged to snag more young volunteers. Recruiters had to learn how to sell technical training to bright, recent high school graduates. To justify the six- to twenty-four months of technical training for these troops, the period of enlistment had to be three years or longer. When the volunteer system came along in 1972, the recruiters had to hustle for every recruit. Moreover, the minimum time of service was three years and many of the jobs offered no training, or training that was not directly applicable to the civilian economy. It was no longer possible to give all these gritty, low-tech jobs to draftees. Through the 1970s, recruiting was a nightmare. It was made somewhat easier by the flawed qualification test that was introduced in the mid-1970s. But this was not much help in the long run as most of the substandard recruits obtained were either poor soldiers or never even completed their training before being tossed out.

As was usually the case, the Army suffered the most. The Navy and Air Force could still offer more attractive deals, and thus obtained most of the better recruits. Fortunately, the Army assigned an extraordinary man with exceptional energy and creativity to be the commander of the Army's Recruiting Command: Maxwell R. Thurman. He focused on the concept of offering young people a true challenge; his theme was "Be all that you can be." Research at the United States Military Academy in the late 1960s had clearly demonstrated that most young people are truly seeking challenges. The key was to be up front with the negative as well as the positive aspects of what these young people were likely to encounter in the Army. By the early 1980s, the Army had developed ways to get the people they needed. But it was a long and costly learning process.

Dealing with Female Troops

The military had been recruiting women on a large scale since World War I. Even so, women rarely made up more than a few percent of troop strength and all of them were in noncombat jobs. The women did their jobs quite well, often outperforming men in the same positions. The end of the draft made recruiting more women an attractive proposition. The higher pay scales and promise of easier (noncombat) duty made recruiting qualified females easier than going after males for the same jobs. By the end of the 1970s, 10 percent of the armed forces was female.

The only downside to this was increasing political pressure to put women into combat jobs. Most female troops wanted none of this, nor did a lot of the male troops want combat jobs either. But the growing number of female officers knew that without access to combat jobs, their chances of promotion to the highest ranks were limited. Supported by some members of Congress and many civilian special-interest groups, the military had to devote a lot of time and effort to dealing with these demands. This had some negative effects on morale, as standards were lowered to accommodate females in some jobs. Many military jobs, particularly those in combat-support areas, require a lot of muscle. When women without the physical ability to do their jobs are placed in a unit, the males have to take up the slack and resentment results. There were also increasing problems with "fraternization" and charges (some justified, some not) of sexual harassment.

Women brought to the armed forces a lot of more easily trained recruits, and competent people in general. There has been, and continues to be, a downside to this with regard to maintaining equal standards for men and women. There is also a lot of pressure from politicians on the matter of women in the military, much of which makes more political than military sense. Politicians tend to forget that combat-support troops carry weapons and often have to act as infantry when the enemy gets too close. No one knows for sure where it will all lead.

TRANSFORMING THE VOLUNTEERS INTO AN ARMY OF EXCELLENCE

The Army of the 1970s was preoccupied with the problems of morale and motivation and the related problems of attracting and retaining volunteers. Exceptionally creative and effective leaders would develop the programs to overcome these challenges.

It would require, however, the Iranian hostage taking and the Soviet invasion of Afghanistan to prompt the administration and the Congress to provide the necessary funding to implement these programs and create an effective Army. But in addition to the funding, it would also require dedication and plain hard work, and above all else, it would require a revolution in thinking. The 1980s saw a shift in the way soldiers and airmen and sailors were commanded and organized. The military recognized that new weapons and equipment had changed warfare and it created an effective mix of forces to be used on a new, much larger battlefield. The battles of the Gulf War were unlike any seen previously. American forces were prepared for this, the Iraqis were not, and the results say it all.

Once the money was available in the early 1980s, it was possible to increase pay levels. A recession in the early 1980s also helped fill the ranks, as did the fading memories of Vietnam and an increasing public concern about the state of the military. The generals and admirals made the right moves. In general, they treated their new troops like professionals and made it clear that anyone who didn't want to be a professional was free to leave. There was a dark side to all this, as there usually is to anything. While most of the additional money went into payrolls, new equipment, and expensive training exercises, corners were cut in some departments. The biggest victim of cut corners was the stocks of ammunition and spare parts needed to actually fight a major war. This was ludicrous, and it was no secret. Yet no one made a move to actually do anything about it. The politics of military budgeting traditionally allowed less visible items like ammunition stocks to slide. More emphasis was always on new and expensive weapons systems. These could be used to get the attention of Congress in ways that warehouses of munitions could not. There was enough stuff on hand to fight the 1991 Gulf War, but that was not the kind of "major war" the U.S. armed forces were being paid to be ready for. Low as the munitions stocks were, they were able to cover the needs of the Gulf War. Fortunately, the Cold War ended before the Army had to confront these deadly shortages. The major war in Central Europe slipped into history without having been fought.

Related to the shell game with the phantom wartime munitions stocks were things like the "Army of Excellence" (AOE). This was a wide-ranging program that encompassed new concepts for practically everything the "new" Army was going to be in the 1980s. The AOE was the right tool for upgrading Army personnel standards as the switch was made from the conscript to the all-volunteer force. In other areas, however, the AOE became a bad joke. For example, the AOE was the cover for the Army plan to field more divisions using less manpower and, in some critical areas, less equipment. While the AOE could work in producing a force with fewer (but better) troops who could do much of the work of the pre–all volunteer force, the AOE could not make up for crucial shortages in equipment and active-duty soldiers.

For example, the AOE was able to expand the number of active divisions by integrating into them many reserve and National Guard units. In peacetime, many active divisions had only about two thirds of their nominal (wartime) size. If war came, the reserve and National Guard units would quickly join the active divisions and off they would go to war. While this looked good on paper, the reserve and National Guard troops did not always have the expected levels of troops, equipment, or training. In many areas, the active units also lacked crucial combat-support equipment. In particular, the heavy trucks needed to support combat operations were not there. All this came out into the open during the 1990–1991 Gulf War when the Army refused to send the National Guard brigades to the Gulf. Fortunately, that was a "medium-sized war" and there were enough (in some areas, barely enough) troops and equipment to fill the gaps.

One of the aftereffects of the Gulf War was that the media rubbed everyone's face in this AOE sleight of hand. The Navy and Air Force had similar problems. This does not mean that they will be solved in the future, just that everyone got a wake-up call. These situations are not new, but actually rather ancient. There will always be some discrepancy between what the military says it has ready for war, and what can actually be sent into action when the shooting starts. No one seems able to consistently find an answer.

CHAPTER

10

New Ideas

The reform of the Army was carried along by an increasing number of new ideas. Once the word got out that new ideas were wanted, a trickle turned into a flood. While some of the new ideas were off the wall, most were right on target. The flood continues, and the atmosphere in the Army is still one that encourages new thinking.

It was ideas, new and rather radical ideas, that sparked the 1970s reform of the U.S. military. New ideas, especially ideas that imply major changes, are not normally very popular in the military. More important to soldiers is the ability to expertly perform a lot of simple, traditional things. Experience shows that even getting the simple down pat in combat is not easy. Soldiers are always faced with the prospect of death, and this has a lot to do with their cautious approach to dealing with change and untried new ideas. There is also the highly structured organization of the armed forces. The hierarchy of ranks for officials and troops is there to provide a modicum of stability in the chaos of combat. The ranks are rigid, with discipline and prompt execution of orders seen as lifesaving virtues. Also, doctrine provides a common way of thinking that helps training, communications, and operating under stressful conditions of combat. But when rapid change is required, this common way of looking at things can often get in the way of new ideas.

The Vietnam experience forced the Army to take a hard look at how it functioned, creating a fundamental shift in every aspect of operations. This was to be the fifth major shift in Army thinking since World War II. The other four were:

1946. Disbanding of World War II armed forces, the largest in U.S. history. By 1950, forces were being restructured for possible mechanized war with the Soviets in Europe. But then the Korean War broke out and produced a hard-fought infantry war. This was not the kind of "Next War" America was preparing for in the late 1940s. Through all this, it was largely the divisional organization and weapons of World War II that were used.

1954. In the wake of the Korean War, U.S. policy shifted to the idea that nuclear warfare would be the common form of combat. This left the Army without much of a mission and Army thinking drifted all over the lot. A radical new division organization was introduced (the "Pentomic Division") for fighting on the nuclear battlefield and research favored missiles and nuclear weapons.

1962. Despite a public show of support, most Army officers were not keen on the pentomic concepts and the critics became louder and more persuasive. By 1960, the criticism was becoming public (via the media) and by 1962 the changes began as it was realized that all future warfare would not be nuclear. The divisions were reorganized to the form that is still the standard. New weapons research emphasized conventional warfare. Work had also been ongoing since the mid-1950s on the problems of "Unconventional (Guerrilla) Warfare" and this led to the establishment of the Special Forces ("Green Berets") in 1957. This was just in time for the Vietnam War. The Special Forces caught the attention, and patronage, of President Kennedy early in his term of office. This led to their being one of the first groups sent to Vietnam (1963). Before that there had been military advisers, but none as specifically trained for this kind of work as were the Green Berets. However, Special Forces were then, and still are today, even with a unified command for special operations, seen as outside the mainstream of Army thought and operations.

1960s. Once the Army got involved in Vietnam, most work on preparing for European combat came to a halt. From 1964 to 1972, most Army mental and material resources were directed at unconventional (guerrilla) warfare in Vietnam. There was not a lot of enthusiasm for unconventional warfare, as it was a lot murkier and vaguer than the conventional warfare troops are accustomed to. Guerrillas did not come out and fight like regular troops, but preferred ambush and terrorism. At first, the withdrawal of resources from Europe did not cause too much alarm in the Pentagon. The Soviets had actually reduced their armed forces in the late 1950s and early 1960s. But then the Soviet leader (Khrushchev) who had pushed these troop reductions past his generals was himself replaced in late 1964. The new leader, Brezhnev, was beholden to the armed forces for his new job, and repaid their support by giving them a blank check on the Soviet Union's economic resources. Thus began a quarter-century arms race. However, the extent of this Soviet arms buildup was not immediately known to the United States. Distracted by Vietnam, the Army didn't really take note of the Soviet buildup until 1970. As the chart below demonstrates, by 1970 the extent of the Soviet buildup was evident. It didn't take long for Pentagon analysts to fill in the rest of the historical numbers.

The U.S./USSR Arms Race (Ground Forces)

Year/Nation	Ground Forces Troops	Tanks	Troops Ratio	Tanks Ratio
1960/USSR	2,250,000	35,000	2.15:1	2.69:1
1960/US	1,043,000	13,000		
1970/USSR	2,150,000	38,000	1.35:1	3.80:1
1970/US	1,590,000	10,000		
1975/USSR	2,390,000	42,000	2.46:1	4.82:1
1975/US	970,000	8,700		
1980/USSR	2,400,000	48,000	2.49:1	4.49:1
1980/US	964,000	10,700		
1985/USSR	3,040,000	52,000	3.10:1	3.88:1
1980/US	980,000	13,400		

U.S. forces include Army and Marines. The Soviets had one division for every 16,000 to 17,000 troops. The U.S. ratio was one division for every 30,000 to 35,000. Both sides had reserve troops to fill out divisions in wartime and provide replacements. The ratios show the number of Soviet troops or tanks for each U.S. one. The favorable U.S. troop ratio in 1970 is deceiving, as most of the troops were tied up in Vietnam, and not available to oppose the Soviet forces in Europe.

The Soviets made similar strides in their naval and air forces. But it was the ground forces that naturally concerned the U.S. Army. Moreover, ground forces were a historical Soviet strength, while the United States had a similar track record for naval and air forces.

In 1960, the USSR outnumbered the United States over two to one in the key areas of manpower and tanks. But the Soviets had to cover other fronts, especially the Middle East and China. The Soviet troop reductions of the late 1950s were still going on in 1960. Moreover, the European NATO countries were rearming at a rapid clip and the 1956 rebellion in Hungary had demonstrated an obvious weakness in the Soviets' Eastern European "allies."

By 1970, much had changed. Although U.S. troop strength was higher, most of that was committed to Vietnam and demobilization was already in the works. The tank ratio was the most telling, standing at nearly four to one. This was indicative of the Soviets' vastly increased arms production. The falling number of U.S. tanks demonstrated how much the Vietnam fighting was detracting from the mechanized forces committed to European defense.

Few 1970 Pentagon forecasts of the 1980s situation were as bad as the reality. The Soviets were on a roll, even though some Western economists correctly deduced that the Soviet arms buildup was crippling their economy. This message had a difficult time getting a hearing. Soviet experts in the government and academia knew that the Pentagon preferred to hear the worst about Soviet intentions and capabilities. This attitude was partially one of prudence. Military people tend to get ready for the worst, as that's what they'll often encounter on the battlefield. A more mundane reason was that a Red Army perceived as strong and getting stronger made it easier to get larger defense budgets. In the aftermath of the Cold War, former Soviet defense officials remarked that they used the same technique.

Even the Pentagon optimists got a shock in 1979 when the Soviets invaded Afghanistan. At the same time, the end of U.S. conscription had cut manpower to lower levels than before Vietnam. Even in the numbers of tanks, the United States could not keep the Soviet ratio from increasing. All this was obvious to most senior Army commanders in the early 1970s. Some new ideas were needed. Some radically new ideas, at least as far as U.S. Army thinking was concerned.

One of the new ideas the Army adopted was centralized selection of unit commanders. This would have a profound impact on improving the quality of leadership in the Army. The Army began selecting its battalion and brigade commanders from a centralized list of the Army's highest-quality officers. Prior to the centralized selection process, who you knew was often the primary factor for receiving command positions.

At TRADOC, the search for new ideas was led by General Bill DePuy and his cohorts. The first thing they did was hit the books. They realized that while new technology required new tactics, there are many constants in warfare that have not changed in thousands of years. The new ideas that molded the present U.S. Army can be summarized thus:

1. Training. Throughout history, the victors were almost invariably better trained. The Macedonians, Romans, Swiss pikemen, Frederick's grenadiers, Napoleon's grognards, and the Germans in the twentieth century are all examples of troops that were very difficult to beat on the battlefield, even when they were outnumbered. Several ancient armies had the same saying on this: "The more you sweat in peace, the less you bleed in war." From this came the increased emphasis on effective training. The NTC and other programs were the result.
2. Mobility. Whether attacking or defending, successful armies tended to be more mobile than their adversaries. This included speed in getting to the battlefield as well as speed on the battlefield. The increased emphasis on helicopters, cross-country trucks, and the M-1 tank were all results of this. The record-breaking advances during the 1991 Gulf War would not have been possible without the preparations that began in the early 1970s.
3. Command, Control, Communications, and Intelligence (or C^3I). While this category is thought to mean lots of electronic gear, the most important part of C^3I is ideas. The best form of command and control of military units is when you don't have to communicate with them. That means your subordinates have all been well trained on how to react to typical battlefield situations. Thus prepared, a commander requires a lot less communication because he knows what his subordinates are likely to do. Also, subordinates require a lot less communication because they have been trained to understand the intent of the commander and can adapt on their own to unexpected changes. In addition to new battlefield techniques and more training for commanders, there was also a flood of new communications gear. The intelligence people also received a lot of new gadgets.

The new ideas for the Army were rarely put as simply as that. Instead, there was much concern and debate over catchy new buzzwords like "Active Defense," "AirLand Battle," "Win First Battle," "Come As You Are,"

"Target Servicing," "Deep Attack," "Bounding Overwatch" and "the Army of Excellence." While these were ideas, they were not the core ideas but rather the concepts through which the Army attempted to express the three ideas above.

To their credit, the officers leading the Army into the realm of new ideas did not let the debates over the buzzwords and interpretations of concepts distract them from getting the three key ideas into action. Meanwhile, a number of interesting debates occurred as new doctrine was hammered out through the late 1970s to the present. These debates unfolded in the following order:

1976: Active Defense and First Battle (FM 100-5, 1976 edition)

Although few dared to say so at the time, this was very much a reinvention of the German blitzkrieg doctrine as it stood late in World War II. In that period, the Germans were fighting large mechanized Soviet forces and had adopted a doctrine of "active defense" that allowed them to fight many battles outnumbered and still win. The Germans still lost the war, but one cannot ignore the fact that their active defense doctrine enabled them to win many battles they otherwise would have lost. The key to the German active defense, and FM 100-5's 1976 version, was the use of mobile firepower, terrain, and well-trained troops to break up and weaken attacking Soviet units. At that point, the Germans could often launch their own counteroffensive to retake important positions or to complete the destruction of the attacker. The Germans developed a number of special antitank weapons (assault guns, portable antitank rockets, antitank aircraft, etc.). The Germans were also very methodical in preparing the battlefield. That is, they selected the best firing positions for their antitank guns and used mines and obstacles to channel enemy forces into killing zones.

The 1970s saw a resurgence in the study of military history in all the services. But even with the increased interest in the subject, few officers had studied in detail the German tactics used in World War II. Fortunately, most of the doctrine developers were well versed in them. Many of the doctrinal techniques offered in FM 100-5 were straight out of the German cookbook. For example, General DePuy was fond of personally advocating the "DePuy foxhole." This was a firing position in which the weapon was fired at an angle, leaving the oncoming enemy to see only the wall or berm the weapon was behind. Naturally, several weapons had to operate together to provide interlocking fire to cover each other's position. This technique was standard for the Germans in World War II. Ironically, many of the tactical ideas in FM 100-5 were attributed to the Israelis. Yet the Israelis made no secret of the fact (which they did not play up loudly for obvious reasons) that they developed much of their doctrine from German World War II experience. For those who were aware of the details of late World War II doctrine, it was amusing to watch the debate over these "new" tactics. The debate did get the creative and reflective juices flowing. This was sorely needed, for while many World War II techniques were useful, the battlefield had changed in the ensuing thirty years because of the technological developments in weapons systems and other equipment.

1977: What *Was* the Soviet Doctrine?

It wasn't long after the debate over FM 100-5 began that questions were raised about Soviet doctrine. It was Soviet weapons and tactics that came up second best in the 1973 Arab-Israeli War and the Soviets had reached their own conclusions as to what had to be changed. In actuality, the Soviets changed very little. Much later it was discovered that the Soviets had decided that their weapons and doctrine were all right as is. The Soviets blamed the Arab soldiers.

Meanwhile, there was an ongoing debate within the Soviet military on how they were going to deal with all these new American weapons, and what FM 100-5 meant for them. The Soviets had also learned much from the German World War II experience. Even though the Red Army ultimately beat the Germans, it was only after a long string of battles that were lost because of superior German organization and technique. Since World War II, Russian doctrine had been based on all-out offensive, even if they were defending. Many Western analysts took this at face value, ignoring the many problems the Soviets have had launching offensives without battle-hardened troops. The experience of the Soviets from 1941 to 1945 provides ample examples. By the 1950s, the Soviet army of World War II was gone, replaced by new equipment and inexperienced leadership at the lower levels. Examples of what this meant were not really noticed until the Red Army fumbled through the 1968 invasion of Czechoslovakia and then really stumbled during the 1979 Afghanistan invasion. From the 1970s on, more articles appeared in the Soviet military press bemoaning the low level of readiness for major combat. But in the West, the Soviets had become ten feet tall. As a result, the "Soviet Doctrine" debate concluded that hordes of well-trained Soviet divisions would descend on Western Europe in any future war and NATO had to prepare accordingly. The net result was concentration on using artillery and air power to hit the oncoming Soviet divisions before they engaged NATO ground forces.

1977: The Central Battle Calculation

Trying to cut through all the talk, this entry into the debate was another throwback to a World War II era technique. Put simply, the Army decided to analyze the potential European battlefield in detail. In other words, they went and wargamed the situation at the lowest level. Wargaming was coming back into fashion in the late 1970s, although the Central Battle Calculation also covered a lot of what the Soviets customarily did with their "correlation of forces" technique. What this effort produced was confirmation that NATO forces would indeed be outnumbered, but that if the expected situation were tweaked a little this way and that, the Soviets would have a much harder time of it. What was amazing about this planning on how to fight was that it pointed out the lack of training, and thought, about how commanders would actually run a battle. Before the 1970s most battalion commanders would admit that their principal command skills were "in running mess halls and motor pools." The troops had to be fed and the equipment maintained at all times, but a unit was rarely in combat. From this point on through the present, battalion commanders are trained in how to use their units on the battlefield.

1978: The Use of Reserves

This became an issue for both U.S. and Soviet forces. The "active defense" and "winning the first battle" were initially thought to require every unit to be in action. Critics were quick to invoke the lessons of history, pointing out that armies had rarely been successful without benefit of some reserves. Into the midst of this debate came the issue of how the Soviets would handle reserves. It was known, from World War II practice and current writings in the Soviet military journals, that the Soviets had a different concept of reserves. Basically, the Soviets attacked in waves (or "echelons") of divisions. There might be three or more waves. As one was shot up, another would take its place. Typically, the Soviet divisions had scant (if any) reserves. The next echelon would perform as the reserve. As all of this got debated, U.S. commanders realized they would need some reserves, even at the expense of firepower at the front. This also got everyone thinking of ways to take care of those second and third echelon Soviet divisions before they got into combat with outnumbered NATO forces.

1979: Interdiction, Corps 86, Division 86, and the Deep Battle Area

For most of this century, America had led the world in artillery technology. The Army also now had the world's largest fleet of attack helicopters. Thus even without the Air Force, the Army was able to deliver firepower over a large distance. Once everyone got focused on the issue of those waves of Soviet divisions heading west, the next question was how to stop them before they reached outnumbered NATO units. It was noted that these advancing Soviet units would be strung out along roads and in no position to defend themselves as well as they could once they reached the front lines. The U.S. Army and Air Force began cooperating on a plan to jointly go after these approaching Soviet divisions, as the farther away the Soviets were stopped, the better. At the same time, the Army began to take steps of its own. Conventional warheads with cluster bombs were developed for Army long-range missiles. A new multiple rocket launcher (the MLRS of Gulf War fame) was developed. Small mines that could disable a tank were developed. These "trackbuster" mines could be delivered by artillery or missile twenty or more kilometers behind enemy lines. The Defense Advance Research Project Agency (DARPA) aided the Army and Air Force in their work on interdiction by sponsoring the Assault Breaker Program in the late 1970s. This program introduced an entire new family of smart mines and smart submunitions for attacking Warsaw Pact units while they were still moving toward the combat zone. Apparently, the Soviets found the threat of these long-range antitank weapons intractable. By 1980, the Army was planning on providing the corps commander with interdiction capabilities over a hundred kilometers into the enemy rear. All this talk of interdiction bothered the Soviets no end and cost them huge sums of money just to search for a solution.

1979: The Integrated Battlefield

Once people started to really think about all the things that were happening (or should be happening) on the modern battlefield, the issue of organization and control arose. At this point, the Air Force was being brought into the picture, and that added an entire new bureaucracy to the cacophony. But the item that was thought to need the most attention was integrating the heretofore separate plans for nuclear-weapon use and nonnuclear battle. The Air Force issue would be dealt with later as "AirLand Battle" doctrine. The integrated battlefield ideas would finally bring together all the diverse nuclear and nonnuclear firepower doctrines and weed out the contradictions and suggestions that, on examination, were unlikely to work. When garbled word of this work got out, it became something of a scandal that "the Army was planning to use nuclear weapons early in a war," and so on. But that's just the way the media works. The Army was better prepared.

1980s: The Light Division and Little Wars

While Vietnam had soured the U.S. Army on the prospect of chasing guerrillas through the bush, by the early 1980s it was obvious that most current and potential wars were of the guerrilla variety. Not wanting to be caught short as it had been in Vietnam, the Army began work on having some forces trained and ready should America again get involved in Vietnam-type combat. The result was the Light Infantry Division, of which several were eventually created and, so far, none really used much at all (until Somalia). At the time, critics pointed out that the 82nd and 101st divisions were light infantry. They were, and are, but these are the "fire brigade" divisions. The new Light Infantry Divisions are for sustained use in some future jungle or urban hellhole. These units don't have a lot of armored vehicles or as many heavy antiarmor weapons as mechanized and armored divisions. One aspect of this Light Infantry Division issue is still under debate. What do these guys do if faced with a lot of enemy tanks? The Light Infantry Divisions have yet to be used and are unlikely to be used for the very simple reason that they are likely to endure a lot of casualties. As American politicians have learned during and since Vietnam, dead American soldiers will cost you a lot of votes.

1980s: High Technology Test Bed

In the early 1980s, the Army accepted that high technology had come to ground warfare for good. A program was begun to look into all aspects of high technology that could possibly have some use in land warfare, particularly from the infantryman's perspective. This gave official sanction to a lot of previous activity by officers wanting to make more use of technology. Contracts were freely handed out to experiment with a lot of ground-warfare technology. Many of the gadgets were civilian items, coming off the shelf. The use of armed dune buggies was one of these projects. This relatively modest program paid big dividends toward the end of the decade.

1981: AirLand Battle and the Deep Attack

Since the early 1970s, TRADOC officers had been meeting regularly with Air Force officers to develop better ways for the Army and Air Force to work together. At first, not a lot came of these discussions. But by the late 1970s, with Army generals talking about long-range interdiction and Army combat units dashing deep into enemy territory, it was time to merge the efforts of the two services. This was not an easy chore, as the Air Force had been increasingly developing its own agenda since it became a separate service in 1947. But an increasing number of Army officers assigned to work with the Air Force made an increasingly persuasive case for a battle plan that integrated Army and Air Force efforts. The doctrine came to be known as AirLand Battle (the capital L was intentional). General Donn A. Starry, the TRADOC commander in 1981, selected the term AirLand Battle to capture the emerging concepts of extending the battlefield and integrating air and land operations.

At its core, AirLand Battle sought to simultaneously use Air Force and Army combat units to quickly and decisively take apart an enemy force. What happened in the 1991 Gulf War was no fluke; it was an application of AirLand Battle doctrine. The Army people convinced the Air Force leaders that it was just not good enough to disrupt the arrival of enemy forces into the battle by using aircraft to destroy distant Soviet divisions. To win the battle required the coordination of the air interdiction with the ground battle so that the Army would have enough combat superiority at the front line to go on the offensive and break through into the enemy rear area and basically destroy the enemy's ability to fight. In other words, use the deep interdiction to set the terms of the future battles by shaping the battlefield and creating opportunity for the ground forces to gain and maintain the initiative and actually get inside the decision cycle of the enemy. The "inside the decision cycle" bit is nothing more than moving faster than the enemy can react, much like one boxer hammering another so quickly that the victim can't effectively react. Again, this is nothing new. This was the essence of the World War II blitzkrieg, and was a devastating combination.

To demonstrate the degree of cooperation in the Gulf between the Air Force and Army, consider the JSTARS aircraft. The *J* stands for *Joint* as in cooperation between Army and Air Force. JSTARS was a four-engine Air Force radar aircraft, similar to the AWACS, but designed to show only what was on the ground. The information was transmitted to ground forces and Air Force commanders on the ground and both used the data to coordinate ground and air operations. After over thirty years of pulling apart, the two services finally began to pull together with the Air Force working hard with the Army to make the AirLand Battle doctrine viable. While the Air Force never accepted all aspects of this doctrine, there was agreement on enough of it to achieve an unprecedented level of cooperation and coordination. The Air Force always considered AirLand Battle doctrine an ''Army'' doctrine. The Air Force saw elements of AirLand Battle that were consistent with its doctrine and that's as far as the cooperation went. This was farther than cooperation had gone in the past, and this was a major achievement.

1982 (and 1986) Editions of Army's FM 100-5

The 1976 edition of FM 100-5 (with its ''Active Defense'') had touched off a massive debate on just what that edition really meant. There were many new (for the Army) concepts. The 1982 edition provided the Army with a sound intellectual basis for how it could fight outnumbered and win. It emphasized maneuver much more, as well as attacking deep into the enemy's rear area and the use of long-range firepower and how to control combat units on the battlefield. There was more emphasis on the human dimension of warfare, a more global outlook, and it added more emphasis on the operational level of war (how to plan and fight at the senior levels of command—division and above). The doctrine developers prepared and presented briefings to clarify the major thrusts of the doctrine and delivered these briefings throughout the entire national security system including the Congress, the White House, the other services, and industry. By carefully listening to all the comments and criticism from inside and outside the Army that was directed toward the 1976 edition, the 1982 version came out as something everyone could understand and work with. The 1986 version clarified many points and is considered a well-reasoned treatise on how modern warfare should be conducted.

1984: Competitive Strategies

Now that everyone was thinking about the details of how U.S. and Soviet units operated on the battlefield, it became clear that these were two very different ways of fighting. This gave rise to the concept of Competitive Strategies. That was a ten-dollar term for concentrating on tactics and technology that the Soviets were less capable of resisting. In practice, this meant more electronic devices, both in weapons and sensors. The Soviets knew they were generally behind the West in technology and sought to make up for this with quantity. As the Soviets were fond of saying: "Quantity has a quality of its own." But the United States used both its technological edge as well as its doctrine and training edge to overwhelm the Soviets in the Cold War and the Iraqis in Desert Storm. The United States used its new doctrine to drive weapons requirements that resulted in the marriage of smart munitions, modern target-acquisition systems including space-based systems, modern communication systems, and stealth delivery systems.

This combination of battlefield systems is proving to be as powerful as, and perhaps having a greater impact on the evolution of warfare than, the German integration of tanks and airplanes to create the blitzkrieg concept of war. The Soviets recognized this, foreseeing accurate long-range sensors and weapons that could quickly find and hit distant targets. But the Soviets realized that the West would probably get these new systems first, which would put the Soviets at a big disadvantage. Systems emerging out of SDI (precision bombing, stealth aircraft, and an abundance of electronic gadgets from personal computers to GPS navigation devices) are all part of this new form of warfare. But most of the technology for the systems seen in the Gulf War was developed ten to fifteen years ago. The next edge that the United States will most likely employ will be the integration of bombs with their own guidance systems and sensors, the B-2 bomber delivering very accurate smart munitions, and smart mines that talk to each other and the troops controlling them. All of this is being integrated into a real-time command and control system. This new collection of advance systems is revolutionizing conventional warfare just as the nuclear intercontinental ballistic missile revolutionized strategic warfare.

CHAPTER

11

Innovative Training

How does a large Army retool itself for a new form of warfare? Mainly by coming up with innovative ways to train the troops. The Army rewrote the book on combat training during the 1970s and the 1980s, producing some of the best-trained peacetime troops ever.

Consider the training problems faced by the Army in the wake of Vietnam:

- How does it go from fighting primarily an infantry war for over a decade in Vietnam to creating an Army capable of fighting the highly mobile armor warfare required for Europe and the Middle East? This was accomplished by throwing out most of the pre-Vietnam concepts and essentially starting from scratch. For example, time-oriented (two hours of this, six hours of that) training was tossed out in favor of more practical methods. This was an uncharacteristically bold move for a peacetime military establishment and one generally motivated by unsatisfactory performance in the last war. In other words, the bitter Vietnam experience provided the needed motivation to reform the military, especially the Army.
- How does it go from a conscript Army to an all-volunteer Army? In a painful succession of learning experiences. It would take the military, and especially the Army, a decade to get the volunteer force working satisfactorily.
- How does it go from spending over a decade on fighting unconventional warfare in the jungles and rice paddies of Southeast Asia against an undeveloped country to being capable of fighting at any level of intensity of war anywhere in the world and against any country that threatens the vital interest of the United States? The NATO obligations, the 1973 Arab-

170

Israeli War, and increasing instability in the Persian Gulf forced the military to learn to deal with multiple commitments. The concept of greater commitments was not as important as developing the means to effectively deal with the potential hot spots.

- In a period of severely constrained resources, how does it rectify a failure to modernize equipment in order to support the costs of Vietnam while at the same time the Soviets were modernizing their military at an unprecedented rate? Through the 1970s, the money simply wasn't there to keep up with Soviet arms building. Thus the 1970s saw an emphasis on something that could be done: changing the way the Army (and the other services) thought about waging war. While most of the money in the 1980s went to buying new weapons and equipment, there was enough carryover of people-oriented thinking from the 1970s to fund new training concepts like field training centers that were instrumented to provide feedback to the troops and the use of wargames and simulations.
- How does an Army restore its morale and keep from falling into a cycle of self-defeating scapegoating and politician bashing, when the years of sacrifices in blood appeared to have all been in vain? To its credit, the military did not dwell on the implications of being misused by politicians in Vietnam. The troops concentrated on being better at what they did, being more inclined to tell the politicians straight out what was and was not possible, and preparing to come out of the next Vietnam in a lot better shape than the last one.
- How do you create an Army with a spirit of initiative and with an offensive orientation while the national policy is emphasizing détente and restraint? The experience in Vietnam taught the military that an inability to execute the details of its job (destroying enemy's ability to fight) was a sure road to failure. While the national policy might be peace, the nation retained armed forces in case peace failed. The military's renewed study of history in the 1970s revealed that the most successful armies were the ones that could, when needed, "generate maximum violence." This became a catchphrase for the military after Vietnam, because to "generate maximum violence" required well-trained professionals. Not a lot of them, but with an all-volunteer force there was more likelihood that all the troops would be at the top of their game when called upon to fight. It was also noticed that, historically, short wars tended to be ones where the winner came on like gangbusters and blew the opposition away.
- How does an Army create a winning spirit, one that's capable not only of

victory but of winning decisively from the very first battle? This is something that the U.S. Army had not traditionally done before. This required a leap of faith to accomplish. But with the volunteer Army, the halfhearted attitudes of the draftee force could be discarded. More important, this change in attitude required determined leadership from the officers who came out of Vietnam. The leadership was there, which is an important thing to remember. For if it hadn't been there, the chance of significant change would have been remote.

Many senior officers in 1976 thought the Army's key doctrinal handbook, Field Manual 100-5 (1976 edition, based on the lessons gathered from the 1973 Mideast War), would be the unifying force that could turn the Army around. To a great extent it served its purpose. Its clearly written concepts provided the underlying structure for major initiatives in revolutionary changes in training, command and control, reorganizations, and weapons. But the debate over its firepower-intensive tactics for the active defense would serve to generate a revolutionary change in the way the Army viewed the time and space relationships of the battlefield. Providing increased emphasis on campaign planning and the concept of extending the battlefield to over the horizon, while balancing maneuver and attrition, were just some of the advancements that were a result of this intense and personal debate. It would take hard work by many successions of exceptionally outstanding people in and out of the military to make this new way of viewing the battlefield viable, and to translate it into doctrine, planning, equipment, training, and organizations.

One of the driving forces behind this new view of the battlefield was General Donn Starry. He had returned from Europe in the summer of 1977, where he had been the commander of V Corps, to assume command of TRADOC. Starry took over from General DePuy, who had got the ball rolling by being the first commander of the newly created TRADOC a few years earlier. DePuy had personally pushed through the 1976 edition of FM 100-5 and Starry had been a key ally while FM 100-5 was being created. At that time Starry was the commandant of the Army Armor School and it was the work of his Armor officers that put most of the attack and mobility concepts into FM 100-5.

The new thinking of FM 100-5, and new technology now available, created a revolution in training. General DePuy attributed much of the credit for this revolution in training to General Paul Gorman, who was the deputy chief of staff for training at TRADOC from 1974 to 1977. For most of the Army's history, it used a time-oriented process for moving both the troops and units through the training program. After completing a scheduled period of time on a task, men and units normally advanced to the next task with the assumption that they had been trained regardless of their level of performance. In 1975, General Gorman instituted performance-oriented training for both individuals and units. This approach requires that troops and units demonstrate their ability to competently perform one task in the training program before taking on the next one. For example, soldiers would have to demonstrate their proficiency with their weapons before going on to learning how to use them in tactical training. This was a development that was unique in military history and was largely responsible for the outstanding performance in the Gulf.

INSPIRATION FROM ABOVE

While General DePuy and his team solved a lot of conceptual problems with regard to how the U.S. Army could successfully fight outnumbered, there still remained the problem of how to prepare the troops to do the job. DePuy, like most of the 1970s and 1980s generals, had commanded troops in Vietnam. Many of the Vietnam generals had also commanded troops in Korea. These officers could not help but notice the truth of one of the maxims that came out of Vietnam: "The Army went into Korea weak and came out strong, but went into Vietnam strong and came out weak." Most officers knew what the problem was—the troops weren't properly prepared for combat. There was no single reason why they weren't prepared. Part of it was the thirteen-month tour of duty and the use of two-year conscripts. Another problem was coming up with the right kind of training for a war the Army never decided exactly how to fight. While many officers, and troops, wanted to put Vietnam behind them, people like DePuy and Starry knew that out of failure came inspiration. Salvation came from above, in the form of Navy and Air Force aircraft using electronic tag as a way to train effectively.

After a few years of air combat during the Vietnam war, the Navy became concerned that its pilots were not able to shoot down as many enemy aircraft for each U.S. plane lost as they had during World War II and Korea. After studying the problem, naval leaders realized the primary reason was the kind of training their pilots had received. During World War II, it was taken for granted that you trained your pilots to outfly and outshoot enemy aircraft. Naturally, the enemy pilots did not operate the same way U.S. pilots did and these differences were taught during aviator training. Most of the Korean War pilots were World War II veterans and they used the same successful training techniques. But in the eleven years between the end of the Korean War and the beginning of the Vietnam conflict this bit of wisdom managed to get buried in a mountain of "new and improved" training methods. Going into Vietnam, U.S. pilots knew only how to fight other U.S. aircraft. It was assumed that the enemy would not be that different. This assumption was wrong, as Vietnamese, Chinese, and Russian pilots quickly demonstrated. There were also significant differences between the Russian and U.S. aircraft used. The Navy solution was the creation of the "Top Gun" school in 1969. This was actually the existing Naval Fighter Weapon School. The new curriculum now emphasized realistic training against instructors who operated like enemy pilots and flew aircraft modified to perform likewise. It worked. By the early 1970s, the Navy pilots were doing as much damage as they had during the Korean War.

The Air Force pilots were also aware of the problem, but were not as quick off the mark as the naval aviators. Once the results of Top Gun were seen, however, the Air Force came up with its own twist on the situation. The Air Force had a Top Gun–type program since 1964, but it lacked the necessary realism. The revised Air Force program was called Red Flag and began in 1975. Being second didn't hurt the Air Force. If anything, one can say that Air Force efforts in this area have been more productive than the Navy's for the past fifteen years. One thing the Air Force research highlighted, and the Navy agreed with, was that a pilot's chances of survival went up considerably after as few as ten combat missions. New pilots, who had never been in combat, had a 60 percent chance of surviving their first ten missions. After that, their chances of surviving any additional missions went to 90 percent. The primary purpose of Top Gun and Red Flag, even though this was not intended at first, was to get new pilots through those first ten missions without using live ammunition.

The Air Force concept saw the Red Flag program as a substitute for those crucial first ten missions. This meant that the Red Flag setup had to be much more realistic. The Air Force did this by using many electronic devices that could accurately mimic the various air-to-air weapons. Like the Navy Top Gun program, it used instructor pilots who were specially trained in the doctrine, tactics, and organizations of likely enemies. Eventually this was extended to include ground-to-air weapons (guns and missiles) and air-to-ground weapons (bombs and missiles).

While all of this activity among the Navy and Air Force aviators was described in some detail in the general and professional media, the Army did not immediately pick up on the implications. What finally made the connection in the Army was the network of former Army air corps officers who now led the Air Force. Many of these officers had even attended the Army officers' academy at West Point. The Air Force did not have its own academy fully functional until the late 1950s and West Point cadets often transferred to the Air Force in the years before that. The former cadets stayed in touch, and when they did they often talked proudly and enthusiastically of their favorite projects. Red Flag was a hot item in the Air Force in the late 1970s, and before long many senior Army officers were aware of what Red Flag was, what it could do, and how it was done.

Creating a ground-combat version of Red Flag required first overcoming a number of conceptual, technical, and fiscal problems. The problems were solved, and are still being refined. This led to the establishment of the Army's National Training Center in October 1980.

THE NATIONAL TRAINING CENTER (NTC)

While the NTC could arguably be called "Son of Red Flag," much of what eventually became the NTC had to be invented out of whole cloth. The aviators' concept of training against aircraft that mimicked enemy techniques is nearly as old as air combat itself. The fact of the matter is that such training is relatively simple and inexpensive to do. The principal chore is training the "enemy" pilots to fly and fight as the enemy does. The hardest point of this is remaining aware that the enemy are not simply clones of your own pilots and aircraft. Not an impossible task, but one America managed to flub in the 1950s.

But the American aviators did more than remember what their fathers had practiced in World War II; they improved on it. In earlier times, the only record one had of these exercises was the memories of the participants and, at times, some fuzzy still or motion pictures. Great training, but lousy record keeping. This was OK during a war when you had a steady stream of recent combat veterans coming back as instructors. The fresh memories of these vets would serve as an ongoing reality check to the training exercises. What

Top Gun and Red Flag did was to set up electronic systems that recorded every aspect of the training flights. This data could be played back to refresh memories of trainees who had suffered minor, or major, lapses. More important, the data could be systematically analyzed and studied. Just as this type of analysis has allowed coaches to train more capable athletes, so pilots used the analyzed data to make minor, but crucial, adjustments to their technique. It worked as well for pilots as it has for football teams and boxers. It was the recording and analysis features of Red Flag that the Army wanted to duplicate on the ground. It wasn't going to be easy.

Now that the Army accepted that they would not be fighting other Americans in a future war, they were faced with the formidable task of actually re-creating land combat with real troops and equipment. And recording all that they did in sufficient detail to enable them to see what they were doing later on. The Army accomplished this task by taking advantage of recent advances in electronic and laser technology.

Laser Tag

The technological key to success of the NTC was a military version of the civilian "laser tag" device. (This was a toy gun that "shot" an infrared light at sensors other players wore. When the infrared light hit one of the sensors, a buzzer went off to signal the hit.) The Army version was called MILES (Military Integrated Laser Engagement System) and was first put to use for infantry weapons in 1981. The principal difference between MILES and civilian laser-tag equipment was that MILES was attached to existing Army weapons and it sent out a coded laser beam so that the receivers on the target knew what kind of weapon had hit them. When hit, the MILES equipment on the target (an individual or a vehicle) calculated if it was a near-miss (a "wounding hit") or fatal hit (and disabled the victim's weapons). While the early MILES units were restricted to infantry and tank weapons, they added a tremendous shot of reality to training. For the first time since gunpowder weapons replaced swords, spears, and bows, troops could train against each other realistically. Before gunpowder came along, realistic training could be obtained by using blunted swords, spears, and even arrows (if the troops were wearing armor). Until MILES came along, there was no way to take the deadly sting out of gunpowder-propelled projectiles. MILES was used by the troops at their home bases before they got to the NTC, where a more elaborate version awaited them.

Big Brother Is Watching—and Recording

At the NTC all the troops and their vehicles carried devices that emitted a signal that a system of receivers captured and relayed to NTC headquarters. There the signals were sorted out and a record of the ongoing operation preserved for later critique and analysis. In addition, there were roving videocamera teams who caught as much of the action as they could on film. This was integrated with the electronic information to provide an unprecedentedly thorough look at realistic training operations. Thus, while the troops were out there trying to kill each other, their activities were being recorded. This was one of the keys to NTC's success, for in the heat of even simulated battle it was difficult to sort out what you did right, or wrong. The NTC system kept a record of it all. This made it possible to conduct extremely useful debriefings for the participating officers and troops. In the later 1980s, TRADOC began to systematically analyze the nearly one hundred battalion-training cycles it had recorded. Much useful information was obtained this way, and history-minded analysts noted how closely NTC results resembled real battles.

Finding a Playground Big Enough

Training individual combat battalions takes a lot of space. In addition to the maneuvering and laser tag, provision had to be made for live-fire exercises. Initially, the Army wanted to use an area with characteristics similar to Western Europe. At the time, the most likely opponent was the Soviet Armies in East Germany, not Iraqis in the desert. But there was no available area large enough, or with sufficiently thin population density. The local population had to be considered because these combat exercises would be noisy and round the clock. There would also be aircraft and helicopters involved. What the Army ended up using was Fort Irwin, in the Mohave Desert midway between Los Angeles and Las Vegas. The area contained a thousand square miles of usable space. It was divided into one live-fire area and two maneuver areas. Even with a thousand square miles available, this barely left sufficient space for the units to move and fight. The two maneuver areas provided areas about ten by fifty kilometers. Since the maximum range of tank guns was over three kilometers, this was pretty tight. Moreover, a mechanized force could easily move over fifty kilometers in a night march; thus the fighting could be simulated, but not the long and frequent marches that led up to the battles.

While Fort Irwin was in a desert, it was not the same kind of desert found in Saudi Arabia. The Mohave Desert is what is known as "high desert." In other words, it's mountainous highlands that get little rain. It's not quite as hot as the Arabian desert on a summer day, although temperatures over 110 degrees are not unknown. At night it's colder than the Arabian desert, with a lot of freezing weather in winter. Fort Irwin is sandy, windy, rocky, and a real challenge to the troops and equipment. Getting used to rotten weather and terrain is very good preparation for combat.

While the Army officially focused on fighting the Soviets in Europe, many officers knew that there were also plans to go to the Persian Gulf if the need arose. It did, they did, and over 100,000 Army veterans of the NTC landed in Saudi Arabia as desert veterans. This helped—this helped a lot—even if it didn't get much play in the media.

THE 32ND GUARDS REGIMENT

The first year of NTC operation had the participating troops divided into opposing forces and training in the manner troops have traditionally trained. When NTC was put together, there was also a plan to have a realistic opposing force (or "OPFOR") that would look and operate like a Soviet mechanized regiment. By 1982 this force, designated the "32nd Guards Regiment," was ready for action. The designation was in line with Soviet practice. Guards units were generally the best in the Russian Army (before and after both revolutions), having achieved their special status because of exemplary performance during combat. In reality, the 32nd Guards was the 6/31st Mechanized Infantry Battalion and the 1/73rd Armor Battalion. For those not familiar with the terminology, "6/31st" means the 6th battalion of the 31st infantry regiment. The thousand or so troops in the 32nd Guards OPFOR were specially selected and served at the NTC for four years. They were drilled in the Soviet way of making war and used modified (and obsolete) Sheridan light tanks so that they appeared to be also using Soviet equipment.

Winning by Losing

The 32nd Guards did more than just provide an opposing force; they provided an OPFOR that rarely lost in these live wargames. Their success rate was partially attributable to their greater experience, as the 32nd Guards troops spent four years exercising at the NTC while the average soldier would spend from two to six weeks at the NTC in that same four years. But the second reason why the OPFOR usually won was because they were using Soviet tactics on American troops who had never experienced the Soviet army up close and personal. This was a break with tradition in an important way; the good guys were not automatically assured a win. Historically, most wargames and field exercises of this type were not "free play," but followed a script of sorts of which always ended with the good guys winning. At the NTC the good guys could win only if they were very, very good. Some U.S. battalions did beat the 32nd Guards, and walked a little taller afterward for having pulled it off. But the purpose of the NTC was to show a worst-case situation. The theory was that if the troops could handle the NTC without going completely to pieces, they would be much more effective on a future battlefield where real bullets are used.

Despite the lethal appearance of these exercises, and the sometimes reckless fervor that the troops worked up, there were few deaths or injuries. All field exercises are dangerous, largely because of the nature of the equipment and the frequent number of night operations.

STRAIGHT TALK

The payoff at the NTC went beyond getting out in the field and doing some realistic training. The post-battle briefings were, for many, the most valuable part of the exercise. Nowhere else was so much information collected on what units had done in a training exercise, and the NTC rubbed the troops' faces in it big time as they dissected good, and bad, performance.

Each unit going through the NTC took part in six to ten separate exercises during about eight days of actual field operations. Units used weapons and equipment maintained at the NTC for that purpose. Two battalions from a division were sent to the NTC together with the divisional support troops that normally support a brigade in combat. Units were given six to nine months' warning before being sent to NTC, so they could prepare as much as possible for "battle." Thus prepared, most of the troops were eager to strut their stuff, despite the awesome reputation of the 32nd Guards. However, each exercise was so similar to actual combat that it was often difficult to determine who had "won" without benefit of the after-action briefings given by the NTC staff.

Immediately after each of these exercises there was a briefing by the NTC staff on how the unit had performed, complete with details and illustrations. There were separate briefings for the commanders, and additional briefings right down to the troop level. At the end of the two-week NTC tour, there was a final briefing for the commanders and their staffs. This was where yet another NTC innovation came into play, for the commanders were critiqued in front of their subordinates. Historically, this was hardly ever done in peacetime, and was not common in wartime either. The reasoning behind this was that to maintain the discipline of a military force, it was necessary to preserve a "can do no wrong" image of commanders. Naturally, such commanders were frequently chewed out one on one by their bosses, and often removed from command for incompetence.

But the NTC experience was unique in the history of warfare. Never before had there been such realistic training, and such a complete electronic and video record of who did what. The NTC staff realized that while they could conduct critiques in the traditional fashion, it would be counterproductive to keep all the data on the exercise from the other officers and troops in a unit. To gain from their NTC experience, everyone had to know what they did right, and wrong. In the face of strong opposition, but with the backing of senior generals, NTC proceeded to give the NTC after-action briefings to unit commanders in the presence of the unit's officers. The NTC officers were brutally frank in their appraisal of commander, and unit, performance. It worked, although it was rough on many commanders who had a hard time getting used to having their shortcomings spotlighted in front of their subordinates.

As part of the "criticize the commander in front of his troops" approach, the NTC established the policy of regarding performance at NTC not as "winning" or "losing" but rather as "training." The NTC analysis of each unit's experience did not include a score that could be compared to that of others that went through NTC. The briefings concentrated on how units performed hundreds of individual tasks. Issues like how often units used their radios, or how long it took them to move or get into position were discussed. Especially interesting to the troops was the electronic record of who shot what and to what effect. There was discussion of who "won" each of the engagements with the 32nd Guards, but no box score was provided. The official Army policy was that NTC was training, not a test of the unit commander's capability. However, it was very much the commander's ultimate responsibility how well his units did at NTC. The old adage "There are no bad troops, only bad officers'' applies very much to battalion commanders. These officers have tremendous power and authority to prepare their battalions for war. The capabilities of battalion commanders make a marked difference in the performance of battalions in combat. General DuPuy's experience with the 90th Infantry Division in World War II clearly shows the impact of the battalion commander on his unit: "The secret of success lies in the selection and training of leaders before the first battle so that the seasoning process can stay ahead of the casualty process."

Although there were no official scores for commanders at the NTC, or for troops to compare with other units, the word did get around. Despite strenuous efforts on the part of NTC and the Army to downplay overall performance of commanders at NTC, it was generally known who did well and who did not so well. Since the biggest influence on the progress of an officer's career was the OER (Officers Evaluation Report) prepared periodically by each officer's superior, few commanders were willing to rate someone highly who had reportedly done poorly at NTC. As a result of this, NTC has become something of a final exam for battalion commanders. Considering the experience in Desert Storm, the system works.

TECHNICAL PROBLEMS

Nothing is perfect. Although the MILES equipment is great for direct-fire weapons, the laser still has trouble getting through smoke, dust, and rain. Moreover, the troops (including officers) often become so obsessed with beating the 32nd Guards that they will come up with ingenious ways to cheat the MILES system. The NTC staff is constantly plugging new loopholes the troops find in MILES. There are also the usual technical problems with all the electronic equipment that tracks the combat vehicles. Sometimes a tank will do gown a gully quickly and become "lost" to the tracking system. And so on.

A key element of the NTC's success was the determination of the staff to persist in finding solutions to problems as they arose. Despite the large defense budgets of the 1980s, the NTC did not have a lot of rabid partisans in Congress or the Pentagon budget bureaucracy. NTC had to constantly scrape by on a lot less money than it needed. The NTC engineers and technicians were accustomed to improvising and shooting for the doable rather than the moon. In this light, the tight budgets probably helped NTC avoiding getting bogged down trying to make state-of-the-art technology work. Most of the NTC gear was off-the-shelf technology. Nothing fancy, and all the innovation was in how the stuff was put together. After all, laser-tag kits were being sold as toys for kids.

But there were some areas in which state-of-the-art technology had to be developed. For example, there are no MILES systems for indirect-fire weapons (artillery or mortars), the ones that cause most of the casualties in combat. This could have been a serious limitation on the effectiveness of the NTC. But a field expedient solution was worked out whereby the NTC computer system (which was constantly receiving all the data from the tracking instruments on vehicles and MILES gear) calculated where artillery fire would land. The NTC staff (OCs or Observer Controllers) who accompanied each platoon were then notified and these OCs would start tossing out the required number of artillery simulators (large firecrackers that made a whistling sound, followed by a loud bang and cloud of smoke). Using known probabilities of injuries and vehicle damage for such barrages (from wartime experience and peacetime tests), the OCs would designate which troops and vehicles were injured and to what extent. Although this was a throwback to pre-MILES training, it was not considered as unrealistic as OCs determining who was hit by tank or rifle fire. Artillery is accepted as a random killer, while tank and rifle fire can be controlled by the troops. However, through the 1980s, work continued on developing a MILES-type device to represent the effects of artillery and bombs.

Another missing link in MILES was equipment to represent the effects of air attack and antiaircraft weapons. Part of the problem here was that two different services were involved, the Air Force and the Army. Throughout this period the Air Force was heavily into developing a MILES-like system to allow it to realistically train pilots to attack ground targets. What the Air Force eventually came up with was not compatible with what the Army needed for NTC, and neither service was successful in getting the other to compromise. Thus air attacks would be handled in much the same manner as artillery until a mutually agreeable solution was found in the 1990s.

One shortcoming of the NTC didn't become obvious to a lot of people until Desert Shield, when officers and troops in the desert casually remarked that this was the first time they had ever had sufficient room to train with an entire division at once. The fact that a thousand square miles of land at Fort Irwin was barely adequate for two battalions at a time to train gives you an idea of the scope of the problem. A division has over a dozen combat battalions and there's no training area in the United States large enough to handle a modern combat division (which contains over five thousand vehicles and, under optimum conditions, takes at least thirty minutes to pass by). The Army plans to acquire more land adjacent to Fort Irwin, wire it up, and provide sufficient space to maneuver a brigade, but even this is doubtful because of the cost. Meanwhile, the solution is to use networked computer simulations. This is fine as far as it goes, but it is only as realistic as the situation programmed into the computer. While NTC puts the battalions under realistic combat conditions, a brigade or division has far more coordination problems. Many examples of this were seen in Desert Storm, where NTC-trained battalions were understandably inexperienced in sharing a fast-moving battlefield with other friendly battalions. Many of the friendly-fire incidents resulted from this.

TECHNICAL SOLUTIONS

In the case of NTC, success begets progress. Not content with the payoff of the NTC of the 1980s, the staff has been adding new features throughout the 1990s.

One of the first improvements was a system to represent artillery and aerial firepower. It uses radios linked with MILES units. When artillery or aircraft fire is used, the NTC computers calculate where the explosions will take place and whether there are any MILES-equipped trainees in the area. If there are, they calculate who is dead or wounded. The MILES units in question would be activated.

These improved artillery/air-power systems are being replaced in the mid-1990s with MILES II. This new MILES system will be able to deal with smoke, and provide more accurate information on when, where, and to what extent MILES-equipped troops and equipment were killed or injured during the training exercise.

The scoring system will be upgraded to allow the computerized scoring systems to decide if the target was destroyed, immobilized, had its communications knocked out, or was undamaged. GPS will be included to better pinpoint where the troops are for after-action reviews. MILES II will also be able to deal with the effects of nuclear warheads, chemical weapons, aircraft bombs, and mines.

The Army and Air Force finally agreed on how to deal with aircraft at

NTC, to everyone's satisfaction. Pilots will be able to realistically evade (or not evade) ground fire while delivering fire on ground targets. All of the air and ground interaction will be controlled by the NTC computers.

The OPFOR (the 32nd Guards Regiment) will get new equipment that will more accurately represent Russian-made gear. There are also plans to change the doctrine of the OPFOR to reflect the more variable use of Soviet doctrine in the wake of the Soviet Union's breakup.

VIRTUAL NTC

The expense of sending units to the NTC led to the creation of a "virtual" NTC using personal computers and phone lines. This was SIMNET (SIMulator NETwork), a system that had its origins in some late 1970s brainstorming. The concept, which took nearly ten years to bring to the troops, was a bunch of armored vehicle interior mock-ups that used personal computers to display what the troops in the vehicles could see outside. The different vehicles were linked together by phone lines (either at the same base, or in another country) and the troops would play out a computer-moderated wargame. As personal computers became more powerful, cheap, and effective, so did SIMNET. A $2,000 PC in 1993 has more computing power than a multimillion-dollar machine of the 1970s, and this provided all sorts of simulation opportunities heretofore impossible. By the early 1990s, SIMNET was an inexpensive alternative to NTC. While not as gut-wrenching and exciting as NTC, SIMNET was realistic enough. The troops got into it, and got valuable training out of it.

BEYOND NTC

By the mid-1980s it was obvious that NTC was working. While NTC was expensive, costing over $20,000 for each soldier put through the two-week exercise, the basic idea behind NTC was proposed for smaller training areas in Europe (CMTC, Combat Maneuver Training Complex) and for a "light forces" (infantry and commandoes) center in Arkansas (JRTC, Joint Readiness Training Center). Most of the U.S.- and European-based units and commanders who deployed to Operations Desert Shield and Desert Storm had trained at the combat training centers during the year before the war.

Another spin-off of the concept of combat training centers is a program that was begun in the late 1980s to improve the combat proficiency of division and corps commanders and their staffs. It relies on an extensive use of computer simulations to exercise the doctrine against a realistic opposing force and to get practice in coordinating many levels of command. This program is very similar to the Fleet Readiness Program that was begun in the Navy in the mid-1970s, and is called BCTP (Battle Command Training Program). This system uses minicomputer-based wargame software and telephone or satellite communications that can link hundreds of commanders and staff officers anywhere in the world, or the entire exercise can be conducted at the BCTP center at Fort Leavenworth, Kansas. Unlike the NTC, the BCTP is largely dependent on its wargame software to maintain its connection with reality. While this is always a potential problem, since the mid-1970s the Army has come to embrace history and field experience as the primary sources for its computer wargames. As a result, there were not too many surprises for BCTP-trained commanders and their staffs when they found themselves in a real war during the 1990–1991 Persian Gulf operations. As a result, the Persian Gulf experience was used to modify many of the military's computerized wargames. NTC field experience is also constantly analyzed and used in the same manner.

The training of commanders and their staffs with exercises that simulate actual combat has a long history going back over a century. Actual maneuvers with the divisions and larger units to provide commanders with opportunities to increase their proficiency in command and control is too expensive to give them and their staff officers any significant training. The computer was seen early on as an ideal means to provide these staff exercises. Before computers came along, it required about as many "controllers" as people being trained to provide realistic information and to calculate the results of participants' decisions. Often these exercises degenerated into little more than highly scripted drills. These shortcomings in earlier command exercises led to bloody disasters in wartime, as officers believed the outcomes of their peacetime drills and often ignored what was really happening on the battlefield. There was a certain amount of "command blindness" in Vietnam, and the veterans of those incidents are senior commanders today. During Vietnam, these officers were leading platoons and companies and they don't want their current lieutenants and captains to go through the same nonsense.

Wargaming Readiness

The BCTP was actually the result of three different trends in the post-Vietnam army. First came the study of military history, which had been largely ignored since World War II. About the same, it was remembered that the Army had used wargames for training up through the early 1960s and maybe it wasn't a bad idea to try using wargames again. These two trends were in support of more realistic training and standards for readiness. This last term, "readiness," is a catchall phrase in the military that encompasses the quality and quantity of preparations for war. In most peacetime armies, "readiness" becomes little more than a phrase, until the brutal realities in combat demonstrate what readiness really is and how badly it is needed. The commanders in the 1970s wanted to be more ready in the future than they had been before and during Vietnam. DePuy and trainers like Gorman led the way in revitalizing the development and use of wargames for the troops.

But what about combat simulations to increase the "combat readiness" of the senior commanders and their staffs? Studies of the early battles involving U.S. forces since 1776 indicated that one of the primary reasons for the bloody failures of these battles was the poor training and preparation of commanders and staffs above the battalion level. The lack of experience in conducting realistic large-scale operational-level exercises before the first battle was a major cause of many of these failures. Traditionally, commanders and their staffs spend most of their time on peacetime requirements and not on keeping their edge in warfighting skills. Even at the Army War College, there was a constant struggle over whether the instruction should focus on what most generals do most of their time—budgeting, management, personnel problems, procurement, etc.—or the remote (it is normally assumed that war is not expected for at least the next five years) probability of war that will require combat skills. Consequently, historically, the troops even with poor training and equipment were often readier for war than the senior officers and staffs who led and supervised them.

The Navy actually led the way with its Fleet Readiness Program, which was established at the Naval War College in the mid-1970s. The Navy built one of the most modernized computerized wargaming simulation centers in the world at the time and included on the center staff a group of intelligence specialists who could realistically portray the actions/reactions of opposing forces. The Navy's objective was to give fleet commanders a cost-effective way of keeping combat-ready. This was done by leading senior commanders and their staffs in computerized combat simulations that used the fleet's actual wartime plans. The program included a learning phase that helped increase the professional competence of the participants.

A Review of Education and Training for Officers (RETO) was conducted by the Army in 1978. In the review of formal educational programs for general offices, the study recommended that the Army should establish something similar to the Navy's Fleet Readiness Program. A test program was established at the Army War College in 1979. It was given the name Tactical Command Readiness Program (TCRP). The emphasis of the TCRP was on keeping senior tactical commanders and their staffs abreast of operational considerations by providing programmed learning computerized wargaming support. General Meyer (the Army Chief of Staff at the time) was a major proponent of the TCRP and he later added contingency planning support to do it. It was the strong belief of General Meyer that poor planning, especially in the area of systematically developing effective concepts of operations, was a major contributing factor to many of the early battle defeats. Many revolutionary combat-simulation models and simulation techniques came out of the TCRP test program.

When the Army's Battle Command Training Program (BCTP) was actually initiated at Fort Leavenworth, Kansas, in 1987, some even more distinctive features were added. The exercises for the corps and divisions are normally conducted in two phases. The Army tries to conduct the first phases early in the corps or division commander's tour. During the first phase there are seminar games designed to assist the commander in team building with his key commanders and staff. Following this by two to six months is a command-post exercise called WARFIGHTER. The emphasis is on using realistic situations. The simulation models included digitized terrain maps for most of the world where U.S. forces are likely to fight. The BCTP also uses senior retired officers as leadership consultants. From the very beginning of the test TCRP, finding effective ways of bringing lessons learned to the attention of the senior commander was a problem. The use of distinguished retired senior officers has worked well in interjecting lessons for the BCTP. These exercises last as long as the commander wants, but the usual time is five days. Just as the NTC provides for the battalion-level troops, the goal of the BCTP is that if and when U.S. corps and division commanders have to fight their first real battle, they will have the confidence and the edge that comes from already having fought it. Desert Storm was not only proof of the success of the BCTP, it validated the value of all the services' combat training centers.

MY REALITY VERSUS YOUR REALITY

All of this change did not get by without a good deal of criticism, particularly from civilians. This turned out to be a case of the blind trying to tell the half blind what 20/20 vision was like. The 1976 edition of FM 100-5 got the brawl rolling because this, the Army's new "how to fight" manual, proposed a concept called "active defense." The term, and the concept, was easily reinterpreted to mean whatever critics wanted it to mean. While the reality of the situation was being worked out in wargames and training exercises like the NTC's, critics could make just about any statement they wanted and call it "reasonable."

Meantime, the Army's wargamers were crunching their history and numbers to try to determine just what would happen if large-scale combat broke out in Europe. The punch line to all this did not appear until the Soviet Union began to collapse between 1989 and 1991. At that point, a flood of hard information on the true nature and capabilities of the Soviet armed forces began to reach the West. These revelations showed the 1976 FM 100-5 to be pretty much on the money as a technique for countering Soviet-style ground combat. The Red (Soviet) Army had not changed all that much from its World War II days. FM 100-5, by advocating essentially the same doctrine that had allowed the Germans to beat the Soviets, proved to be militarily correct.

What may never be officially admitted was that implicit in FM 100-5 was a technique that worked for the Germans in World War II but was politically taboo in any official NATO war plans. That is, NATO forces were not supposed to talk about giving up any terrain to attacking Soviet armies. But in many a training and staff exercise, this was done in order to play upon the weaknesses in the Soviet style of warfare. As one World War II German general told some 1980s U.S. generals about successfully fighting the Soviets, "Let them run past you and then kick them in the ass; they won't know what hit them or what to do about it." Critics would point out that the Germans lost the war doing whatever they did, but the critics would have missed the point that, man for man, the Germans inflicted more casualties on their enemies and lost in Russia largely because of strategic errors and political interference in military operations. As details about Soviet operations in Afghanistan began to come into the open, it became obvious to even slow learners that the Red Army was still the same old Red Army. While the Soviets were still building more weapons, the U.S. Army was building much better ways to fight and training the troops accordingly.

Civilian critics of the new Army doctrine and training policies had more success in questioning Army spending habits. Basically, the Army (and the armed forces in general) had to justify every penny and in great detail. That made the Army bear down and do its homework. This war of paper bullets also served to make the Army commanders battle-savvy in a bureaucratic battleground.

Toward the end of the Carter administration and through the 1980s, there was increased awareness of the growing arms race between the Soviet bloc and the West. While this caused more critics to come out of the woodwork, it also gave the military more leeway to get on with their reforms. All of a sudden, the military was needed once more. The lingering feeling that we came out of Vietnam with less capable armed forces than we went in with created support for any moves that would increase their effectiveness. The 1979 taking of American Iranian embassy staff as hostages, and the subsequent failure to effect a military rescue in 1980, made change in the military appear as something desirable. At around the same time, the threat of a Russian invasion of Poland, war between Iraq and Iran, and several smaller incidents merely enhanced the view that change for the better in the military was a good thing and should not be hindered. By and large, the reform efforts were not hindered and were often assisted by the politicians.

CHAPTER

12

The Fat 80s

After uncharacteristically low defense budgets in the 1970s, military spending skyrocketed in the 1980s. Some of this money was wasted, but most of
it was put to good use. And what would have happened if all that money
had not been available?

The 1980s saw an unprecedented growth in defense spending, with average
annual outlays of nearly $290 billion (in 1990 dollars). In contrast, the
1970s averaged $210 billion a year, the 1960s (including Vietnam costs)
$240 billion, and the 1950s (including Korea costs) $195 billion. The 1940s,
including World War II expenses, averaged only $240 billion a year. If the
1980s are to be considered the decade in which we won the Cold War, then
it was more expensive, at least in dollars, than winning World War II.

The large military budgets of the 1980s did not loom as large as one
would think in increasing the Army's, or other services', capabilities for the
future. Much of the money was spent on weapons and equipment that was
then, and is still now, of questionable usefulness for the rest of the 1990s.
Other costs were unique to the armed forces of the 1980s:

- Ever-increasing pension costs (approaching 10 percent of the defense
  budget). The United States established large peacetime forces after World
  War II and provided for half pay (after twenty years) and two-thirds pay
  (after thirty years). Retirees also have access to other benefits. In addition,
  troops wounded in action can be retired at a pay level commensurate with
  their degree of disability and rank at the time of retirement. The cost of

these pensions has gone from under 1 percent of the defense budget in 1947 to over 10 percent in the 1990s.

- Higher personnel costs because of the voluntary Army. Before the voluntary Army was introduced, most of the enlisted troops were paid very low wages, wages that were not at all competitive with civilian pay scales. This was possible because most of the troops were conscripts. After 1975, all the troops were volunteers and pay levels had to be increased so that they were competitive with comparable civilian jobs the troops could obtain. Thus payroll costs increased over 25 percent after the all-volunteer armed forces were introduced in the 1970s.

- Increased spending for strategic weapons. The original heyday for strategic-weapons spending was the 1960s, when most of the first generation were built. The annual costs for this in the 1960s ran to about $30 billion. But in the 1970s and early 1980s, these annual costs fell by more than half. But when the big defense budgets again appeared in the 1980s, so did calls for more spending on new strategic weapons. Annual spending quickly returned to 1960s levels. This surge in strategic-weapons spending was a key factor in ending the Cold War, as it was one area in which the Russians soon felt no longer able to compete.

- Increased spending on research and development (R&D). Spending in this area averaged between $15 and $20 billion a year through the 1960s and 1970s. When the big defense budgets returned in the 1980s, R&D increased to levels to 40 to 50 percent higher than the previous two decades. This was another key to Cold War victory. Russia could turn out lots of weapons, but it was less capable of developing new ones as fast and as reliably as the Western nations.

- Increased spending for the National Guard and reserves. This was primarily an Army initiative. Through the 1960s and 1970s, spending in this area averaged $10 to $15 billion a year. Because the Army had promised Congress it would increase its number of divisions in the 1980s without increasing active-duty manpower, the manpower shortfall had to come from reserve and National Guard units. Thus, overall annual spending in this area increased about 25 percent.

The additional $80 billion a year the military had in the 1980s was cut down by over $50 billion a year for the above items. The remaining $30 to $40 billion went to other improvements, which had the major impact on Gulf

War performance. The major impacts of the additional 1980s defense spending were:

- Rebuilding of the inventory. While most military spending goes for payroll and maintaining forces, some of it goes for buying new weapons and equipment. This material is inventory for any military operations the troops will have to engage in. Most of this stuff will last, on average, about twenty years before it is useless. Coming out of World War II, U.S. forces had an enormous inventory of weapons and equipment. It was this World War II legacy that comprised the bulk of Army equipment until the early 1960s. Indeed, just before the Vietnam War, it was not unusual for troops to be using weapons and equipment that had been manufactured in 1944 or 1945. In 1960, this inventory had a value of over $600 billion. Then came Vietnam and the lean 1970s. Not much was spent on procurement, and the value of the inventory plummeted. When the big budgets of the 1980s arrived, a lot of money was poured into procurement. The following chart shows the impact of all this.

Year	Inventory (Millions of 1990 $)
1960	635,435
1965	561,376
1970	503,424
1975	423,981
1980	412,604
1985	536,922
1990	701,846

The end of the Cold War has begun to shrink defense budgets once more, so the growth of the inventory will level off and, most likely, begin to shrink in the next ten years. One advantage of the inventory shrinking so much by 1980 and then increasing enormously through the 1980s was seen in the Gulf War. The American forces had the largest amount of relatively new equipment of any major nation in the world.

- Allowing sufficient resources to make the jump to high technology. The Army had not really gotten the technology bug big time until the 1980s.

This was more than just buying weapons with a lot of bells and whistles attached. The Army had to change its attitude toward technology. This meant first understanding technology better, then knowing what you wanted, and finally giving the troops high-tech weapons that would be used effectively. The three best examples of this are the M-1 tank, the Apache attack helicopter, and the new generation of command and control (C^2) equipment. Both the M-1 tank and the Apache helicopter were systems comparable (in cost, complexity, and effectiveness) to contemporary high-performance combat aircraft. Both of these weapons made extensive use of computers and sensors and required carefully selected and trained crews to get the most out of them. The C^2 developments included a wide range of communications equipment, computers, and new ideas on how to keep in touch with and keep track of the troops in combat. All of this technology was something the Air Force and Navy had been doing for several decades, but until the 1980s, the Army had not really believed that the ground pounders could also make effective use of all these gadgets. By the end of the 1980s, the Army had institutionalized the acceptance, development, and use of new technologies. When future histories of land warfare are written, the U.S. Army of the late twentieth century will get most of the credit for making ground combat high-tech.

- Allowing sufficient resources for training. When money is short and items must be cut from the budget, training expenses are generally the first to go. Training is very expensive and the results don't show up unless there's a war. Since most nations rarely spend much time at war, it's a reasonable gamble for generals to shortchange the training budget when money is tight. This was the case in America after Vietnam. But when the defense budgets began to increase in the late 1970s, the veterans of Vietnam who now comprised the bulk of armed forces leadership saw to it that training was increased. Not only were training budgets vastly increased, but the quality of the training was higher than ever before. One of the legacies of Vietnam was the realization that poor training is expensive on the battlefield.

- Creation of a totally professional force. This was initially created by the pay increases of the 1970s, but really came of age with the larger training budgets of the 1980s. In practice, the pre-Vietnam, largely conscript force was quite professional. The military had such a large pool of potential conscripts to draw from that it could afford to be picky. As a result, the pre-Vietnam ranks were full of well-educated, physically fit troops. Vietnam forced the military to reach deeper into the barrel. Not only did the military need more troops during Vietnam, but its better-educated potential conscripts increasingly evaded service. By the end of the Vietnam War, morale and discipline had collapsed. Worse, the younger NCOs were not up to the higher standards of the pre-Vietnam generation. The NCOs come from the ranks, and if the troop quality declines, so does that of your next generation of NCOs. The increased training budget and several years to weed out the lower-quality NCOs and officers enabled the armed forces to enter the 1980s with a reformed attitude toward personnel quality. By the early 1980s the troops saw themselves as professionals and embraced a dedication toward being the best. By the end of the decade, they were, and in 1991, they proved it.

WHERE THE BIG BUDGETS CAME FROM

The marked increase of defense budgets was actually started by President Carter, although it was carried forward with a vengeance by President Reagan. Reagan got most of the credit. Carter, however, was a former military man and, although his Democratic party was generally hostile to larger defense budgets, was able to make the case to Congress that more money was needed. While Jimmy Carter is generally, and accurately, regarded as a politician more interested in social than military affairs, he did have unique military experience. Carter was a Naval Academy graduate and his military background was with Admiral Rickover's nuclear submarine program. Rickover was a perfectionist, and he personally selected officers to crew the nuclear subs. Carter was selected, and under Rickover's leadership he acquired a keen insight into how the military worked, and what was required to make it work well. No matter how low other segments of the military declined, Rickover's nuclear subs were always crewed with a highly professional and competent elite. When the generals and admirals came to Carter requesting more money, Carter was able to sort out the necessary from the unnecessary and get a hefty defense-budget increase through the Democratic-controlled Congress. When Ronald Reagan defeated Carter in the 1979 election, he did it partially by convincing the voters that Carter had not been supportive enough of the military. This was ironic, because while Carter was a veteran, Reagan was not (although Reagan was put in the Army Air Force to make training films during the war). Moreover, Carter had provided the money and civilian leadership to get the long-sought military reforms going. While Reagan made good on his promise to obtain even more money for the Defense Department, he did this perhaps too well. A case can be made that too much money was poured into defense without proper planning by Reagan (and his close associates), and therefore a lot of it was misapplied.

The United States spent nearly $3 trillion (1990) on defense during the 1980s. This was nearly $800 billion more than what was spent in the 1970s. America did receive tangible benefits from this additional spending, but most of it went to weapons and technology that had little bearing on the Gulf War victory and will likely have small impact on post–Cold War needs.

But at the time the money was being authorized, no one knew the Cold War would come to an abrupt end, nor that at about the same time the United States would find itself involved in a major land campaign with Iraq's large army. The spending on strategic weapons and research and development was seen as a viable strategy for countering the Soviet Union's continued ability to produce more weapons than the United States. Until 1989, the possibility of a land battle in Central Europe was still considered real. Thus anything that might cause the Soviet defense establishment problems was considered money well spent.

While the larger defense budgets of the 1980s were welcomed by the military, the additional funds came with political strings attached. This had always been the case, but in the 1980s it was even more so. The largest, and most expensive, political string was attached to the Strategic Defense Initiative (SDI or "Star Wars"). SDI was an ambitious, expensive, and problematic project to develop and build a defensive system that could shoot down enemy ICBMs before they could land on American targets. On the political side, this was a pet project of President Reagan and he used it to show how concerned he was about defending America from the one Soviet weapon system that could definitely reach North America.

Along with the funding for SDI went a green light for a lot of other high-tech research and development. Many of these projects didn't survive simply because, when it came time to run some field test, the new systems couldn't perform to even a minimal standard. This in itself was not unusual; it is typical with new weapons and equipment that push the state of the art. It's not for nothing that people in the research and development business privately recast the common term "leading edge technology" into "bleeding edge technology." It was somewhat worse in the 1980s because there had been something of a drought in research and development during the 1960s and particularly the 1970s. The commonly accepted fear was that the Soviet Union was in the process of wiping out America's technical lead. This proved not to be the case, but no one on this side of the Iron Curtain knew that at the time.

PUTTING IT ALL INTO PERSPECTIVE

The defense-spending binge of the 1980s is history now and we can only speculate on what might have happened if it had been done differently. We have examined three alternative scenarios for different spending strategies in the 1980s:

1. Spending less (continuing 1970s levels). There would have been a tremendous political debate over this. Remember, even the Democratic president of the late 1970s, Jimmy Carter, was in favor of increasing the defense budget. And Carter did not beat his Republican opponent, Gerald Ford, by a landslide. But then, anything is possible, and if the defense budgets had stayed at 1970s levels, the military would have adapted. The principal adaption would have been cuts in personnel (largely because payroll costs still had to go up to support the new volunteer force) and research and development, and smaller increases in procurement. There had to be some procurement, as the World War II and Korean War era equipment still being used by many troops was on its last legs. The difference between annual defense budgets in the 1970s and 1980s was about $70 billion a year. A little over half of that difference was new procurement. While procurement would not have been as much as under the actual 1970s budgets it could have been increased. SDI would most likely not have gotten under way at all. The call for a six-hundred-ship navy would not have been heard and the Air Force would have lost several of its secret (and very expensive) development projects (like the B-2 bomber and the SR-71 replacement, as well as the more expensive Navy ships and Army helicopters). A lot of the new weapons you saw in the Gulf War would still have been there, but not in the same quantities. The biggest hit would have been taken in the training and readiness departments. The specialized training centers of the Army and Air Force would probably have lost a lot of their funding. Moreover, there just wouldn't be much money to send the pilots and units to them anyway. The Navy would have spent less time at sea. On the positive side, there would still have been a professional attitude among the now all-volunteer force. This would have led to innovations to overcome the shortage of funding.

2. Spending the same (but spending differently). When all that additional money went to the military in the 1980s, there was no single spending plan for using it. The way the money was put to use was subject to an ongoing debate. In addition to the services, and the branches within the services, there were also political considerations. Both Congress and the president had pet projects that the military had to consider, and often implement, even if the troops didn't want or need what the politicians were demanding. The primary impetus of the higher defense spending of the 1980s was the perceived need to meet the growing Soviet military threat. Another constant was the difficulty of increasing personnel levels in the U.S. armed forces. This meant that the traditional (since the 1950s) U.S. approach to better defense would continue to be a search for better battlefield technology. Going into different directions with technology was difficult in the late 1970s, primarily because so many current technology projects were being barely kept alive at low spending levels in the expectation that bigger budgets would arrive. For example, the Army's new surface-to-surface air missile system (the Patriot) had been in development since the early 1960s. Many Air Force and Navy high-tech systems were also stalled in research and development, awaiting sufficient funds to begin manufacturing.

The various doctrinal debates of the late 1970s and early 1980s over what the Russians were up to and what we should do about it could have created significant changes in direction. For example, the Air Force might have embraced precision bombing even more enthusiastically and this might have led to the Navy's adopting precision bombing on a larger scale. The Air Force might have been more aggressive in expanding its air-transport capability. The Navy might have been more enthusiastic about smart munitions and buying more fast transports for moving Army and Marine units. In actual fact, the Navy had to be forced by Congress to purchase what few transports it had to use for the 1990 Persian Gulf crisis. The Navy might have also expanded its mine-clearing capability more quickly and extensively. Traditionally, the Navy has never been enthusiastic about cutting back warship building in favor of transports, mine clearing, and better aircraft munitions for attacking land targets. Old traditions die hard.

3. Spending even more (unlikely, but possible). Had the Soviets not invaded Afghanistan in 1979, the state of the Russian armed forces would have been more of a mystery in the 1980s. As it was, the flaws of the Red Army became more obvious because of the Afghan War and this shaped the spending decisions in America during the 1980s. Without Afghanistan to show how decrepit the Soviet ground forces had become, more money might have gone into upgrading and expanding U.S. ground forces and Air Force ground-attack capability. Increased defense spending would probably have resulted in more spending for space-based systems. These would be for communications and information gathering. The Afghanistan invasion also made it clear to many that the Soviets still had imperialistic ambitions. On the other side of this coin, the invasion was one reason why the U.S. defense buildup began during the Carter administration. Jimmy Carter was trying hard to get the Soviets to cooperate in world peace efforts and he felt a bit of personal shock when the Soviets up and invaded one of their neighbors.

The ''spending it differently'' angle can be twisted into many shapes to produce hundreds of different scenarios. But we can simplify this by looking at different spending levels and strategies in terms of how they would have:

1. Changed the performance and outcome of the 1991 Gulf War. Less spending would have resulted in increased casualties. Without the well-trained pilots, and the number of aircraft with precision-bombing equipment, the damage to the Iraqis would not have been as great. More aircraft would have been lost, although probably not a whole lot more. Less money spent on technical upgrades and aircraft procurement would have made the American AWACS aircraft (of which there were actually ten) less abundant and capable and the two JSTARS would not have been there at all. The same number of U.S. troops could have been put into the area, but not as quickly, as there would have been fewer cargo aircraft and fast naval transports. The tanks and armored vehicles would not have been as capable; GPS would not have been ready. Instead of a few hundred casualties, there would have been a few thousand. The fighting would have lasted longer. If 1980s defense spending had been the same, but distributed differently, or if spending levels were higher, the outcome in the Gulf War would not have been much different. If less money had been spent on training and/or the GPS system were not ready, there would have been much higher casualties and a few more days of fighting.

2. Changed the outcome of the Cold War. Wouldn't have made much difference how much, or how little, the United States spent. The Soviet military-industrial complex worked on long-term planning goals. Five-, ten-, and twenty-year planning cycles were used for many major items (like nuclear reactors for submarines and new weapons systems designs in general). There was sufficient flexibility in the system to take care of newly discovered (or stolen) technologies, but overall, the system had a life of its own that was relatively oblivious to external events. Thus the system would have continued to pour out weapons, and cripple the Soviet economy, with little regard to what other nations were doing. The Soviets set their course for an economic debacle in the 1960s and their government system had little or no capacity to change that course. Lower U.S. defense spending still left the West with what the Soviets considered a technologically superior military capability. It was Western military technology, more than Western battlefield prowess, that frightened the Soviets. SDI, and continued enthusiasm for high-technology weapons in America, was what kept the Soviets spending, and spending. This was suspected during the Cold War, but wasn't confirmed until later. So this is all hindsight.

3. Changed the situation of the American forces in the post–Cold War world. If we had spent less, the military would have been in a more experienced frame of mind to deal with lower post–Cold War budgets. Never underestimate frame of mind. It's now a more wrenching experience to go from the Fat 80s to the Lean 90s. Time and opportunity will be lost while the gears are more painfully shifted. Had more money been spent in the 1980s, the lean 1990s would have seen the post–Cold War military better equipped and facing a more painful disposal of relatively new weapons and equipment. Much of it could be sold to allies, as is happening now with Saudi Arabia and Kuwait. There would also have been a larger pile of technology with which to upgrade systems through a decade of low transition from development to production. This is a very popular proposal in the 1990s, putting a lot of resources into research and development but little into production.

THE ETERNAL DEBATE: WHO GETS HOW MUCH FOR WHAT?

Every nation has to deal with money squabbles among the various factions in its armed forces. In addition to the three traditional services (Army, Air Force, and Navy), there are many different branches within the services.

The Army has branches for armor, infantry, artillery, logistics, signal, engineers, intelligence, and so on. The Navy has surface ships, subs, and naval aviation (carrier- or land-based). The Air Force has fighters, bombers, ICBMs, and transports. There are several reasons for this ongoing budget battle. In no particular order (because it varies from nation to nation and time to time) there is:

- Self-preservation. More money means you are better prepared to survive combat. Superior, more numerous, and better-maintained weapons give you an edge.
- Pride. Everyone feels that his or her branch or service is the most important (or at least more important than some of the others). In peacetime, this can be best demonstrated by that branch or service receiving more money.
- Power. Peacetime armed forces are bureaucracies and any bureaucracy calculates its power by how much money it has to play with.
- Patriotism. Most people in the military are there to "defend the nation." One can more effectively do that with more money, and such officers see it as their patriotic duty to get that money any way they can. Even at the expense of another branch or service.
- Pragmatism. Each service and branch makes a detailed, logical, and impassioned case for its share of the pie. Often the details are dubious, the logic flawed, and the passions turned way up.

The budget battles in the American military have always been fierce. After decades of wrangling, the late Cold War pattern came down to the Air Force and Navy each getting 20 to 25 percent more than the Army. Consider this the high-tech bonus, since the Air Force and Navy use more technology than the Army. This ratio is now up for renegotiation in the post–Cold War world. After having the Cold War to frame arguments for nearly five decades, the participants have to put their thinking caps on to develop a new set of arguments. The environment has changed faster and to a larger extent than anyone anticipated, which will make the budget debates of the 1990s interesting and entertaining to watch.

To put all this in perspective, consider what might have happened if the budgetary largess of the 1980s had been distributed differently.

The Army wanted more divisions and more high-tech weapons, particularly helicopters and antiaircraft weapons. The Army's new M-1 tank, first delivered in the early 1980s, came with a long list of "future enhancements." These improvements would have come faster had there been more money. It was unlikely that the Army would have gotten less money during the Cold War period, because all services recognized that the feared Central Front battle would have required a lot of divisions and tanks. Going into the post–Cold War world, this rationale is gone and with it goes most of the Army's hopes of grabbing a larger slice of the defense budget.

The Air Force had the missions that were bottomless pits for funding. They wanted fighters and strike aircraft to defeat enemy air forces and achieve air superiority. In the late 1970s, the Air Force got its new generation of combat aircraft (F-16, F-15, and A-10). But it had to try several times to get a new bomber (the B-1, which Jimmy Carter got canceled and Ronald Reagan later resurrected). Meanwhile, the Air Force built the F-117A and B-2 stealth aircraft in secret (from the public, not the president). As a result of all these machinations with bombers, the United States ended up spending more on bombers in the 1980s than on strategic missiles. Had the Air Force had more money it would have built more bombers more quickly and built a new generation of strategic missiles (the MX or "Peacekeeper"). The Air Force also wanted a new mobile strategic missile. If the political clout and the money had been there, the Air Force would have gone after this also. (The Soviets already had these systems.) Any money left over would have gone to more fighters and strike aircraft (like the F-15E version of the F-15). With the impressive Air Force performance in the 1991 Gulf War, the Air Force enters the post–Cold War budget battles with a strong hand. The new national focus on regional crises and rapid response also enhances the budget position of the Air Force because of the inherent versatility that the speed and range of aircraft provide.

The Navy, in contrast, imposed some limits on itself. Rather high limits as it turned out, but limits nonetheless. The Navy's budget battle cry from the mid-1970s through the 1980s was the "six-hundred-ship Navy." The Navy came out of the 1960s with nearly a thousand ships. But the Navy, more than the Army and Air Force, was still living off the building boom of World War II. Over six hundred of these ships would have to be retired by the end of the 1970s. Replacement ships were much more expensive, and the Navy felt that getting ship strength back to six hundred would be an achievable goal. If there was money left over, the carriers could also use some new aircraft, the Marines always wanted new weapons, and, gee, a new attack submarine would be swell too. In the post–Cold War world, the Navy finds its chief rival, the Soviet navy, gone. The Soviet navy has not only disappeared as an organization, its ships have been left to rot from lack of maintenance or professional crews and many of its key naval bases are now in foreign countries. The Navy has therefore begun to switch its thinking from the high seas to emphasizing "littoral" (coastal) operations. The Navy has also recently created a new Doctrine Command to write doctrine that will include maneuver operations from the sea onto land. Perhaps we will soon see "AirLandNavy" Battle doctrine.

And finally, we have the eternal trade-offs. Any armed force, especially in peacetime, has several directions it can go with the funds it is provided. There's no clear formula for how much should be spent on the following needs:

Payroll. This generally has first priority in a volunteer force. Armies with a lot of conscripts (such as the Soviets and their successor states) have to worry only about the cadres (officers and senior NCOs). U.S. forces are tempted to slight this area until they start to lose good people to the civilian workforce; then there is a furious battle in Congress to get a "catch-up" pay raise.

Hardware. This is the easiest to sell to Congress, as it means jobs in many congressional districts. However, the tail often wags the dog as Congress decides it wants a particular weapon not because the military wants it but because Congress wants it to make some members of Congress look better. This often backfires. Once production of a weapon is begun, it's difficult to stop unless a new weapon immediately replaces the old one in the same plant, or you keep producing old weapons even though the armed forces say they don't need it. This is a frequent occurrence with aircraft. The Navy and Air Force are constantly told by Congress to keep producing aircraft they don't want or need because the legislators don't want to see the jobs lost in their districts.

Maintenance. Expensive and easy to ignore in peacetime. This is more than just changing the oil and keeping the cobwebs out of equipment. It also means buying sufficient spare parts to keep equipment going and to support heavy use of equipment for training purposes. Not providing enough trained technicians to perform maintenance is another way to cut costs. When budgets get tight, there is a strong temptation to go cheap on upkeep. The results of shortchanging repair and maintenance of equipment are hard to spot in peacetime, but they are painfully obvious in wartime. Look for this temptation to become unbearable in the 1990s.

Combat Service Support. This includes units that support the combat troops by moving supplies to them, repairing their equipment, tending the wounded, providing communications, and a host of other activities. Along with maintenance, this is another big favorite for cutting when budgets are tight. In the 1991 Gulf War, the U.S. Army was caught short by its policy of tight spending on combat support units. Maintenance of equipment was better funded, but money for all that the Army wanted to do in the 1980s was tight and combat service support was one area where dangerous economies were made.

Training. If you cut maintenance, it's almost automatic to cut training also. Without properly supported equipment, realistic training is difficult and not really worth the effort. This is particularly true with the expensive "dissimilar training" (where you train and equip some of your units as realistic enemy for your troops to train against). So if you see a nation that goes cheap on upkeep, it probably doesn't spend much on training either. In peacetime this is not much noted; in wartime it is.

Reserves. This is a recent innovation, as only in the last century or so could nations afford to equip units that were staffed by part-time soldiers. This was still expensive, but not nearly as expensive as active units. The combat performance of reserve units has been mixed. Some have performed very well; more have performed much less well. The level of performance depends on how much money, attention, and effort the nation puts into its reserve forces. As with most items whose quality is not verified until wartime, the reserves often bear the brunt of budget cuts. All the while, the press releases go out claiming what great shape the reserves are in.

Ammunition Stocks. You can't fight a war effectively without large stocks of munitions. But it's expensive to stockpile this stuff. It costs money to buy the munitions and still more expense to store it safely. Moreover, munitions do not have an indefinite shelf life. Depending on the type, most munitions have to be used or discarded within ten years. You also have the problem of their becoming obsolete. The typical solution is to say publicly that you have sufficient munitions stocks, but that you can't reveal the numbers because that's a military secret. Meanwhile, the reality usually translates to pitifully low stocks for wartime needs. The people who manage the supply stocks know that if war breaks out they can often escape punishment in the mad drive to produce more munitions. Only the historians will identify and properly vilify the real culprits. But by then it's too late to damn the rabid bean counters or spineless generals who left the troops without the means to fight.

CHAPTER

13

Proof of Performance

The 1990–1991 Gulf War was something of a final exam for the reformed Army. Anyone who had followed the path of Army reform in the 1970s and 1980s would not have been surprised. But most people were unaware of these reforms, and what they meant. At least until Kuwait was liberated.

U.S. armed forces were in action eight times between the end of the Vietnam War and the 1991 Gulf War. These were all small operations, and total casualties were fewer then twelve hundred. Two of these operations, the 1980 Iran hostage rescue and the 1983 Beirut occupation, were failures. The other six (Mayaguez rescue, Gulf of Sidra, Grenada, Achille Lauro terrorist capture, Libya bombing, and Panama) were successes, to one degree or another. But operations like these did not make a truly favorable impression on most Americans. It wasn't until the 1991 Gulf War that the American public (and many of the troops) realized just how dramatically the U.S. armed forces had reformed themselves since Vietnam.

The Gulf War was the first large-scale combat operation for American armed forces since Vietnam. Not all the services performed to the same level. The Air Force put on the most sustained and dramatic performance. The subsequent dramatic three-day ground offensive led many to believe that the Air Force had done all the work. However, when you look at the Army's operations in detail, you realize that the ground forces put on just as stunning a performance as the Air Force's.

There were two American ground forces in action, eight divisions from the Army and two divisions of U.S. Marines, plus nearly another division of Marines afloat in the Gulf. The Marines were as effective as the Army troops, but then, the Marines' reputation had not sunk nearly as low as the

Army's in the post-Vietnam miasma. The Marines used their amphibious-assault training to develop an effective attack through the Iraqi defenses. Supported by an Army armored brigade and Marine tank units, the Marines were able to pierce the Iraqi fortifications and then head straight for Kuwait City.

The Navy had the most problems when it came to picking up praise in the post–Gulf War analysis. This was not the Navy's element, as their ships are optimized for naval combat on the high seas. But support of land operations has always been a Navy mission, and its troops performed competently in the Gulf. During the blockade phase of the operation, the Navy performed the primary role. In particular, the Marine aviation units gave their usual efficient support to Marine ground units.

But what is the real story in the Gulf in terms of what the Army expected and what actually happened? The officers and troops were actually pretty confident that they would do well in the Gulf. Yet few soldiers believed they would do as well as they actually did. There was still the ghost of Vietnam hanging over everyone.

The Vietnam experience played a major role in motivating the troops, especially the older NCOs and officers who had served in Vietnam. Although most soldiers who actually served in Vietnam felt that the Army had often done a competent job, they had a hard time convincing anyone outside the Army. Such was the strange nature of the Vietnam experience to most American civilians. For even though American soldiers in Vietnam could see with their own eyes the competence of many U.S. troops in that war, these same soldiers were still part of the general American public that simply didn't believe what the troops had actually done. This has always been an American tradition and it had some strange effects on the post-Vietnam Army.

The troops, once back in the United States, were bombarded by press reports of "what really happened in Vietnam." The media version of the war became the "conventional wisdom." Only the million or so troops who actually saw combat in Vietnam knew better, and after a while, most of them got tired of arguing with those whose Vietnam experience consisted of the media version. The troops were there and knew that they usually overcame communist advantages in the field and killed far more enemy troops than they lost. Specially trained patrol units regularly beat the communists at their own game. But the media concentrated on American problems and defeats. The constant drumbeat of "what everybody knew happened in Vietnam" made many of the U.S. Gulf troops less sure than they should have been of their own capabilities. In their hearts they knew they were the best, but their ears and heads were full of a rather different version of their prospects.

For most of the six-month buildup to the counteroffensive in the Gulf War, the press was full of stories of how the battle would certainly go badly for the American troops. Casualties would be heavy and military victory might not be possible, or so the pundits said. The media preferred to showcase "experts" who expounded these dire forecasts. While the troops were out in the desert getting ready for the battle, they weren't getting much news from back home. This no doubt helped their morale. In any event, when some of the press accounts did reach the combat units, the men and women in uniform often wondered which American Army the journalists were reporting on.

THE OFFICIAL ESTIMATE

When asked by the media what it expected to happen in the coming war, the Pentagon played its cards close to its vest. Largely, this was because the prewar preparations for dealing with the press were based on damage control: not giving the ink-stained wretches any ammunition. So the press ran after their worst-case stories unhindered by any official predictions from the Pentagon.

The Pentagon did have an "official estimate" of the situation and how it expected it to turn out. In fact, it had dozens of them. While this may appear confusing, it wasn't at the time. For while many different study groups in the military were working out what was going to happen in the coming battle, they all agreed that Iraq was going to lose. The major difference among all the official studies was how long the fighting would last and how many American casualties there would be. This last point was one that got the most attention from the president and his advisers. No one wanted a lot of American casualties. In fact, the aversion to U.S. casualties drove most of the military decision making throughout the buildup.

Fortunately, this commendable attitude toward U.S. casualties was not allowed to get in the way of the military commanders' plans and preparations. The generals in charge had been commanding troops at the battalion and company level during the Vietnam War and were equally ardent in wanting to avoid U.S. casualties. But even the most optimistic U.S. commanders did not expect casualties to be as low as they were. The troops were ready, the commanders were ready, but no one was getting his hopes up too high.

How did the Army evaluate its performance, and that of the other services, in the Gulf? Once the shock of the war's outcome wore off, Army analysts began to look at the campaign more closely. Although much went amazingly well, they also found to their initial surprise that many things had not gone as well as many people thought. For example:

- The Army had been woefully ill equipped to fight a large-scale mobile battle in the desert. The biggest deficiencies were in transportation. There were not enough cross-country trucks in the Army inventory. The Army bought, borrowed, and rented additional trucks during the months before the ground campaign. However, the truck support available was not sufficient to take the offensive much farther than it actually went.
- Doctrine and tactics were found wanting in some areas. Despite GPS and plentiful communications equipment, units still got intermingled. Aside from the increased control problems, this also led to a lot of the friendly-fire situations. Since doctrine is derived from experience, it's best to look at the bright side of the Army's Gulf War performance. The U.S. Army had not operated large units in a desert since 1943. The current doctrine was developed during the 1970s and 1980s from the experience of foreign armies in World War II and the Arab-Israeli wars. The several months before the ground battle began were used largely to train smaller units and get the troops accustomed to the harsh desert environment. Future doctrine will no doubt take into account many of these factors. Army doctrine will be changed throughout the 1990s based on further analysis of the Gulf War experience.
- Cooperation between the Air Force and Army could have been much better. The Air Force officers assigned to ground units were not sufficiently familiar with what the ground units were doing. The Air Force was not eager to place a lot of aircraft under the control of an officer up front with the troops. The Marines, having their own aircraft, flown by Marine officers, did a much better job. This shows that the creation of the separate

Air Force from the Army air corps in 1948 has created an interservice problem that continues to defy resolution.

• Some highly valued weapons were not nearly as impressive in action. Most U.S. artillery ammunition was the new DPICM (Dual Purpose, Improved Conventional Munitions). These shells contained combinations of antivehicle and antipersonnel bomblets. Others contained antivehicle mines. What was discovered on the battlefield was that there were not enough old-fashioned HE (High Explosive) shells to root enemy troops out of fortification. Moreover, the DPICM bomblets had an unexpectedly high dud rate, leaving the battlefield littered with bomblets that caused a lot of friendly casualties later. Since it was not possible to do realistic training with these munitions in peacetime, any flaws they might have had quickly became obvious on the battlefield. A lot of maintenance procedures were changed as a result of the Gulf War, and many minor modifications are being done on existing weapons.

There were a number of lessons learned in the Gulf War, and several of them promptly became part of the Army's way of doing things.

• Training pays big dividends. The realistic training received in the combat training centers and related training exercises brought the troops up to a level of performance that surprised even some of the unit commanders. This is in itself would not have been so notable were it not for the fact that this had never happened before in the U.S. Army. While American troops had trained hard for the first battles in some previous wars, they had never been trained so effectively. The NTC type of training proved as realistic as many participants had suspected. The other individual and unit training also turned out to be very comprehensive and effective. One rarely noticed outcome of the Gulf War was that U.S. casualties were, proportionately, fewer than any of the other (less well-trained) coalition armies'. It will be difficult, but not impossible, for the Army to return to its old bad habits of shortchanging training requirements. However, that does not mean that budget pressures in the 1990s won't hit training funds particularly hard. But at least there will be more resistance to such budgetary shell games.

• Simulation works. Wargames and simulations were used increasingly from the late 1970s on. Most people in the Army were taking it on faith that these tools would prove useful. The faith was well placed. Wargames were used successfully before Iraq invaded Kuwait, during the buildup of coalition forces in the Gulf, while the fighting was going on, and after the fighting was over. This last use of wargames was important to sort out what happened and why. Before lessons from the Gulf War are applied to future wars they must be gone over carefully to make sure they are really lessons and not just quirks. Post–Gulf War wargames can separate the two.

• Rehearsals and battlefield preparation are more important than previously realized. Because most coalition divisions had several months to prepare after getting to the Gulf, there was ample opportunity to train and rehearse. Once ground-combat operations began, it was discovered that this training and rehearsal time paid big dividends. Division-size units rarely train together in peacetime and it's easy to forget how difficult it is to maneuver these large units around. Once U.S. and coalition divisions began to exercise in the Saudi desert they realized that they would have been in big trouble had they been forced to go into combat without these exercises. The coalition already knew that it would have to prepare the desert battlefield with support dumps, roads, defensive works, and the like. Unlike the Central European battlefield U.S. forces had long been preparing to operate in, the desert was literally a wilderness. There was nothing there except heat, sand, disease, and no water. U.S. staff planning had anticipated problems, and the problems turned out to be worse than anticipated.

• Having professionals at all levels makes a big difference. All the U.S. troops in the Gulf were volunteers; they had made a commitment to becoming professional soldiers. While there were many unforeseen, or underestimated, problems in the Gulf War, the troops were able to quickly overcome them. This was largely a result of this professionalism. Because the average time of service was more than twice what it would be in a conscript Army, there was more experience. The combination of experience, voluntary service, and professionalism has in the past, as it did in the Gulf, given the army possessing these traits an enormous advantage.

• Rapid movement works. The ground battle was won by rapid movement of large coalition units. The speed of these units charging through the Iraqi desert completely broke up any organized Iraqi resistance. The U.S. 24th Mechanized Infantry Division set a new world record for sustained movement in a combat operation. This should not be surprising, as the previous speed records in this century were made in similar situations.

Top Eight Twentieth-Century Combat Movement Records

Force	Location	Opponent	Year	Distance Covered	Duration	Kilometers Per Day
U.S.	Iraq	Iraq	1991	368km	4 days	92km
Russia	Manchuria	Japan	1945	820km	10 days	82km
Britain	Sinai	Turkey	1918	167km	3 days	56km
Israel	Sinai	Egypt	1967	220km	4 days	55km
Russia	Russia	Germany	1944	400km	8 days	50km
Germany	France	France	1940	368km	12 days	31km
Germany	Russia	Russia	1941	700km	24 days	29km
Allies	France	Germany	1944	880km	32 days	28km

All but two of these speed records (the ones in France) were achieved in flat, featureless terrain. Half of them were in Middle Eastern deserts. In all cases, the attacker was moving against a demoralized enemy. In all but one of these operations, the attacking forces were veteran troops. Only the 24th Infantry Division's record-breaking drive into southern Iraq was accomplished by troops in their first combat operation. In all the other operations listed, the attacking troops had one or more recent campaigns under their belts. Most of the Russians in the 1945 Manchurian operation had several years of experience before they were moved east. The Germans in 1940 had campaigned in Poland the previous year, and so on. Put another way, the U.S. ground forces in the Gulf accomplished what no other army in the twentieth century has been able to do—they won a striking victory in their first battle.

Credit for some of this goes to the Air Force and Saddam Hussein. But in most of the other battles, the attacker had air superiority and massive support from friendly ground-attack aircraft. What was unique about the Gulf War was that the defending army sat still for six weeks while the coalition air forces pounded them around the clock. We can thank Saddam Hussein for this. But the losers in most of the above battles were also led by commanders who had a tenuous hold on the reality of the situation. In any event, the Iraqis were not the perfect opponents; they were simply in the same league with the losers in the other seven battles noted in the above chart.

Note that the 24th Infantry Division that did so well in the Gulf War was the same one that, forty-one years earlier, had been humiliated when North Korean troops ran right over Task Force Smith in the opening days of the Korean War.

CHAPTER
14

The Other Services

While this book concentrates on the Army, which was most in need of reform and undertook the most far-reaching changes, the other services also changed between Vietnam and the Gulf War. The Navy didn't reform much at all, but the Air Force went through nearly as many changes as the Army.

The Navy and Air Force were in a different situation, compared to the Army, when it came to post-Vietnam reform. Put simply, the Air Force and Navy were not as desperately in need of reform because of the differences between the services and the varied experience they had in Vietnam. These differences can be summarized as follows:

1. Form of warfare. The Army encountered most of the dirty work in Vietnam, took most of the casualties, and confronted the major paradoxes head-on. On the other hand, the Air Force and Navy were not facing as unusual a situation as the Army. The Air Force was given targets, which it bombed. Like the Army, the Air Force was prepared to fight a Soviet mechanized army and modern air force in Central Europe. What the aviators had to do in Vietnam was not much different from what they expected to face. If anything, the pilots had an easier time in Vietnam than they would have had in Europe. The opposition in the air and from ground fire were less (with a few exceptions) than what they expected from the Soviets. Since the communists were using Russian weapons, the Air Force saw its Vietnam operations as a chance to gain valuable experience against Soviet equipment. The Air Force flew all the types of missions it expected to fly in a European war,

although not in the same proportion and over a different landscape and in a different climate.

The Navy had a similar experience in Vietnam, although the vast bulk of its efforts were centered around carrier operations in support of the air war. There were also a lot of offshore patrolling and coastal commando operations (using Marines and SEALs). The Marines ran into the same problems in the ground fighting that the Army encountered, but were less in need of reform in the first place. The Marines had not made any 1950s detours through the Pentomic Army, and had stuck to the basics of land combat. The Marines came out of Vietnam in better shape than the Army because they were better prepared going in.

2. Training. The Air Force and Navy always had an advantage in training because simply getting the aircraft into the air or the ships out to sea comprised most of what the pilots and sailors would do in wartime. Army peacetime training is a much more difficult situation since army units sprawl all over the place and cost a fortune to move. While Air Force squadrons and larger units regularly train in peacetime, as do Navy task forces, it's rare for Army divisions or corps to do this. In fact, even battalions and brigades get very little training together. There are literally no training areas available for deploying an entire Army division, let alone a corps, for peacetime training. And tight peacetime budgets have always restricted such expensive exercises even when space was available. Until the 1980s, the Air Force and Navy had better training simulators than the Army, largely because their operations were simpler to simulate. Going into Vietnam, the Air Force and Navy were better trained than the Army and this made the war far less traumatic for the sailors and aviators.

3. Simpler battlefield. Compared to ground forces, the pilots and sailors have a much simpler battlefield. This is why the Air Force and Navy are able to make such good use of sensors (radar, sonar, etc.). The guerrilla nature of the Vietnam War made the Army's tribulations even worse. In most land wars there is at least a "front line"; in Vietnam there was not even that. This made it more of a sporting proposition for Air Force and Navy pilots coming in low to hit enemy units fighting U.S. troops. But this type of aircraft operation is always tricky in the best of situations.

4. A different class of opponents. While hundreds of Air Force and Navy pilots were shot down over Vietnam, they were not facing nearly as much opposition as they had trained for. The Navy ships had even less of a challenge to their defensive capabilities. The Army (and Marines) had the opponents from hell. The Army never came up with a way to completely suppress its communist opponents. These communist troops were given due respect (called "Mister Charlie") as fanatical, resourceful, and skilled infantry. The communists knew how to use the terrain to maintain the mobility advantage. You kill a bunch of them, and more show up, undismayed by the fate of their predecessors. Many Army officers came out of Vietnam with the taste of defeat in their mouths, something pilots and sailors did not feel nearly as much. The Air Force and Navy pilots dropped their bombs, took their occasional losses, and considered their job done. But the Army troops stared frustration and resistance in the face daily. For the ground pounder, there was no end to it.

The Air Force did some development and use of smart weapons and specialized counterinsurgency aircraft and tactics, and came out of the war feeling that these efforts were successful and worthy of future use. The Air Force had been working on guided bombs since World War II, so its successful use of such weapons in the last few years of the Vietnam War should not come as a surprise. Its counterinsurgency aircraft are less well known. The one type to survive to this day is a cargo aircraft equipped with a lot of sensors and guns. Circling around an area where guerrillas were suspected to be operating, these gunships (called "Spooky" and "Puff" during Vietnam) were able to pinpoint the enemy and deliver devastating cannon and machine-gun fire. On the ground, the Marines had experiences similar to the Army's, but they did not feel they were "defeated" to the extent the Army did. The Marines had fewer discipline and leadership problems in Vietnam, and this had a lot to do with their better attitude.

Air Force and Navy aviators did get one reality check over North Vietnam when they discovered they were unable to get the same kill ratio (number of enemy planes destroyed for each U.S. aircraft) they had obtained in Korea twelve years earlier. As a result, first the Navy and then the Air Force changed their training methods.

All the services came out of Vietnam with challenges to face. The racial animosities that grew up among the troops during the war affected the entire armed forces. The end of conscription and the need to recruit all troops had considerable impact. Looming larger were the lower defense budgets in the 1970s. The Navy was particularly hard hit as many of its World War II era ships were in need of replacement, and during the 1970s the money wasn't there to do it.

All the services went through some reform between Vietnam and the Persian Gulf. In terms of overall reforms, the Air Force came in second to the Army and the Navy made the least progress. The other services also underwent less reform, largely because they were less in need of it. The Army was, in a historical sense, much worse off after Vietnam than it had been at the end of earlier wars. The Army did rise to the challenge, more so than in any other postwar period. The Air Force and Navy situations were more normal. Some reform was needed, and some reform was undertaken.

NAVY REFORMS

The Navy did go through some reform after Vietnam, and a substantial amount during the war. The 1967 Arab-Israeli War included an Israeli destroyer sunk by a Soviet-made cruise missile. This prompted the U.S. Navy to quickly develop and produce its own antiship missiles. The Navy also spent considerable resources on weapons and sensors to defeat enemy missiles. During the air war over North Vietnam, the Navy discovered that its peacetime pilot training was lacking in realism. This was remedied while the Vietnam War was still going on and the improved (Top Gun) training program continues to this day.

In many respects, however, the Navy did not have as many problems to overcome as the Army. There were the Vietnam-era racial tensions and the need to adapt Navy customs and regulations to a new generation of sailors. The end of conscription also presented some problems. The Navy handled these changes about as well as the other services.

Many of the issues the Army had to cope with after Vietnam, the Navy had already dealt with. For example, the Navy had made the intellectual breakthrough in World War II in using advanced technology to extend warfare over the horizon with the development of its aircraft-carrier combat doctrine. From 1942 on, the Navy was accustomed to fighting battles with an enemy force that was hundreds of miles away. In contrast to the Army, the Navy has always had a maritime emphasis. America has always been a nation dependent on access to the oceans. Much of the reason for the renewed interest in strategic thinking after Vietnam can be traced to Admiral Stansfield Turner, who in the mid-1970s initiated at the Naval War College a rigorous program to study the writings of classical strategists such as Carl von Clausewitz. In retrospect, Vietnam was seen as getting tied up in a sideshow, while America's true strategic interests were being slighted. The Navy was eager and able to refocus American thinking on its strategic interests: the control of the high seas.

The Fleet Readiness Program previously discussed in the training section was another major reform program that the Navy initiated after the Vietnam War to improve the professionalism of its senior commanders. This program was established at the Naval War College. The Navy built one of the most modern wargaming facilities in the world to support the Fleet Readiness Program. The Navy, unlike the Army, had not lost its long wargaming tradition after World War II. Moreover, the staff of the Navy's Center for War Gaming greatly assisted the Army when a similar program was established at the Army War College.

Naval wargames were somewhat different from the Army variety, but not as different as one might think. Wargames for land combat, the most common kind, are similar to very elaborate chess games, with the following differences:

- The playing board is much larger, containing thousands of spaces rather than sixty-four (as in chess).
- Instead of squares, hexagons are used. This provides more accurate representation of movement. On squares, you actually progress farther in a diagonal move than in a horizontal or vertical one.
- The hexagons contain terrain that has an effect on movement and combat. Some terrain is harder to move over than others. Some terrain types are also easier to defend from.
- There are far more playing pieces, to represent the many units in an army. There are different types, to represent infantry, armor, artillery, etc. Each has different characteristics, principally to represent movement and combat ability.
- Combat is not "all or nothing" as in chess. As in real combat, the

outcome depends on which side is stronger and usually weakens both sides. Combat outcome is based on probability, and this degree of chance is based on historical experience.

Naval wargames are very similar to the land variety, but differ in the following ways:

- The game map shows far less detail, simply because the ocean does not have as many different characteristics as the land.
- There are relatively fewer units in play, because there are fewer ships in a fleet than battalions in an army.
- There is more emphasis on the details of each ship. Naval vessels are very complex machines, and fleet leaders have to keep track of what shape each is in.
- There is more emphasis on aircraft and, unique to naval warfare, submarines. Electronic warfare (using radar, sonar, and attempts to block their use) is more prominent.
- The pace of combat is much faster. While land battles can drag out for days, naval actions are often over in less than an hour. Thus naval wargaming is more intense, and more games can be played.

One of the major achievements of the Naval Center for War Gaming was to make certain that the naval planning process took fully into account the basic truth that military and political factors are inseparable and that the wargaming also reflected this reality. The chief of naval operations had the Naval Center for War Gaming made available to fleet commanders at least six months of the year. After 1975, it was typical for the Commander in Chief of the Atlantic fleet to conduct at least four wargames annually to test his plans and to train and educate his commanders and staff. The tutorials of Admiral Kidd, Commander in Chief of the Atlantic Fleet in the mid-1970s, as he critiqued his commanders after wargaming exercises at the center, became legendary. Atlantic Fleet commanders also tested their current war plans annually. From 1975 to 1979, over ten thousand naval officers participated in exercises at the Naval Center for War Gaming. The interesting part of all this was that most of these exercises increased commanders' combat skills for a battle that was never fought. The Navy spent forty years preparing for naval clashes with the Soviet fleet. The U.S. Navy was ready, and all indications were that the American fleet would have won spectacular victories. But the Soviet fleet is gone now, never to meet American warships in combat.

Such is the fate of the well-prepared American sailors. They were ready, the Soviets knew it, and this also contributed to the end of the Cold War. Few Americans will know, much less give proper credit to, the enormous efforts and sacrifices American sailors made to prepare for, and win, the war that never was. But then, the situation can also be considered one of the greatest naval victories ever won. The planet's second-largest fleet was vanquished by the U.S. Navy without a shot being fired.

One of the naval reforms that resulted in especially high payoffs in Desert Storm was the Navy's Top Gun program. A study conducted in 1968 indicated that the poor exchange ratio of U.S. Navy aviators in Vietnam could be attributed to a great extent to inadequate training in air-to-air combat. Navy pilots had done much better in Korea and World War II. To correct this deficiency, the Navy established the special Naval Fighter Weapons School. The purpose of the school was to provide tough and realistic training to fighter-interceptor crews in close combat between jets. After this program was initiated, the kill ratios in Vietnam from 1969 to 1972 went up from 2.1 to 12 enemy jets lost for every American jet shot down. In many respects, the Navy led the way in developing more realistic training facilities. Soon the Air Force improved upon its combat training centers and the Army followed with the creation of the National Training Center. These combat training centers would be key to the success of U.S. forces in Iraq.

Through the 1980s, the Navy introduced wargames at all levels, including individual ships. Simulators were developed that allowed ships in port to link their sensors and other systems to dockside trailers loaded with wargame-equipped computers so that the crews could train without leaving port. The Marines also developed their own wargames and new training methods.

Where the Navy fell behind was in cooperation with the other services. The Navy had always been a force apart. Possessing its own air force and army (200,000 Marines), the Navy was accustomed to thinking in terms of operating alone. Therefore, little work was done during the 1980s to prepare for joint operations with the Air Force and Army. The problems this policy created were much in evidence during the Gulf War. Not only was naval aviation unable to work efficiently with the Air Force-developed and -controlled battle-management system (the ATO, or Air Tasking Order), but it became obvious that the Air Force had made the right moves during the

1980s, and the Navy had not, in developing and fielding a new generation of aircraft bombing systems. The Air Force had the F-117A, the F-15E, and a large array of smart-bomb systems; the Navy didn't. While the sailors had done some work in this area, the Air Force effort was superior, and in retrospect the Navy would have been better off with a more cooperative approach with the Air Force. In the wake of the Gulf War, the Navy embarked on a course that does make "joint" cooperation with the other services a central item in its strategy. Only time will tell how successful this strategy will prove.

The Navy is a much more diverse organization than the Air Force or the Army. Part of this is tradition, but mostly it is the nature of naval operations. The unique nature of the U.S. Navy springs from four sources:

Branches

The major branches of the Navy don't get along very well. The Navy has three "unions," or four, if you count the Marines, which are practically separate services. There is the traditional surface Navy, plus the two twentieth-century developments: submarines ("squids") and aviation ("airedales"). A century ago, the surface Navy was supreme, and all by itself save for a minuscule Marine Corps. The battleship (or "ship of the line," as battleships still fought in a line of ships) had changed physically since the seventeenth century, but its role as the arbiter of naval warfare had not. In World War I the modern submarine put in its appearance and began a fundamental change in naval warfare that reached its culmination with the widespread introduction of nuclear subs in the 1960s. While it is still largely untested in a major war, most sailors acknowledge that the nuclear attack submarine will loom large in any extensive naval conflict. But before the submarine matured, naval aviation became predominant. Starting in the 1920s, aircraft carriers grew potent enough to replace the battleship as the "capital ship" of the Navy during the 1940s. Proven in combat, the naval aviators wait to see which will be decisive, aviation or submarines, in a future war. Meanwhile, aircraft carriers have a lot of uses in smaller wars where submarines are not a major factor. The Gulf War was an excellent example. Indeed, the only war where nuclear subs played a decisive role was the 1982 Falklands War, where a lack of British aircraft carriers made the British nukes decisive in keeping Argentinean warships out of the fighting.

Among the Navy branches, there is a more visible pecking order than in the Army. The nuclear sailors see themselves as an elite, and in many ways they are. More highly trained and carefully selected, the submarine crews feel there are only two kinds of ships: subs and targets. They might be right. Next come the carrier sailors, represented by the pilots. As select a group as the submariners, the pilots' elitism is diluted by the enormous crews of the carriers themselves (some twenty carrier sailors for every pilot). Carriers are still the major ship type in the Navy, do most of the work, and get most of the glory. Last, in every sense of the word, are the surface-ship sailors. Most of them serve primarily as escorts for the carriers. Although U.S. surface-ship sailors are arguably the best in the world, they suffer from comparison to the airedales and squids. The naval press is constantly running stories about the "sorry state of the surface Navy" and how "something should be done."

Theaters of Operation

The Navy has always thought globally, more than the Army or Air Force ever have. Equipped with the different forces needed to fight a distant war all by themselves, the Navy has tended to look on the Army and Air Force as just supporting forces. The fleet (or large parts of it) is always at sea, and often in far-flung locations. Should there be trouble overseas, the Navy will likely be the first American force on the scene. Moreover, if the event is one of the numerous small disturbances that litter the political landscape, the Navy will be the only U.S. force involved. Another little-known characteristic of the Navy is the differences that have arisen over the decades between the Atlantic and Pacific fleets.

The U.S. Navy is, in effect, two navies, one for each major ocean. This situation has existed for over a century and has resulted in two organizations that operate, and some say think, quite differently from one another. The Pacific is a different ocean from the Atlantic. The distance from California to Asia is far larger than from New York to Europe. The potential opponents in the two oceans are different. As a result, these two parts of the Navy are also quite different. Overall, the Navy has tended to look on itself as a truly independent service. The Army and Air Force might work together, but sailors have rarely seen any pressing need for the Navy to get involved in such joint operations. The Navy's new strategy for moving emphasis from the high seas to coastal areas may require a major change in thinking as well as operating with the other services.

Naval Operations

Being a naval commander means being able to take care of yourself, by yourself. The naval mind-set is of independence, and action, without a lot of second-guessing from the folks back home. A naval task force is trained and equipped to operate by itself for months at a time. Supplies are carried by special cargo ships that chase after the task force and provide whatever is needed to keep the ships going. No other service operates like this. The key to promotion in the Navy is the ability to think independently while you're way out there all by yourself. A ship's captain has powers that no other military officer has, and during crises at sea, the captains are rated on their ability to handle these problems promptly without seeking a second opinion from anyone else. This is still true even through naval commanders are now reachable instantly via satellite communications. The Army and Air Force, in contrast, are still trained to operate as if at the end of a long leash.

The Sea

For as long as sailors have gone down to the sea in ships, they have been recognized as a special group. The sea is a force unto itself. Aside from the sheer expanse of the high seas, there are many other factors that make it a hostile environment. It is like a vast desert; there is nothing for sailors to eat or drink. If you lose your ship, you can't walk home. The undrinkable salt water is also highly corrosive, debilitating both sailors and ships. The weather is an implacable and potent foe. Even today, the largest warship can be brought low by the typhoons and gales that frequent most of the world's oceans. Sailors who stay at sea a lot, as American sailors do, are toughened by the experience. They are different—they have to be.

After Vietnam, the Navy focused on dealing with the growing Soviet fleet. During the Vietnam War, U.S. naval appropriations were largely spent on thousands of carrier aircraft sorties each month, and replacing the aircraft that didn't come back. There was no money to match Soviet shipbuilding. By the early 1970s, there was a lot of catching up to do and at that moment the Navy's budget was cut. It wasn't until the late 1970s that more money became available, and it wasn't until the 1980s that the U.S. shipbuilding program really got going. While much effort went into upgrading electronics and weapons, the Navy was basically fixated on getting new ships into the water. The Navy had to build a lot just to stay even, since most World War II era ships had reached the end of their useful lives. As older ships were retired (often to serve on in foreign navies), new ones had to be launched, and then even more in order to go from the "four-hundred-ship Navy" of the 1970s to the "six-hundred-ship Navy" of the 1990s.

In a word, the post-Vietnam Navy did not so much reform as spend most of its energies on expanding. The Navy was not as hard hit by the end of the draft as was the Army. The Navy generally got a lot of volunteers who simply wanted to avoid going into the Army. The volunteer force caused the Navy some problems, but by the time the number of ships expanded in the 1980s, it was becoming easier to recruit. The new ships were more automated and required fewer sailors.

As the growing Soviet Navy loomed larger and larger on the horizon, the Navy did some creative thinking on how to deal with this, its only real threat at sea. Antisubmarine warfare (ASW) became a major effort, as Soviet submarines were seen as the greatest threat to the fleet as well as to the crucial merchant ships that would supply the Navy and ground air forces in Europe and Asia. The ASW program included hundreds of long-range (P-3) patrol aircraft as well as building nearly a hundred attack submarines. New surface ships had improved ASW sensors and ASW helicopters on board.

Someone had to lose out in all this and it was the carrier people. While new carriers were still built, the 1970s and 1980s experienced a noticeable slowdown in the post–World War II carrier building program that had started in 1955 with the commissioning of the *Forrestal*. What kept the carrier building program going at all was the carrier experience during the Vietnam War and the recognition of how valuable carrier aviation could be in support of far-distant land combat. Nevertheless, older World War II carriers had to be retired eventually. Thus the Navy went from thirty-one carriers in 1968 to twenty-one in 1978. The new carriers were larger and more efficient and needed relatively smaller crews.

While the Navy was able to keep the carrier production going, much less work was done on developing new aircraft. Going into the 1990s, most carrier aircraft are the same types in use during the Vietnam War. As a result of this, the Navy put in a less impressive performance during the Gulf War. Carrier aircraft did not have the electronics that the Air Force had invested so much money in during the past twenty years.

The end of the Cold War hit the Navy particularly hard. Much of what the Navy had worked so hard to create since the 1960s had now sharply declined in value. The Soviet Navy melted away far more quickly than anyone had ever imagined, and with it went the Navy's justification for many of its ships, sailors, weapons, and tactics.

The carriers were still useful for unavoidable little wars in out-of-the-way places. But now, in light of the Gulf War experience, the Navy would have to scramble to make its carrier-based bombers as effective as Air Force planes. The submarine force was particularly hard hit, in proportion to the rapid demise of the Soviet submarine fleet and the "blue water" threat. After over a century of following a strategy that emphasized battles on the high seas, the Navy is now faced with a new world where it must emphasize coastal and amphibious operations. It is going to be interesting to see where this new tack will take the Navy.

AIR FORCE REFORMS

Vietnam also had a few surprises for the Air Force, but not nearly as many as the Army encountered. The Air Force learned that it had been chasing some of the wrong goals during peacetime, and it used Vietnam as a testing ground for many of the innovations it pioneered in the next twenty years. These programs (and some problems) tell the tale of how the Air Force was every bit as reform-minded as the Army in the same period.

Red Flag and Follow-ons

Seeing the Navy's success with new training methods, the Air Force improved its training centers in 1975 to make them more realistic and with greater feedback for the pilots. At that point, the Air Force even had some MiG fighters to use, rather than using U.S. aircraft modified and flown to act like enemy aircraft. The Air Force's Red Flag program showed the same results as the Navy Top Gun school, although this was not proven until Air Force pilots were able to strut their stuff in the Gulf War.

Precision Bombing

The Air Force, unlike the Navy, was determined to improve bombing accuracy even during the Vietnam War. Before that conflict was over, it had developed and used the first of its guided-bomb systems. This was used to good effect in attacking pinpoint targets that had previously resisted conventional attacks (and had gotten many Air Force bombers shot down by dense defenses). The Air Force continued working on better bombing systems throughout the 1970s and 1980s. This was an expensive proposition, but then, the Air Force spends more of its budget on research and development than the other services. The wisdom of this effort did not become obvious until the Gulf War when it was found that the Navy aircraft, lacking such systems, were much less effective.

To put this into perspective, consider what it took—in three wars, over the past fifty years—to achieve a 90 percent probability of destroying a target measuring sixty feet by one hundred feet (a building, usually housing a headquarters, factory, or whatever). In the 1940s (World War II) this required 1,500 heavy bomber (B-17) sorties dropping 9,000 one-ton bombs (half of which would land more than 3,300 feet from the target). In the 1960s (Vietnam) more accurate bombing systems allowed the same target to be destroyed with 176 jet fighter-bomber (F-4 Phantom) sorties, each carrying one bomb (half of which would land more than 400 feet from the target). In the 1990s (Iraq) this required one sortie by a light bomber (the F-117A Stealth), carrying a single one-ton bomb that will land within ten feet of where it is aimed.

Stealth

A painful lesson from Vietnam was the high cost of attacking heavily defended targets. These losses could be reduced by sending along swarms of electronic-warfare aircraft and bombers to destroy the enemy radars and antiaircraft weapons. Precision bombing systems also made the losses more tolerable. The Air Force theorized that it would be even more efficient to develop aircraft that would be relatively invisible to enemy radar. Thus these "stealth" aircraft (designed to be nearly invisible to enemy radar) could go in alone and either bomb high-value targets or destroy the enemy air defenses. Also, when they were loaded with precision guided bombs, the Air Force would have a practically invulnerable bomber that would not only reduce friendly losses but also reduce the losses of enemy civilians. The first of these stealth aircraft was the F-117. Built in secret to deny potential opponents the opportunity to develop countermeasures, the F-117 became operational in the early 1980s and did not get its first real trial by combat until the Gulf War. While the F-117A was called the "stealth fighter," it was actually designed and used as a light bomber. The mission it was designed for was to penetrate thick Soviet air defenses in Central Europe and attack key targets and air-defense systems (radars, command centers, and missile launchers). The Iraqi air-defense system was built with Soviet assistance and largely with Soviet equipment. The F-117A had little trouble dealing with it. Production of the initial batch of F-117As was completed in the late 1980s.

Meanwhile, another "black" (secret) project, the B-2 bomber, was also built using stealth technology and was scheduled to become operational in the early 1990s. The B-2 is an enormously expensive aircraft as it contains even more advanced stealth technology, carries much more weight in bombs, and has a much longer range. The cost of this program makes it difficult for the Air Force to justify building more than a handful of B-2s. The Air Force has other stealth projects that deal with reconnaissance work.

AirLand Battle

A major breakthrough in cooperation between the Air Force and Army was achieved with the publication of the Army's AirLand Battle doctrine in 1982. This was a doctrine that tightly integrated Air Force and Army combat operations. The Air Force revised its basic doctrine in 1984 to reflect its increased cooperation with the Army. For example, the doctrine explicitly called for the air commander to coordinate air interdiction with the ground commander. The doctrine recognized that "the weight, phasing, and most importantly, the timing of interdiction can provide outnumbered ground forces the time or opportunity to seize and maintain the initiative and win." The Air Force and Army began meeting to work out such a doctrine right after the Vietnam War.

The reasoning behind such a doctrine is fairly obvious when you realize that the Army has a large fleet of attack helicopters that duplicate many of the functions of Air Force fighter-bombers. The Army also has long-range missiles that further complicate the targeting process behind enemy lines. AirLand Battle provided "rules" for Air Force and Army commanders to determine who would attack what. There were also procedures for the use of Air Force bombers to provide front-line support of Army units. Generally, the Air Force prefers to go after enemy targets far distant from friendly troops. But "Close Air Support" (CAS) is generally considered an emergency resource when friendly ground units are hard pressed. The problem has always been, who defines the "emergency"? AirLand Battle set down guidelines to eliminate turf battles over when and where CAS would be used.

AWACS, Son of Moonbeam

During Vietnam, the Air Force developed the use of airborne command centers for coordinating air (and to a limited extent, ground) operations. These slow-moving transports, laden with electronics and communications gear (the call sign of one was "Moonbeam"), would cruise back and forth along border areas and keep tabs on friendly aircraft entering and exiting North Vietnam. Based on that experience, AWACS (Airborne Warning and Control System) was developed as an airborne control center that carried its own long-range radar. The first AWACS units were deployed in the early 1980s, and by 1990 there was a full complement of them in Europe and the Persian Gulf. The Soviets rushed to copy the idea, although they never caught up with the capabilities of the U.S. original. AWACS proved a revolutionary and successful battlefield tool in the Gulf War. For one thing, AWACS ensured that there were no air-to-air collisions among friendly aircraft. This in itself was unprecedented in such a large air campaign. The ability of AWACS on-board staff to see all enemy and friendly aircraft at once also prevented friendly-fire losses between aircraft. As intended, AWACS made the large-scale Gulf War air operations a lot easier to manage.

JSTARS

The immediate success of AWACS got the Air Force (and the Army) to thinking about a similar system that could track, and control, ground units. This resulted in JSTARS (Joint Surveillance and Target Attack Radar System). Radars that can pick up a lot of vehicles on the ground are a recent development, being dependent on enough computer power to sort out all the clutter found when a radar is pointed at the ground. In the 1980s, computers became powerful enough and small enough, that a sufficient amount of data-processing capability could be loaded onto a large (AWACS-size) aircraft. Actually, both the AWACS and JSTARS aircraft are military versions of the 1950s-vintage Boeing-707 jet transport (which is itself a civilian version of the original KC-135 tanker aircraft). The JSTARS radar is built into the underbelly of the aircraft. The radar has two modes: wide area (showing a twenty-five-by-twenty-kilometer area) and detailed (four by five kilometers). Each aircraft has radar displays on board plus more on the ground with Army headquarters units. All the radar displays can communicate with each other. The radar simultaneously supports both modes and several different chunks of terrain being watched, storing large quantities of scanned data in its computers.

While an operator might have to wait a minute or two for an update on his screen, this would not be a problem because of the relatively slow pace of ground operations. The radar could see out to several hundred kilometers and data was most useful when saved and brought back later to compare to a more recent view. In this manner, operators could track movement of ground units. Operators could also use the detail mode to pick out specific elements of ground units (fortifications, buildings, vehicle deployments, etc.). For the first time in history, commanders were able to see and control mechanized forces over a wide area in real time. Some Army commanders had seen the power of JSTARS during tests in maneuvers conducted in Europe, but the other Army commanders, who first saw the system in action during the Gulf War, were astounded. One never got to see that many ground-combat units maneuvering in peacetime, so the Gulf War was the first time JSTARS got a look at these many troops in action. The Air Force had wanted JSTARS for other reasons: to better spot targets for its bombers. JSTARS was also used for this during the Gulf War. The ground commanders maneuvered their units via the JSTARS screens, while Air Force commanders sent their bombers ahead to soften up the enemy units starkly exposed on the same JSTARS displays.

Battle Management

As aircraft became more reliable in the 1960s and 1970s, they also became more expensive. Fewer could be bought, so the Air Force had to get more out of each aircraft. Modern aircraft are more durable than their pilots, and squadrons have more pilots than planes, so a "fresh" pilot can jump into the cockpit of a plane that has just landed from a mission and been quickly refueled and rearmed. Missions became more complex, with "strike packages" comprising dozens of different aircraft sent out after several targets at once. Management of all this activity became a major task in itself and this gave rise to demands for increased efficiency in Battle Management. After Vietnam, this problem was attacked from two directions, both using computers. Mission management (getting the pilot, and the aircrafts' increasing number of computers, all the information they needed) was accomplished by using yet another computer that allowed the pilots to simulate their mission, make all the mission-planning decisions, and then make a tape that would be read into the aircrafts' computers. The pilot then had a knowledgeable electronic copilot in the form of aircraft computers containing all the many bits of mission information. This technique has already gone through several generations since the 1970s. The second solution was the ATO (Air Tasking Order). This technique took all the requests for air missions (from the Air Force intel people and other services, particularly the Army) and information on all aircraft available and calculated the most efficient mix of missions. The ATO was then transmitted to all aircraft units and the missions were flown. The ATO system has also gone through more than one generation since it came into use in the 1980s.

Bombers in the 1980s

One curious development of the larger defense budgets of the 1980s was the Air Force spending more on bombers in that decade than on ICBMs. Ballistic missiles are a more efficient, and cheaper, way to deliver nuclear missiles and there was much clamor during the 1980s to upgrade and expand America's ICBM arsenal, yet more was spent on bombers in that decade. The reason for this was both political and operational. Bombers have more versatility and flexibility than missiles in that they can also be used in nonnuclear combat, an important consideration militarily (no bomber has dropped a nuclear weapon in anger since 1945) and politically (a purely nuclear system like ICBMs generates more political opposition). Within the Air Force, bombers are more popular because bombers have pilots and nearly all the senior Air Force leadership are pilots. There's also more command and leadership involved with bombers. With ICBMs, you press a button and that's it. At the end of the 1980s, the Air Force had four long-range bombers (B-52, FB-111, B-1, and B-2). Also, one of these projects, the B-2, was secret, so the work on the B-2 was only suspected until the late 1980s. The stealth, speed, and range of the B-2 provide it with the capability to fly directly over targets without detection, eliminating the need for supporting aircraft and thereby increasing its flexibility.

With the changes in the national strategy that now place the priority on regional problems, the Air Force has restructured to ensure that the vast capabilities of its bombers are fully utilized in the new security strategy. To be able to rapidly respond to any region on the globe with massive firepower in implementing national strategy, the Air Force in 1992 deactivated its Tactical Air Command and its Strategic Air Command and created the Air Combat Command (ACC). The ACC provides air-combat forces to the major combat commands including all fighter, bomber, reconnaissance, and command, control, communications, and intelligence aircraft. It also provides air-defense forces to the North American Aerospace Defense Command. The Air Force has streamlined its organizations and has revamped its doctrine to help prepare itself for the challenges of the post–Cold War.

ECM for Every Occasion

ECM stands for Electronic Countermeasures, the major part of the electronic battle that is a component of every air campaign. Electronic warfare is something that aircraft got into big time during World War II. Work continued after 1945, particularly when surface-to-air missiles began to proliferate in the early 1960s. As more powerful, and cheaper, computers became available, it became theoretically possible to build into aircraft ECM systems that could protect against nearly all electronic threats an aircraft might encounter. While the theory was fine, the reality was very expensive and not all that easy to implement. The end of the Cold War brought the cancellation or scaling back of several major ECM projects. All this cost the Air Force and Navy a lot of money. Although most of the Soviet-made radars and missiles that these projects were designed to protect against were still around, it was obvious that the shrinking defense budgets could not sustain moving ahead with these costly plans. However, computers continue to get cheaper and faster, so the next decade will probably see cheaper and more reliable versions of the 1980s "blue sky" ECM efforts. Future ECM projects will go forward with the knowledge that it isn't as easy as it looks.

BVR and Making the Missiles Work

BVR is Beyond Visual Range, using missiles to attack enemy aircraft too far away to be seen visually. This has been the "tactic of the future" for over twenty years. It is still not quite here yet. Airborne guided missiles were first used in World War II, by the Germans, with some success. But these were basically radio-guided bombs used to attack ships. Work on these devices, and other types of airborne missiles, continued after 1945, and by the early 1960s there were several types in service. Unfortunately, the Vietnam War demonstrated that what worked in peacetime tests had a much more difficult time when faced with combat situations. Coming out of Vietnam, air-to-air missiles (the most common kind) had a mixed reputation. Some said it was a tarnished reputation, but Air Force weapons developers had a sense of history and knew that the future belonged to those who kept trying until they got it right. As is often the case, it wasn't until the Gulf War that everyone was convinced that air-to-air missiles were the superior weapon for aerial warfare.

Meanwhile, the missile developers were pushing ahead with more capable and reliable BVR missile systems. The biggest problem with BVR missiles is the uncertainty over what the potential target has up his sleeve. The original air-to-air weapons, machine guns and cannon, were unambiguous. You saw the target, you fired, and you saw the results. The most successful (to date) air-to-air missiles (heat-seekers like the Sidewinder) took over twenty years and more than a dozen models before they finally displaced cannon. With BVR missiles, you are never sure if the "enemy" aircraft isn't one of your own with a broken electronic IFF (Identification, Friend or Foe) device. Moreover, a legitimate enemy target may have some effective countermeasures to your BVR missile that you don't know about. But, then, maybe not. This makes BVR technology something that has always been just out of reach, and may continue that way for some time.

Sensor Supremacy

The 1980s was the decade in which the Air Force finally got a clear look at what was on the ground. From the beginning, pilots depended on their eyes to find and pursue targets in the air and on the ground. Airborne radar gave pilots an opportunity to find the enemy first, and then sneak up on him for an attack. But radar was, until recently, rather useless for spotting ground targets. Pilots had to use their eyes, and in anything but a desert, it was difficult to get a clear view of what was down there. And even during the Gulf War, many pilots brought along a pair of binoculars, the better to confirm their target before making a bombing run. Moreover, each generation of aircraft had a faster minimum speed, meaning that pilots had even less time to spot something and successfully attack it. Bad weather and darkness made it practically impossible for pilots to attack ground targets.

In the last twenty years, the Air Force (and Navy) have made great strides in remedying this problem through the development of "vision enhancement devices," or, as they are more commonly called, sensors. Not only can pilots now see targets through fog, dust, and darkness, but these sensors allow magnification of the objects on the ground and a more efficient fire-control system. Guided bombs and missiles are used with these systems to provide an arcade-game approach to hitting targets. Most of these sensors use infrared (heat) detection, which means they can also see the warm parts of armored vehicles and other targets through foliage and camouflage. As the Gulf War demonstrated, these sensors can also see through some sand and dirt.

The Gulf War used 1970s and 1980s technology; the 1990s is producing even more powerful sensors and fire-control systems. The objective is to make the bomber able to hit a greater number of targets per sortie and in all kinds of weather. This was sometimes achieved in the Gulf War, where an aircraft would go out with eight bombs and destroy eight tanks. This is a considerable improvement from past wars, where an aircraft would be lucky to get one tank per sortie. Of course, the Gulf War was a unique situation, where the enemy cooperated by putting thousands of armored vehicles, manned by demoralized troops, out in the perfect target area: a desert. The next test will be to see what results can be achieved in something other than a desert. The Balkans would be an acid test, as the area is wooded, mountainous, and populated by very feisty troops. Most sensor testing and training is done in desert areas of the United States, although pilots who have trained in these areas and then operated in places like Korea note that things on the ground become much more difficult to spot, or hit, when you add mountains and foliage. The improved sensors are much degraded by the higher speed of aircraft when there are no wide-open spaces to fly over while approaching the target. Coming in at over two hundred meters a second in a desert is one thing when you have twenty to thirty seconds (because of the range of your sensors) to spot the target and prepare to hit it. With hilly, tree-clad terrain, you can have less than ten seconds to spot the target in a busier environment. Solving this problem will be one of the major efforts for the Air Force in the 1990s.

The Fighter Mafia

The upper ranks of the Air Force are dominated by pilots, and this august group is further dominated by fighter pilots (to the exclusion of bomber and transport pilots). This shouldn't be surprising, as pilots are the cutting edge of the Air Force's combat capability. But fewer than one in a hundred Air

Force personnel is a fighter pilot. This small community of some five thousand fighter pilots not only does most of the fighting but generally sets the policy for the entire Air Force. The fighter pilot's aggressive outlook helps the Air Force keep out front in many areas, but this aggressiveness sometimes creates problems in cooperation with the other services. With the military being drastically reduced and future defense budgets being severely constrained, cooperation and unity of effort among the services become crucial. The Air Force must fight as an integrated joint force to actually win a major land or naval war. Air superiority is a valuable military asset, but it still takes ships (particularly submarines) to guarantee control of the sea and only ground forces can obtain absolute control on the ground. Overcoming the fighter pilot's competitive spirit while finding ways to make the most of the new political landscape will be a key task for the Air Force, and the other services, in the 1990s.

BLUE AND GREEN TOGETHER

Much has been accomplished in forging closer links between the Army and the Air Force during the 1980s. And this goes far beyond the assistance that the Air Force gave the Army when it was developing its AirLand Battle doctrine. Ever since the U.S. Army air corps was split off as the independent Air Force in 1947, cooperation between the two services had its problems. After Vietnam, this began to change. The placing of the Army's Training and Doctrine Command only a few miles from the Air Force's Tactical Air Command fostered increased cooperation. Then, there was the Goldwater-Nichols Act (GNA) of 1986 that made the Chairman of the Joint Chiefs of Staff the senior military officer. GNA not only increased his position relative to the chiefs of services but also gave him responsibility and authority to develop joint doctrine to improve joint operations among the services. Previously, the Chairman was just a fifth wheel, unable to resolve the many interservice disputes. Now the Chairman has real power to settle most of the disputes. Actually, it's not always that simple, but it was a big improvement. Another major boost for Army-Air Force cooperation was a three-year period when the commanders of the Army and Air Force were officers who had been roommates when both were attending West Point in the late 1940s.

These two officers, generals Gabriel (Air Force) and Wickham (Army), were also both of the post–World War II generation. In 1982, General

234 GETTING IT RIGHT

Gabriel became head of the Air Force (Chief of Staff) and in 1983 General Wickham became head of the Army. Both these officers had stayed in touch and remained friends throughout their careers and agreed on a lot of the things both services needed to do to get the most out of their budgets and joint operations. They came up with a list of some thirty items the two services could focus on together and proceeded to make this program a reality. The instructions that both General Gabriel and General Wickham gave their staffs were to select the course of action that was best for the nation and not necessarily best for their own service. Among other things, duplicate programs were eliminated (the Army was working on its own version of JSTARS, which was dropped in favor of the Air Force version) and increased cooperation at all levels in the two services. All these things were going on to one degree or another before the two West Point room-mates achieved command of their respective services. But after this duo got going, the pace of cooperation increased enormously. The momentum that was gained in this period continues to this day. The list of about thirty items has grown and is still being worked on, as some of the items on it will never truly be completed.

The Long Arm, and Who Owns It

The Army has an increasing number of long-range missile systems and the Air Force is beginning to suggest that all long-range systems should belong to them. When missile systems began to proliferate in the 1960s, there was talk that the Air Force's would soon be out of business. Like most quick predictions, that one was false but did contain a grain of truth. Missile systems have continued to proliferate and have gotten more effective and cheaper in the process. The Army now has several missile systems with a range of over one hundred kilometers and has changed its doctrine to include "taking charge" of the battle area that far behind enemy lines. Hundreds of Army attack helicopters can also operate over a hundred kilometers inside enemy territory, although it's safer to send missiles into such an area against the numerous antiaircraft weapons it usually includes.

This situation—the Army staking out a claim on the one-hundred-to-two-hundred-kilometer zone behind enemy lines—has prompted the Air Force to claim that it should have that control. Thus some Air Force officers insist that the Air Force take charge of Army missiles and long-range antiaircraft missiles. Army helicopters would operate under Air Force direction in such an arrangement. There is a practical problem in all this in that someone has to sort out who is where and doing what in the air space over the battlefield. Since the Air Force became a separate service, various arrangements have been made to sort out Air Force aircraft, Army antiaircraft missiles, and everyone's helicopters and transports. But the Gulf War demonstrated such a dominating influence by Air Force combat power and control (via the AWACS, JSTARS, and ATO), that many Air Force officers are clamoring for the Air Force to have formal control of the air and those weapons that operate up there. This brings us right back to the arguments heard in many nations over which service should control which aircraft. Russia, for example, has (or had, at one time or another) separate services for long-range bombers and missiles, for antiaircraft missiles and interceptors, and yet another service (under Army control) for ground-attack aircraft. The U.S. Marines have their own Air Force, as does the Navy.

While it would appear more efficient for one service to control "anything that flies," there is also the argument that those flying objects are up there for a lot of different reasons and many of their functions involve direct support to specific people on the ground. Moreover, each service has its partisans and supporters in Congress. Indeed, some branches of the services have their own political power base. The Marines are the classic example; this arm of the Navy has enormous influence in the various branches of government and is quite capable of looking after itself in the legislature as well as on the battlefield. But in the wake of the Gulf War, the Air Force threw down the gauntlet to the other services over who would control things that fly. The outcome of this squabble will resolve yet another of many turf battles between the services.

THE BUDGET MAZE

One problem the Air Force tried, and failed, to wrestle to the ground was the murky nature of its budget. More than is the case with the other services, many secret projects are hidden in the Air Force budget. These include a lot of the satellite reconnaissance operations and a number of secret aircraft and electronics development projects. Just how much of a problem these hidden items were became quite obvious when the Army and Air Force tried to work out which projects would be dropped, merged, or otherwise modified in their newfound spirit of post-Vietnam cooperation. The secret projects would be added to a nonsecret project in such a way as to not make it look obvious. At least it didn't look obvious until you dug into that item and then discovered that all was not what it appeared to be. Moreover, the Department of Defense has hundreds of different accounting systems, all having slightly different ways of doing addition and subtraction.

The addition of secret items has made it a very sporting proposition for any two services to determine what a program is really worth when the two (or three) services are horse-trading on who will give up what. Typically, if two services are working on the same (or roughly the same) project, then either the services involved, or someone from Congress, will suggest a merger or trade. One service might run the project and get some of the funds from the other service, which would then share use of the project's technology. A crucial reason why a lot of these cooperative projects don't get under way is the opaque nature of the numbers. Because of the number, and size, of the secret budget items, you don't even hear these aspects discussed openly. For security reasons, obviously. Only after the fact (as in the case of the F-117A and B-2 stealth aircraft) do you discover how long these projects went on and how much they cost.

CHAPTER

15

An Uncertain Future

Reform is like a shark—it has to keep moving or else it will die from lack of oxygen moving through its gills. In the best of times, reform is difficult to promote and is especially difficult in peacetime and after military victory (the Cold War, the Persian Gulf). Constant reform needs incentives, such as defeat or being in the middle of a war. In any other circumstances, keeping reforms going requires very strong leadership. Even a "tradition" of reform will atrophy in the afterglow of victory and the miasma of peacetime soldiering.

The agenda for the future has been set by the end of the Cold War and the Gulf War. The Cold War was the battle that ended not with a bang but a whimper. There were no pictures or parades spotlighting the end of this forty-year war between the largest armed forces ever seen on the planet. It will take a few more years for the full implications of the post–Cold War world to sink in.

The 1991 Persian Gulf War was a different story, and can justifiably be considered "the swan song of the heavy metal crowd." There are unlikely to be any large armor battles involving large U.S. armor forces for the rest of this decade. Yet it is just this kind of battle the United States is still trained and equipped to fight. Indeed, this was the type of combat that the U.S. Army had been preparing for since the end of World War II. While the Army approach to combat must change, it is difficult to get over a million military and civilian Army personnel to turn around rapidly, especially while dragging that forty years of habit.

In the wake of the Gulf War, the Army has to undergo another reformation to get ready for the immediate, and perhaps long-term, future of dif-

237

ferent forms of combat with a new emphasis on joint and combined operations. Even before Iraq invaded Kuwait in 1990, the Army, and the other services, were getting ready for the post–Cold War world. It is one of those historical ironies that as the Cold War ended, the United States should have an opportunity to fight the kind of battle it had been training for since the Iron Curtain came down and sparked over four decades of "armed peace." While this classic, first and last, Cold War battle was fought in a desert against a non-Russian opponent, the Iraqis were lavishly equipped with Russian equipment and doctrine. Moreover, the Iraqis had eight years of recent combat experience. However, this apparently did more to hurt troop morale and restrict initiative than to foster it. Even with the differences, the Army and Air Force saw a lot of their Cold War preparations validated. The Russians saw this also, and while no Russian general would admit it publicly, there must have been a sigh of relief that the battle was fought against Iraqis and not Russians.

As successful as the Gulf War was for U.S. forces, this degree of success would not have been achieved if the battle had been fought ten, twenty, or thirty years earlier. The Army has gone through many equipment and doctrinal revolutions during the Cold War. In the light of its final Cold War form, one can look back and see that earlier versions of the U.S. Army would not have been nearly as successful against a heavily armed Third World opponent.

Up until the mid-1950s, the Army was ready to refight World War II. For five years after that, it really wasn't prepared to fight anybody, having reorganized as a Pentomic Army. That silliness was left behind in the early 1960s, when the Army was reorganized as a somewhat improved World War II Army. Then came Vietnam, with most Army resources going into a guerrilla war in the jungle that the government would not let the troops win. Coming out of Vietnam, after over a decade of forgoing modernization of its mechanized forces, the Army was broke from much-reduced budgets. It wasn't until the early 1980s that the current Army began to take shape.

None of these previous incarnations of the U.S. Army was capable of achieving the 1991 Gulf War victory. These earlier armies could have won, but at much greater loss in men and equipment.

What the Army faces at the end of the Cold War is its most significant reorganization since the modern U.S. Army was created in World War II. This is, in many ways, a curious situation. For example (all dollar figures in 1990 dollars):

1. Before World War II, the U.S. armed forces were much smaller compared to today, with only 3,500 troops per million population in 1940 (at the beginning of the World War II buildup; it had been even lower in the early 1930s). Today it is twice that, and before the volunteer armed forces were introduced in the 1970s, it varied between 13,000 and 21,000 per million population. The World War II peak (1945) was 87,000 troops per million population, with about one in every five adult American males in uniform.

2. Defense costs a lot more today than it did before World War II, even after inflation, average income, and population size are taken into account. In 1940, an American paid 1.5 percent of GNP for defense. To put it in more personal terms, in 1940 Americans were paying 1.5 percent of their incomes for defense. America was just coming out of the 1930s economic Depression, and per capita income was only $6,900 (compared to about $25,000 today). By 1945, the peak year of World War II, Americans were paying 38 percent of GNP for defense. The bright side of this was that the booming war industries had vastly increased the size of the economy. Per capita income was $10,900 in 1945, so the much higher defense costs didn't hurt much. The defense portion of GNP dipped to 4.6 percent by 1950, when the Korean War began and the Cold War arms race began to pick up steam. By 1953, the last, and peak, year of the Korean war, the annual defense bill was 13.7 percent of GNP. Per capita income was still the same as in 1945, and the citizens were complaining. But the Cold War was under way, and the spending stayed at around 9 percent of GNP until Vietnam, when it went as high as 9.2 percent in 1968. But the U.S. economy was booming from the mid-1950s on. By 1970, per capita income was about $16,000. This boom continued until the 1980s, when it leveled off at about $25,000 per capita. Defense spending during the 1970s first shrank to an average of 4.9 to 5.5 percent of GNP and then began to increase as first the Carter and then the Reagan administration vastly increased defense spending. By 1986, we were spending 6.5 percent of GNP, a level not seen since 1972. The spending has since declined, and is now heading for an unprecedented low of 4 percent. This is still more than twice the 1940 level of 1.5 percent, but is the lowest since 1940. Another change in defense spending since 1945 is the portion of the federal budget that defense spending comprises.

Percentage of Budget for Defense and Nondefense Spending

Year	Defense	Nondefense	Defense % of GNP
1940	16	84	1.5
1945	88	12	38.4
1950	31	69	4.6
1960	50	50	9.1
1970	41	59	8.1
1980	23	77	5.2
1990	29	71	5.5

The current debate is over how different the world of the 1990s is from the world of the 1930s.

3. Overseas obligations have increased. World War II was not the beginning of a large peacetime military in the United States. The fallout from the 1898 Spanish-American War created an instant overseas empire for America. Puerto Rico, the Philippines, and sundry Pacific islands suddenly became U.S. possessions. These overseas territories had to be defended, and in the Philippines an insurrection had to be put down in the wake of the war. At the start of the Spanish-American War, the United States had an Army of 28,000, and a militia system (the National Guard) capable of providing (no one was sure of the exact number) over 100,000 troops. By 1899, with the war won but the Philippines insurrection still to be put down, the Army had 80,000 men, plus another 100,000 from the National Guard. The Navy wasn't much better off, with thirty-six capital ships manned by 16,000 sailors and 3,000 Marines. After World War II, the United States gave its major overseas possession, the Philippines, its independence and renounced the acquisition of any more. But at the same time, American commercial, military, and diplomatic obligations overseas grew rapidly. Now the United States has even greater commitments in these areas, and just how much military effort should be devoted to these obligations is the key question to be answered in the 1990s.

4. Potential opponents. Even before its Civil War, the United States had made peace with its neighbors. Mexico and Canada have enjoyed over a century of peaceful coexistence with the United States across unguarded borders (aside from some banditry action). The only enemies

the United States now faces are thousands of miles away. While long-range nuclear missiles bring potential enemies a lot closer, very few nations have such weapons. The overseas allies, most of whom were devastated during World War II, are now possessed of robust economies and substantial armed forces. Most of America's post–World War II enemies are now friends, or at least neutral. Many options, few answers.

5. Murky history of military reform. It wasn't until the Spanish-American War that the U.S. government seriously considered the long-term implications of its armed forces. The scandal over the sorry, although victorious, performance of the ill-trained, -equipped, -supplied, and -led Army troops during that war forced the government to make the first of several twentieth-century attempts at creating professional armed forces. It was obvious then that the twentieth-century was going to be a dangerous place and America needed armed forces capable of efficiently performing any tasks they might reasonably be called upon to perform. This was an effort to move the Army from being frontier Indian fighters to a force capable of defeating the professional armies of the major industrial nations of the twentieth century. Are we now about to make as radical a change in our Army as we move into the new security environment of the twenty-first century?

These first turn-of-the-century reforms paid off when, in 1917, the United States was dragged into World War I. In short order, over four million trained—to varying degrees—troops were sent off to finish the war that had been bleeding Europe dry since 1914. Thus, in thirty years, from 1897 to 1927, the regular Army went from a peacetime strength of 28,000 to 108,000 in 1917 and 140,000 in 1927. But the nation was not enthusiastic about military matters. Despite several hundred thousand enthusiastic amateurs in the state National Guards, most of the population cared little about having a substantial Army, much less about paying for it. But the 1930s brought the threat of another large war. Most Americans vividly remembered the pronouncements about the 1914–1918 war as being "the war to end all wars." The failure of that pronouncement made it difficult for American leaders to get the United States ready for World War II. Americans rose to the challenge when finally dragged into it. But the hopes that the sacrifices of World War II were worthwhile were dashed when the Korean War and Cold War came hard on the heels of the victories in Europe and the

Pacific. The principal military reform for the Cold War was to maintain the largest, and most expensive, peacetime armed forces in American history.

There was indeed a series of American military reforms throughout the Cold War, with the last one, in the 1980s, actually being effective. But with the Cold War now over, many Americans are inclined to revive the 1897 attitudes toward the function, and size, of the military. A tiny Army, a larger Navy, and the newfangled Air Force (of middling size) are proposed by many civilians as the sufficient armed forces for 1997. The military professionals are unsure what they want, because the American people are uncertain what they want to do with their armed forces after the Cold War. The next round of military reform is suffering from a lack of direction or, even worse, too many directions. No one knows where it will go, or what it will lead to.

THE THREAT

Between Vietnam and the end of the Cold War it became customary to refer to the potential enemy as "The Threat." In most cases The Threat wore a Russian uniform. But the only significant Threat troops U.S. forces ever got to fight spoke Arabic and flew Iraqi colors. Unlike the Russian Army, the Iraqis faded fast. Who is The Threat now? That's an important question, as one size doesn't fit all when it comes to doctrine. There are actually only three kinds of military threat the U.S. Army would have to face:

1. A modern mechanized army. Something along the lines of the Iraqis. The U.S. armed forces now have a track record dealing with this sort of thing. But the U.S. force that defeated the Iraqis no longer exists. Some of the divisions have already been disbanded. The doctrine remains, and better knowledge of exactly how it works. For the rest of the 1990s, American troops can still handle this Threat.
2. Irregular light infantry (guerrillas). This is the enemy that bedeviled U.S. forces in Vietnam. This Threat can be beaten, but it takes longer and costs more lives. It is the type of war that does not fit well into the new strategic doctrine of the United States: "the concept of applying decisive force to overwhelm our adversaries and thereby terminate conflicts swiftly with a minimum loss of life." Doctrine for counterinsur-

gency and low-intensity warfare has not generated much enthusiasm since Vietnam. There has been a lot of work done in the 1980s to develop light infantry units and doctrine. But a lack of enthusiasm in the military, and the demonstrated unwillingness of the American public to accept the higher casualty rates of such combat, and the longer campaigns, make progress in this area a dubious proposition. The reluctance to commit U.S. ground troops to areas where this type of combat would be encountered (the Balkans, Somalia, etc.) is indicative of the resistance to this form of warfare.

3. Terrorists. With the collapse of communism and the support communist governments gave to guerrilla movements, the most popular military option left for these opposition movements is terrorism. Combatting terrorists is police work, but it is also work for light infantry, and a very special type of light infantry. Special Operations Forces (SOF, including commandoes, rangers, and the like) are best suited to fighting this kind of war. This approach was enthusiastically embraced by the U.S. armed forces after the end of the Cold War, and even before the Gulf War. However, SOF have never been popular with most senior military leaders in the U.S. military where most of the officers and troops remain oriented and well trained and indoctrinated in mechanized warfare. Along with the public's aversion to seeing U.S. troops fighting guerrillas, there is the perception that U.S. antiterrorist operations could escalate into "another Vietnam," or even become a threat to democracy itself. Moreover, terrorist activity takes place in some very volatile areas like South America, the Middle East, Southeast Asia, and Eastern Europe.

What this changing array of threats reinforces is the political dimension of any future use of American armed forces. The classic Cold War threat was a large mechanized army attacking U.S. forces. This presented no political problems as all Americans would rally around the U.S. use of force to defend itself. The other two threats—guerrillas and terrorists—pose more complex political problems. Guerrillas are usually involved in some kind of civil war, as are many terrorists. The lesson of history, and Vietnam, is to avoid getting into someone else's civil war. Americans are prone to ignore history, but the lessons of Vietnam have become a part of the national memory. Added to this is the traditional isolationism of Americans. The result is a post–Cold War world in which there are plenty of Threats, but none that the American public would support resisting militarily. The legislature makes the obvious connection: Why provide more money for the armed forces if there is no one out there the voters will support using the troops against?

Doctrine can also be political dynamite. It's one thing to publish an FM 100–5 in the 1970s that lectures about defending against invading Russians. It's quite another to live with a new FM 100–5 in the 1990s that talks openly about operations against drug smugglers, terrorists, and taking sides in civil wars overseas. The military's decision to prepare for different threats means putting it in writing publicly, so the troops may study and train according to the new doctrine. This is going to make creating doctrine for the 1990s a tricky endeavor.

In Desert Storm, America did break out of the syndrome that had plagued it in every major war since 1776. For the first time in its history, America not only won its initial battles, but won them decisively, overwhelmingly, and with amazingly few casualties. This was no fluke. It was commitment and hard work by a host of exceptionally outstanding people, both in and out of uniform. For the first time in its history, America created an Army of a highly professional and well-trained officer corps, carefully selected and well-paid volunteer troops, a rigorous and realistic training system, sound and appropriate doctrine and tactics, world-class weapons and equipment, and an armed forces highly motivated to do better. Will America be able to do it again? Will America fall prey to the Victory Disease? Our potential enemies, who have also learned from Desert Storm, are watching. And for these possible opponents, nothing is more instructive than defeat.

THE ONE-THIRD SOLUTION
OR
HOW TO SURVIVE THE BUDGET AX AND AVOID ANOTHER TASK FORCE SMITH

Everyone wants to cut the defense budget. Few can agree on how much and where to cut it. Many wonder if it can be cut at all without exacerbating an outbreak of Victory Disease (by cutting the wrong things). But cuts in the military budget are a reality and the defense budget will probably fall, in the late 1990s, to about 2 percent of GNP. This is less than a third of the defense budget percentage of GNP in the early 1990s. There is no way of reducing the defense budget to some magic number. America's traditional mistrust of large peacetime armed forces has historically led to military spending of less than 2 percent of the GNP.

History has shown that it isn't the size of the defense budget reduction that determines military effectiveness, but the timing and phasing of the cuts. More important is the ability of the political and military leadership to reshape these smaller forces into combat-effective units rather than skeletal leftovers from the Cold War era. American leaders will need to remove their Cold War outlook and view the world differently, and with a new set of priorities.

U.S. defense spending still consumed over $300 billion a year in the early 1990s, or nearly 6 percent of GNP. This includes nuclear and intelligence items that are not found in the Department of Defense budget, but are very much a part of "defense" spending. The traditional defense budget still exceeded $250 billion a year. This is a significant financial burden on the United States.

Before World War II, peacetime defense spending averaged between 1 and 2 percent of GNP. For most of this century, the United States has been the major industrial and trading nation on the planet and has had much the same defense needs it has today. From 1900 on, America has been a major importer and exporter, and has had to deal with terrorism and threats to U.S. citizens overseas. Until the end of World War II, America sought allies to provide for a common defense. However, after World War II, the United States assumed the major defense burden among its allies. This was justified to offset the concentrated military power of the communist nations. Chief among these was the Soviet Union, which was perceived as controlling its allies (and their large armed forces) with an iron fist. As time went on, it became apparent that the communist bloc was not so monolithic. In the late 1980s, this bloc began to crumble and in 1991 the Soviet Union itself disintegrated into more than a dozen nations.

In the last twenty years, many American allies became economic super-powers in their own right, while continuing to depend on America for military security. Thus in the space of a few years (1989–1991) all the rationales for the enormous U.S. military establishment disappeared. For several decades, over half the U.S. defense budget was spent on protecting our allies from the communist threat. In the early 1990s, America still had forces ready and able to fight this war, but the likelihood of such a conflict had disappeared.

What kind of armed forces are now needed when:

- There is no longer a large, hostile fleet posing a potential threat to American use of the oceans. The former Soviet fleet has not only been split up, but years of poor maintenance and shoddy construction have caused many ships to be retired, or simply tied up at a pier and virtually abandoned.
- There is no longer a large mechanized army ready to overrun many of our allies and trading partners. The fifty Soviet and Warsaw Pact divisions that long stood poised to threaten Western Europe are, for the most part, no more.
- Treaties have been signed, and are being carried out, to destroy many of the conventional weapons and nuclear weapons facing us for the last four decades. Nearly half the conventional weapons and two thirds of the nuclear weapons are slated for disposal. This unprecedented disarmament is already under way and shows no sign of being reversed.
- Most of the militarily powerful nations in the world are either long-term U.S. allies or nations that have every incentive to be friendly to America and America's long-term allies (namely, the NATO nations, Japan, and others).

Under these conditions, the size of the armed forces depends on many factors, not all of them military:

- How much you want to, or think you should, use military force. This is up to the voters, usually expressed via media coverage and public opinion polls, rather than waiting for an election. As the taxpayers realize how much operations in Iraq, Bosnia, Somalia, and elsewhere cost, their enthusiasm declines markedly. Iraq's invasion of Kuwait in 1990 was a direct threat to the U.S. economy and support for action was there. Other situations, like Grenada and Panama, are potentially political dynamite if they do not succeed quickly. Declining military budgets also provide less incentive for the civilian leadership to consider a military solution to some of the world's problems. In any event, the current generation of military leaders are the ones who went through Vietnam. They are not eager to even come close to getting mixed up in anything like that again.
- What advantages you think you'll get from using military force versus not using it. As the situations in Bosnia, Iraq (after 1991), and Somalia demonstrated, there is much to risk and little to gain by sending the troops

in. Diplomacy is cheaper and gets fewer Americans killed. The diplomatic approach may be harder on the foreigners in question in the short run, but usually less costly for everyone concerned in the end. For a democracy, diplomacy has the additional advantage of not upsetting the voters, who can become quite unpleasant when many of their fellow citizens come home in body bags. And let us not forget cost. Even with contributions from allies, the 1991 Gulf War cost America the lives of 140 soldiers and over $5 billion. The Somalia operation cost 9 lives and nearly $1 billion in its first six months. As of this writing, the meter was still running on U.S. peace efforts in the Balkans.

- How tolerant (or even aware) you are of taking additional casualties because you were not able to respond immediately with overwhelming force (as could be done through 1991). The alternative is responding more slowly, because of a much smaller defense budget, and getting more U.S. troops killed. This angle is little known, or appreciated, except by professional soldiers and military historians. Desert Storm produced low American casualties because overwhelming force was available, and was used. With a much smaller military, there will be far less force available. Two years after Desert Storm, many units that participated have already been disbanded. However, Desert Storm could still be refought in 1995 if America were willing to send the bulk of its armed forces to the Persian Gulf, rather than the fraction needed in 1990. The alternative is to send fewer troops and experience higher casualties. In the 1990s, especially after Desert Storm, there are far fewer nations likely to attack U.S. allies, and trigger the use of American troops, than was the case in the 1980s. But it can still happen, and smaller armed forces generally mean higher casualties.

- How willing you are to wait for our allies, finding some future conflict in their backyard, to get organized and into action. America has spent much time, effort, and money rebuilding the economies of its allies since 1945. These allies are now rich and well armed. Without another superpower to threaten them, they are militarily capable of taking care of any rambunctious neighbors they might have. However, some of these local problems also have an impact on the United States. The Persian Gulf is the prime example. But many other nations, possessing considerable military power, also depend on Persian Gulf oil and stability. Having the U.S. to lead operations like Desert Storm, and provide most of the troops, is a luxury our allies may be denied in the future by overextended American taxpayers. America has grown accustomed to being a superpower since World War II, and after 1991, the only superpower. While many feel that the United States should take the lead in deciding what other nations should do, we do not yet have a world government. Many nations, including some of our allies, are nervous about "America the world leader." More nations prefer to let the United Nations play the role of "world leader." The UN, for all its faults, is better at obtaining a consensus than the United States, if only because the UN is not a sovereign nation. Trying to be the world leader is not only unpopular, but expensive and dangerous.

- How important it is to maintain a long lead in developed military technology. It's very expensive to be first in military technology. As Desert Storm proved (at least to the military professionals), realistically trained troops were more important than having the most advanced technology.

It also comes down to the "America as World Policeman" question. For most of their history, Americans have been isolationist. The Cold War served as a rallying point for those who backed continuing U.S. involvement overseas from the late 1940s through the early 1990s. The Soviet Union provided a national threat unlike any America had faced previously. But the Cold War is over, voters are focused on economic problems at home, and Americans see few reasons to send, or maintain, large forces overseas, or at home. There are still many who would prefer the United States to serve as the world's police force. Do most Americans want this, and are they willing to pay in dollars and American lives?

After World War I (1918), there was a situation similar to the one we face now. There were no superpowers. The major powers that did exist (Germany, France, Britain) were still recovering from the war when the Great Depression hit them in the 1930s. This double whammy led to low defense budgets worldwide. Russia had turned into the Soviet Union and was rebuilding from the devastation of World War I and the subsequent civil war. The Austro-Hungarian and Ottoman empires had disappeared, leaving behind a score of smaller nations. Only Japan and America emerged from World War I unscathed. Japan was on a war footing through most of the 1920s and 1930s. Japan was a minor industrial power, although it had world-class armed forces. Through these years, America spent about 1 percent of GNP per year on defense. Most European nations were spending 3 percent. When Hitler and the Nazis came to power in 1933, Germany began to rearm. It increased its defense spending steadily each year until it was consuming 17 percent of GNP in 1938. It took several years for Germany's neighbors to react.

In 1936, Britain began to rearm, raising defense spending to 5 percent of GNP. By 1938, Britain's spending was 8 percent of GNP. America didn't begin rearming until 1940, when spending went to 1.5 percent of GNP, and then 5 percent in 1941. America's defense spending peaked at nearly 40 percent of GNP later in the war, a pattern similar to that of the other participants.

Germany lost the war (World War II) that it had been rearming for since 1933. Japan also lost, even though it had been arming for far longer than Germany. Nevertheless, over one hundred million died (most of them Russians and Chinese and most of them civilians). One argument for a strong American military is to achieve sufficient force to deter a future Hitler. Unfortunately, history paraphrases, rather than repeats, itself. If we follow the example of our experience with Nazi Germany, we now have to look nervously at China (a large nation with a long history of occasional aggressive behavior). Russia is another possibility, as are Japan and Germany.

But one big difference between the 1930s and the 1990s is the presence of nuclear weapons. Until nuclear weapons came along, it took a while for a militaristic nation to do a lot of damage. With nukes, a nation of any size can do much harm, in a few minutes, with a handful of nuclear armed missiles or aircraft. Nuclear weapons can be tossed in both directions, which is one reason why none have been used since 1945. Moreover, even the superpowers spent only a small fraction of their defense spending to maintain their nuclear arsenals. Thus massive defense budgets are no longer the primary means of becoming a military threat. More nations are seeking to get nuclear weapons in the 1990s, rather than just starting arms races as in the 1930s. Large armed forces are still useful, as nuclear weapons are more of a diplomatic than military weapon.

Many nations want nukes not only to become the first nation in the region to have them, but also to be able to match a neighbor that is already nuclear-armed. Once two nations in the same region have nukes, they are locked in a standoff. If one uses nukes, the other is likely to, causing massive damage to both nations. During the Cold War, nuclear-armed America and the Soviet Union stared at each other for four decades without using their doomsday weapons. This was largely because these two nations had never been at war with each other, had no past animosities, and were mutually hostile largely because of different political systems. A future nuclear power is more likely to pull the trigger and kick off a nuclear exchange because of far more ancient and heated hatreds. The more nations that have nuclear weapons, the likelier someone will eventually be to use them. Most future nuclear powers have neighbors with whom they have long-standing and intractable disputes. This future use of nuclear weapons would have serious diplomatic repercussions, as most world leaders, and their populations, are properly afraid of any use of nuclear weapons. So while there almost certainly will be another use of nuclear weapons, the user will be a loser. It is very unlikely that America will be the target, but as the premier nuclear power, America will be looked to for leadership in coming up with a diplomatic solution, not a military crusade. At the same time, other nations have to know that America will use its military power when no other choice is available, and that this military power is effective. At the moment, those points are proven. In the future, those points may have to be made again from time to time to remind the slow learners.

Nuclear weapons are, in a break with history, a new weapon that actually limits wars rather than encourages them. Nations know that they can achieve better security with nuclear weapons than with massive buildups of conventional arms. In the 1990s, the major nuclear powers (United States, Russia, Britain, France, China, Israel) have a massive nuclear retaliatory power against any nation that might seriously attack them, especially a nonnuclear power that could not return the nuclear favor. Conventional weapons are still needed for all those situations where it would be diplomatic overkill to nuke an aggressor, but a conventional arms race like that of the 1930s is less likely, particularly among the major military powers. Especially in the wake of the economic ruin America and the Soviets inflicted on themselves during the arms race of the 1970s and 1980s. That's the good news. The bad news is that everyone wants nukes. But that has less to do with cutting the U.S. defense budget down to pre–World War II levels.

What, then, will be the major problems and dangers to lowering the defense budget to historical peacetime levels of 2 percent (or less) of GNP? Most of them are political.

Unemployment and bankruptcies that will accompany the shift of business and workers from military to nonmilitary activity. This has already been happening since the late 1980s. Surplus officers and troops were being forced out of the military even as American units were still pouring into Saudi Arabia in early 1991. These reductions and budget cuts continued while a Republican presidential campaign was being fought, and lost, on the basis of ending a long recession. Through this period, defense contractors were also losing business, profits, and employees. Yes, it can get worse. But even the Republican officials involved in the above drawdowns realized that, eventually, nondefense spending was more beneficial to the economy than military spending. Of course, there's a lot more strain when you cut defense spending by two thirds as opposed to 20 percent. But that is not nearly as severe as the World War II demobilization, where defense spending declined over 90 percent in three years. The result of that was the longest sustained period of prosperity in American history.

Then again, the defense contractors have seen the future and are preparing for the worst. Of course, all concerned want government assistance. Some cry out that the defense industries now are different from those at the end of World War II. The Cold War weapons builders have been at it for decades while the World War II experience lasted only six years. Thus most defense plants had managers and workers who still remembered how to produce consumer and industrial goods in a competitive market. There was also a pent-up demand for consumer goods after World War II, a demand that does not exist today. But the change has to come eventually. It wouldn't be the first time that large segments of the economy had to shift assets and workers. This has been quite common for the last century. One could say it really began when builders of horse-drawn wagons had to adapt to the appearance of automobiles.

Defense spending involves less than 2 percent of the industrial activity in America. The rest of the money goes to firms involved in selling what are essentially civilian goods (food, clothing, industrial equipment, etc.). Those firms that attract the most attention are the few that produce the specialized, high-tech military hardware. Employees in these firms are better educated than those in comparable civilian firms, receive higher pay and are less efficient. The civilian economy, starved for trained employees, could make better use of these people and the above-average amounts of capital they consume in their military activities. Moreover, most of the defense budget goes to payroll.

But there is less to worry about with the troops themselves. Most of the potential ex-soldiers are the lower-ranking ones who tend to get out before they've spent more than three to five years in uniform anyway. The officers and NCOs let go are trained and the result of years of careful selection. It's always a chore to switch careers, but these troops are known as the best America has had in its history. Employers know that, and hire these former soldiers readily. One problem, though, is veterans (usually officers) who don't take a realistic view of their value in the civilian market. Perhaps it's all those salutes they get from enlisted personnel. The hundreds of thousands of Department of Defense civilian employees who would lose their jobs are more of a problem, as these people were not selected and trained with the same care as the troops. However, the rapidly increasing number of government employees (federal and local) is a national problem, not just a military one. Unless one comes right out and labels the Defense Department one big jobs program, there's no reason for having more people on the payroll than you need. Throughout the twentieth century, we have seen nation after nation bankrupt itself by using government jobs as a form of welfare. Workers in the private sector are more productive than those same people serving on the government payroll. It's not easy switching people from the public to the private sector. But in the long run, history suggests it's best for everyone.

There is a fear of losing technical superiority in weapons and specialized military equipment. About a third of the current defense budget goes toward maintaining and developing the "technology base" (researching and creating new weapons and equipment). The Gulf War demonstrated the advantages of technically superior weapons. As a result, many military leaders are more afraid of losing the technical edge than they are of losing anything else (including the training edge American troops had). Then again, much of what drove the development of American military technology during the last few decades was the fear that the Soviets would get there first. Now we know that the Soviets didn't get there first and, typically, were far behind America and our industrialized allies. At the same time, a lot more industrialized, and Third World, nations have gotten into the military technology business. Some of these nations have produced items superior to anything created in the United States. From time to time American troops were equipped with foreign weapons and equipment. But it's expensive to maintain the technology lead America had acquired by the 1980s. The military does not want to lose this technological edge. More to the point, it doesn't want to halt dozens of major R&D projects, some of which have been going on for decades. Moreover, with the Soviet Union gone, most of the military technology being developed outside America is by American allies. Why go to extremes to compete with your own allies? One reason is that we may find ourselves fighting against these weapons in the hands of some third party. Maintaining good relations with these allies should be a key objective of American foreign policy.

But worse yet, the market for military goods collapsed when the Cold War ended. As a result, many nations are now buying weapons from the Russians (and other former USSR states) at bargain prices. Finally, military technology is much cheaper (and quicker) to develop when there is a war going on, or threat of war. This was seen in the Gulf War, where some weapons were developed and fielded in months, rather than years (as is normal). This has happened many times before, and will not change in the future. Military leaders don't like to depend on weapons that haven't been invented yet. History has demonstrated that experimenting on the battlefield with untested weapons is costly in the lives of soldiers. No one can any longer afford the Cold War methods of producing massive amounts of new military technology at a leisurely (and expensive) peacetime pace. Out of this problem comes the suggestion that R&D continue on new weapons, followed by limited production. This may be absolutely necessary, especially if it becomes clear that other nations are developing, and selling, more advanced weapons. Then again, maybe not. It all depends on what the rest of the world does in developing new weapons technology.

Finally, history has demonstrated time and again that it is not technological superiority that is decisive, but the right balance of quality people, training, leadership, doctrine, and equipment. The key to maintaining the balance is tough, realistic training. For the first time in its history, America has the edge in training and leadership. For a long time, American military leaders have depended more on technological superiority. The generals and admirals have to believe in their newfound training and leadership superiority. More important, they must prepare themselves and their subordinates for the day when America will no longer have an overwhelming technological superiority they can no longer afford. The key might very well be more use of simulations, recognizing that simulations for training are only as good as what goes into them.

Loss of security, or fears of such a loss is a natural reaction to the major reductions in the defense budget. But America is well positioned for the new world situation. America is surrounded by vast oceans and much weaker neighbors. No other nation in the world enjoys such an advantageous situation. There were popular fears of enemy invasion at the beginning of World War I (Germans) and World War II (Germans or Japanese). In neither case were there any grounds for such fears and most people quickly realized that when America got involved in those wars. The principal danger during the Cold War was ICBMs. There was, and is, no practical (much less affordable) way to protect the nation from several thousand incoming missile warheads. Protection against a few more primitive missiles from a hostile Third World nation is another matter. The most likely military R&D program to grow after the post–Cold War budget cuts is the SDI ("Star Wars") program.

Before the end of the Cold War, SDI was castigated for being too ambitious. But now, a decade later, parts of it are known to work, and probably work well enough to stop the occasional tyrant's ICBM directed toward America, or an American ally. But before this global SDI comes to life (perhaps in the next decade, perhaps sooner if there is a Third World "ICBM scare"), there are already shorter-range SDI systems nearing completion. Meanwhile, the "threat" of poorly armed and trained Third World troops endangering American interests will get played up from time to time. Some of these ragtag armies are dangerous, as in the Persian Gulf (Iraq and Iran). But that brings up the other question. Persian Gulf oil is vital to many economies other than America's. The next time around, Germany and Japan may have no choice but to send troops and money. It's not just American security that's at stake, but that of U.S. allies as well. Should America spend nearly $100 billion a year, every year, because other nations might not want to do their share when everyone's interests are at stake? That's what it comes down to.

There is concern that the world's finest armed forces are being destroyed. But there's a difference between *destroying* the American armed forces in the post–Cold War drawdown, and simply reducing their size. As most soldiers, and some civilians, noted during the Gulf War, the key to American success was quality soldiers, effective training, and competent leadership rather than technology. Reducing the budgets doesn't automatically reduce troop, training, and leadership quality. But there is always a tendency to cut recruiting efforts, soldiers' pay, and training funds whenever budgets get tight. As well trained as the U.S. military now is, there's no telling how well the training budgets will survive the cuts. If training funds are cut severely, the combat capability of the troops will decline. Moreover, this decline also reduces the effectiveness of future leaders (officers and NCOs), who do not receive the training early in their careers. Such a situation also causes many of the most capable officers and NCOs to quit in disgust, and makes it more difficult to recruit better-quality troops. Cutting training budgets helps a little in the short term but exacts a heavier price in the long term. It is also wise to remember that the reforms that transformed the American armed forces began in the 1970s, when the defense budgets were at their lowest point since World War II. The American military already has some recent experience with creating troop quality in spite of low defense budgets. Cutting the defense budget won't destroy the armed forces; cutting soldiers' pay, recruiting funds, and the training budget will.

What do you get for a third of the peak Cold War budget? Quite a lot. For one thing, we must consider just how massive the last few Cold War budgets were. Of course, our largest annual defense spending was in 1945, with $650 billion (37 percent of GNP—all amounts are 1993 dollars). This was followed in 1953 with the Korean War peak of $265 billion (18 percent of GNP). Then came the Vietnam War peak in 1968 of $325 billion (9 percent of GNP). The Cold War peak came in 1989, at $349 billion (7 percent of GNP). Take a third of this last figure and you have $116 billion (about 2 percent of GNP in the mid-1990s). At the peak of the Cold War, the $325 billion supported 2.1 million troops, nineteen active-duty divisions (three of them Marines), nearly four thousand combat aircraft, fifteen aircraft carriers, and nearly five hundred other warships. Cutting that by two thirds does not automatically cut the combat forces by two thirds. This is because there is much "overhead" in training centers and headquarters that cannot be cut back to the same degree and have them still remain viable. However, if a lot of the troops are brought home (and demobilized), many expensive R&D projects scaled back, and other economies taken, America could approach the end of the decade with:

- About 700,000 soldiers, sailors, airmen, and marines. This is more, in proportion to population, than America ever had in peacetime before 1940. All volunteer, all professional. If we can keep the selection criteria and the training levels high, these will be the most effective troops on the planet. Because these troops now have the degree of professionalism that Americans generally lacked until the 1980s, it is possible to raise a larger force if needed. In other words, a large force of professionals makes it possible to quickly and adequately train large numbers of civilians if a big war occurs.
- Seven active-duty combat divisions. Plus another division's worth of independent brigades and battalions full of such things as rangers and Spe-

cial Forces. How many of these divisions would be Marines and other types, I leave to others to sort out. America is unique in that it has no dangerous neighbors to tie down its troops. Every other major military power on the planet lacks this advantage. Thus America can send nearly all of its troops overseas. This makes those seven divisions go a lot farther.

- About 1,200 combat aircraft. Take what we have now and lop off the older two thirds in most aircraft types, or eliminate some of the older types altogether. Aircraft, missiles, and satellites have, in the past twenty years, come to consume over half the defense spending on weapons. Quality aircraft and well-trained pilots provide a tremendous edge in combat. Again, America does not have to assign aircraft to the defense of the homeland. Most of America's aircraft can be quickly sent overseas and have immediate impact on troublemakers.
- Five to seven aircraft carriers and 140 to 160 other warships. This would include 12 Trident ballistic missile subs, which provide an invulnerable nuclear deterrent (for the foreseeable future, anyway). America is again unique among world nations in that it is simultaneously a "continental power" (having a land area large enough to make it self-sufficient) and a "maritime power" (being dependent on access to the oceans for trade). Unlike Britain and Japan (the principal maritime powers of this century), America could survive loss of naval superiority. While this loss is always possible, it takes a long time to build a fleet and staff it with competent sailors. Even a much reduced U.S. Navy still has a global edge. And anyone trying to challenge this edge will require many years of effort to become a threat. Unless we ignore such a buildup, that will give America time to expand its fleet to meet the challenge.

The above facts are subject to some reshuffling after the "Amateur Force Planning" crowd (politicans, their staffs, media "experts," and assorted special interest groups) are through arguing with the military about what the future threats are. All of this also assumes that America does not lose its "information edge." The increasing importance of electronics and satellite reconnaissance in this century has made information a major military asset. Information was always crucial, but the enormous resources needed to maintain a modern information-gathering system have made the United States the premier power in this area. If this edge is not lost, America will be able to see the future, and the present, more clearly than any potential enemies.

PEERING INTO THE FUTURE

Predicting the future in political and military affairs is a notoriously risky business. Force Planning is the term used to describe this process and it requires a little explanation. While the average citizen (or "Man from Mars") might conclude that the structure of the armed forces is determined by political and lobbyist action, such is not always the case. Professional Force Planning is the complex, and generally thankless, job of figuring out what type of military force will be needed for future military operations. Every commander must do some Force Planning. Even a platoon leader has to decide which of his thirty troops will take what weapons and equipment where to accomplish the mission. At the very top, Force Planning peers into the murky future to sort out what the armed forces of the next five, ten, twenty, or more years will require in order to deal in the best way with future threats. This is an inexact process and often the subject of political influence. Between 1945 and 1991, the Force Planners in both America and the Soviet Union struggled with estimates of the capabilities of their adversaries. Moreover, if one or more senior leaders became fixated on some aspect of their, or their enemy's, armed forces, these senior military (or civilian) folk would let it be known that their Force Planners should bring their plans into line with what the boss was thinking. The official estimate tended to conform to what the national leadership wanted to see. The officers doing the work knew better, and often looked more intently at the more realistic "unofficial estimate" to plan for future combat.

But the official Force Planning estimates have not been totally compromised in the past half century. Force Planners generally get the broad outline of their research out into the open where it can be scrutinized and questioned. Yet it is the details of the Force Planning ("the Soviets will soon have a new tank better than anything the United States has") that drive budget decisions, not the broad outline ("the Soviets will have a lot of tanks, more than the United States"). With the Soviets now gone, and rather suddenly at that, the Force Planners have to come up with a new Major Threat for the future. This does not mean that the Force Planners suddenly invented Iraq, North Korea, Iran, and other current favorite "threats." Through the 1980s, it was accepted that the Soviets were mellowing and the aforementioned countries were becoming more dangerous. Or at least more dangerous compared to the diminishing Soviet menace. This led to an increased interest in light infantry, commandos, and high-speed sea and air transports.

The sudden end of the Cold War and collapse of the Warsaw Pact left the Force Planners in a quandary. The Warsaw Pact had, for decades, been presented as the military threat that dwarfed all others. Much debate raged concerning just how formidable the Warsaw Pact forces were. Western politicians tended to make more of the threat (at least in public) than their generals. This was confirmed, to many citizens and legislators, when the largely NATO army rolled over the Iraqi armed forces in 1991. The Iraqis were pale imitations of their larger and better-armed Warsaw Pact mentors (and suppliers). Nevertheless, American military leaders had grown accustomed to large peacetime forces and generally lavish defense budgets. It was not going to be easy to go on short rations all of a sudden.

With very few exceptions, military leaders accept the fact that the Cold War has now been won by the West and, as after every major war (even a "Cold" one), the troops have to be demobilized. A major debating point is just how many troops will be sent home. Given the curious nature of the Cold War (no general mobilization of the population, nor truly huge armed forces), there was not a large public outcry for immediate demobilization. When you mobilize the entire nation, all those civilians in uniform, and their families, want everyone home quickly once victory is achieved. But the Cold War officer and NCO corps was composed largely of long-term (twenty years' service, then retirement) professionals. So it wasn't just a matter of demobilizing a bunch of uniformed civilians who had spent a few years as officers and NCOs. Many careers were at stake, from sergeant to four-star general. The major problem here, more than in any previous shrinking of the military, was letting people go when no one really wanted to go. In past wars, many officers and NCOs were only in until the war was won. These fellows quickly, and voluntarily, shed their uniforms. It was less of a problem deciding which (if any) of the professional troops to let go. This time, even though many officers and NCOs have their résumés out in anticipation of the cuts, it's a Force Planner's nightmare deciding which types of troops should be encouraged to stay, and which should be offered early retirement.

Every military man throughout history has felt that when it came to troops and weapons, "too much ain't enough." The more you have (in quality and/or quantity), the better the chances of surviving, and winning, any fight you get into. This makes the details of the cuts a very nerve-racking business. The Pentagon Force Planners know that hundreds of thousands of the most competent military professionals in the world have to be demobilized. Exactly how these cuts are made will eventually be a matter of life and death in future wars. Force Planning decisions made now will not be known as inspired, or tragic, until some unknown war takes place in future years.

Predicting the future in political and military affairs is laden with uncertainty. In 1988, who would have believed a prediction that Iraq would invade Kuwait or that the Warsaw Pact and Soviet Union would quickly collapse? You might have gotten a few small bets on Iraq, but beyond that you would have been accused of creating bad fiction. History reeks of similar situations. So what is a Force Planner to do? If Force Planners were brutally frank in their assessments they would offer broad predictions and many caveats. These would not be the sort of assessments that would scare money out of Congress. For example, Iraq and Iran have been troublesome factors in Persian Gulf affairs for decades. These two nations were (and are) known to be potential sources of armed aggression. But the Department of Defense Force Planners are outshouted by White House, State Department, or congressional experts (of the self-appointed variety) who have various reasons for not painting Iraqi and Iranian military capabilities and intentions as they are. The Warsaw Pact was known, from the 1970s, to be increasingly fragile. One could predict that Warsaw Pact military power, because of less reliable East European armies, was in decline. The Soviet Union was also known to be in trouble, although the full extent of its problems was masked by ideologically biased assessments of pro-socialist academics (''We have seen the future and it works'') and congressional defense budget lobbyists (''The Soviets are producing more and better weapons than ours, and don't cut tank production in my district'').

The fact of the matter is that in a situation lacking a large, hostile, aggressive, and heavily armed adversary, there is no way to do highly accurate Force Planning and convince the public that there is a major military threat to America. Add to this America's economic problems and the presence of many economically powerful but militarily timid allies (Germany and Japan, for example), and you have a hard time making a case for realistically organized peacetime forces. The problem here is not with the Pentagon Force Planners, but with all the amateurs in the media and other branches of government. The professionals get drowned out by all those with political and ideological agendas that are better at grabbing headlines— and decisions makers' attention. As always, the troops are prepared to go with what they've got. But with so many cooks in the kitchen, they're never sure what they will have from year to year, much less what hostile force they will be sent to fight.

Cutting the defense budget to one-third its Cold War peak would still mean spending twice as much of the GNP on defense (2 percent) as we did at any other time prior to World War II. This would still leave America with the most competent, versatile, and, arguably, powerful armed forces in the world. The "One Third" solution assumes that reserve and National Guard units, and the ability to mobilize more troops if necessary, would still be available. Some will say that this will make us vulnerable to the kind of problems we had when we entered World War II, with masses of raw recruits led by too few professionals. But the American armed forces of the 1990s are a far different breed from those of the 1930s. Most of this book concentrates on spotlighting those differences (and relentless warnings about the Victory Disease).

Getting ready for a replay of the last war isn't necessary, as there will never be another war like the last one. There never is. The weapons change, the forms of warfare change, and the world changes. There will still be wars, but one must prepare for the wars of the future, not those of the past. And history has shown that those who spend resources on the military at the expense of their economy not only ruin the economy but often come out second best in a war. That was another lesson of World War II. America was the most "unprepared" nation going into World War II. Yet it was America that triumphed. The secret weapon was the American economy.

But how does America ensure that it does not lose its future first battles that could end up being its last battles? The key to preventing the recurrence of the Task Force Smith tragedies is primarily a strong economy. This is the best guarantee of keeping weapons and military equipment modernized. Couple the strong economy with professional soldiers, appropriate doctrine, superior leaders, adequate training, and a new lens for viewing and coping with the post–Cold War world. It's a rare combination, and we've never had it before. If we're not careful, we may not have it again.

Appendices

CHRONOLOGY OF REFORMS

There are always reforms in the military going on, or at least attempts. Mostly attempts. The following chronology of American military reform goes a long way to put the reforms of the 1970–1990 period into perspective.

1776–1972   American reforms to create a ready and trained military have a long history, with many false starts and near-misses. From its very beginning, America had a tradition of being unprepared for its initial battles. Most Americans were suspicious of large standing military forces. The prevailing view was that wars could best be fought by citizen soldiers and sailors called to arms at the time of crisis. In the War of 1812, at Pearl Harbor and Kasserine Pass in World War II, and in the tragic battle conducted by Task Force Smith in Korea we have examples of disastrous early battles where American soldiers have paid a high price in blood for not being trained and ready.

1973   The post-Vietnam U.S. military is faced with major decline in the defense budget, loss of credibility with the American public, crisis of confidence within the officer corps, a broken NCO corps, major reduction in forces, poor morale, lack of resources to attract recruits for volunteer Army, poor public image, and a preoccupation on introspection.

1973   The 1973 Arab-Israeli War provides glimpses into the changing nature of modern warfare and alerts military professionals that much has to be learned and relearned about the complexities of modern land warfare and the effects of the increased speed of maneuver and the increased range, accuracy, and lethality of a new generation of weapons systems.

1973   TRADOC is activated and its first commander, General William E. DePuy, becomes convinced after studying the results of the 1973 Arab-Israeli War that military schools should train their students to be fully proficient in their profession. The troops will have little time to prepare should war come. In his view, the probability is high that there will be no time in the next war for deliberate mobilization. Units will have to "come as you are." At the Command and General Staff College at Fort Leavenworth, the highest-level school under TRADOC, the teaching emphasis is shifted down to the level of the reinforced brigade and the division so that the students taking these courses will be highly prepared for their level of command at graduation.

1974   Aftereffects of the OPEC oil embargo create an oil crisis in the United States. Armed forces begin planning for possible operations in the Persian Gulf. Initially, the danger is seen as Iran or Iraq threatening the smaller Gulf states, or civil disorder in the Gulf states themselves that would interrupt oil supplies.

1975   A revolution in training is instituted in the performance-oriented Army Training and Evaluation Program (ARTEP). Troops and units now have to regularly demonstrate mastery of combat skills, or see their military careers damaged or terminated. The all-volunteer force made this work, as draftees were generally not afraid of being let go before their time was up.

1975   General DePuy writes the Army Chief of Staff, General Fred C. Weyand, and recommends that the organization of the tactical units of the Army be fundamentally changed. In March 1976, the Department of the Army directs TRADOC to proceed formally with a restructuring effort.

1975   The North Vietnamese Army breaks down the gates of the Presidential Palace in Saigon.

1975   The Air Force establishes at Nellis Air Force Base, Nevada, its own version of Top Gun with a force-on-force exercise code-named Operation Red Flag. A major justification for the Air Force was a study that had been conducted by Litton Corporation, using statistics from World War II, Korea, and Vietnam. It showed that pilots in their first engagement had only a 60 percent chance of survival as opposed to a 90 percent chance after ten engagements. Tough realistic training provides pilots with their early engagement experience without the threat of casualties.

1975 Major General DeWitt C. Smith, Jr., initiates a program to increase the study of military operations and the use of wargaming at the U.S. Army War College.

1976 Major General Paul F. Gorman introduces the concept of a Combined Arms Training Center that will eventually become the National Training Center.

1976 New Army doctrine is introduced (Operations FM 100-5). General DePuy and General Donn A. Starry, commandant of the U.S. Armor School, took a personal interest in developing the doctrine. They referred to the new doctrine as Active Defense. Key to the doctrine was fighting outnumbered and winning. The focus was on concentrating combat power at the right time and place at the decisive period in the battle. The concepts worked well in the computer simulations, but shortfalls in communications, intelligence, and the ability to concentrate made it difficult to successfully implement the doctrine in field exercises. Efforts began almost immediately to modify the doctrine and modernize the Army.

1978 Review of Education and Training of Officers (RETO) report is published. It recommends the Army War College place additional emphasis on the study of military operations ("how to fight") and manage an Army-wide Tactical Command Readiness Program to provide continuing education and contingency planning support for senior tactical commanders and their staffs. The importance of using modern educational and training tools to increase the professionalism of the military is emphasized in the RETO report.

1979 On October 18, 1979, the Chief of Staff of the Army approves, in principle, Division 86 as the new Army heavy division. Division 86 was one of four major Army organizational studies. The studies of the light division, the corps, and echelons above corps (army, army group) were still ongoing. The purpose of these four studies was to design and develop a more effective organization for the Army to have in place by 1986.

1979 The Tactical Command Readiness Program (TCRP) is assigned to the Army War College by the Chief of Staff of the Army on May 4. This gave Army generals an opportunity to practice fighting under wartime conditions.

1979   The Iranians take American hostages from the U.S. Embassy.

1979   The Soviets invade Afghanistan and fear of a Soviet invasion of Iran grows.

1980   President Carter announces the Carter Doctrine, which designates the Persian Gulf as an area of vital interest to the United States: ''Any attempt by any outside force to gain control of the Persian Gulf region will be regarded as an assault on the vital interests of the USA and will be repelled by any means necessary, including military force.''

1980   The Rapid Deployment Joint Task Force (RDJTF) is established to determine ways to protect U.S. national interests in the Persian Gulf area.

1980   William Lind discusses in the March 1980 edition of the *Marine Corps Gazette* the theory of maneuver warfare set forth by Colonel John Boyd, USAF (Ret.) (Boyd Theory). To facilitate his discussion of maneuver warfare, Lind uses a scenario that has American forces coming to the aid of the Saudi forces when Iraq forces attack Saudi Arabia.

1980   At the request of Lieutenant Colonel Gordon Sullivan (division operations officer of the 1st Infantry Division, Fort Riley, Kansas; became Chief of Staff of Army in 1991), TRCP is first tested in a highly successful exercise that employs lessons extracted from the hundreds of Jim Dunnigan's simulations and exercises at the Naval War College. The core of the simulation would involve a strategic deployment exercise to Europe. The TRCP team was headed by Colonel Kermit Gates, an Army officer with extensive experience in combat simulations. The Naval War College had worked with the Army War College since the mid-1970s on this, and Dunnigan had made dozens of trips to the Army War College (on a volunteer basis) to help get things moving. One of the unique features of this program was the use of the programmed learning texts and techniques developed by the Ketron Corporation. These methods were used to ensure that everyone participating in the exercises had a clear understanding of their responsibilities before going into the exercise.

1980   The Army's National Training Center (NTC) is officially activated at Fort Irwin, California. The NTC provided tough realistic training that afforded Army troops the opportunity to train the way they would fight, using an instrumented battlefield that provided feedback to commanders so they could better structure training programs at their home stations. In addition, during Desert Shield/Desert Storm the NTC evaluated Iraqi capabilities and developed and structured operational techniques that could be used in Desert Storm to defeat Iraqi tactics.

1980   Desert One disaster (failed attempt to rescue the Tehran hostages). One result was that, under the direction of General Meyer (Chief of Staff of the Army), faculty members at the Army War College used wargaming and modeling to develop a new contingency planning process. This would assist senior commanders in developing better ways to deal with situations like the Iran rescue mission.

1980   Ronald Reagan elected president with the belief he has a mandate to build up the military.

1981   The Department of the Army approves the establishment of an Army War College ''Department of War Gaming'' and a ''Center for War Gaming'' to provide development programs for planners for higher-level joint and Army staffs and contingency planning support to senior tactical commanders. Colonel Macedonia would be appointed as the first chairman of the War Gaming Department and director of the Contingency Planning Program.

1981   A group of historians is added to the faculty in the Department of War Gaming at the Army War College. This was to place more emphasis on the principles of war, and to add more emphasis on the theory of grand strategy, in the use of combat simulations at the level of corps and above.

1981   Colonel Sullivan is assigned to VII Corps in Europe and from there requests support under the TRCP program for assistance in employing simulations to conduct corps warfighting exercises to test war plans.

1982   The AirLand Battle Doctrine (Field Manual 100-5, 1982 edition) is issued. It involves a major revolution in doctrine from attrition warfare to a balancing between maneuver and attrition as well as reintroduction of the operational art of war and over-the-horizon warfare for ground forces. The shift of attention of the Army to the operational level of war will have a profound change on the entire military. The operational art is the employment of military forces to attain strategic goals in a theater of operations through the design, organization, and conduct of campaigns and major operations.

1982   General Starry uses the Army War Gaming Model (a wargame) for evaluating contingency plans of the Readiness Command as they apply in the Joint Process (working with the Air Force and Navy). That is, to practice planning for future military operations with Army, Navy, and Air Force participation. Up to this point, there was not enough joint planning among the three services. This lack of planning would show up only when war came, at which time it would be too late.

1982   Colonel Harry G. Summer, Jr.'s landmark work, *On Strategy: The Vietnam War in Context,* highlights the principles of war and the importance of understanding the interaction of the strategic, operational, and tactical levels of war.

1982   The AirLand Battle Study is conducted to determine required technology and equipment for the future.

1982   General Meyer states, in a speech at West Point, that the United States is not currently organized to go to war. He calls for a strong Chairman of the Joint Chiefs of Staff who would have the power to direct strategy and decide priorities rather than be limited to chairing a deliberative body of the heads of the services.

1983   General John A. Wickham is made Chief of Staff of the Army. He is a close friend of General Charles A. Gabriel (Chief of Staff of the Air Force; they were roommates at West Point as cadets). Both realize that they have a historical and unprecedented opportunity to advance the cooperation of their services. Together they establish the Army-Air Force Joint Force Development Process using officers from their staffs. Their initial staff efforts alone identified over thirty programs where Air Force and Army efforts appeared to be duplicated, and where joint doctrine needed development or clarification. It was through their close coordination and efforts that Air Force support to the Army's National Training Center was finally obtained.

1983   Increased interest in realistic field training and increased flying hours and realistic simulations begin to have an effect in increasing readiness and combat capability.

1983   U.S. forces invade Grenada. There are still a lot of problems getting the services to work efficiently together. Although this operation was executed with only a few days' warning, it was a clear demonstration of how much more work was needed among the services.

1983   CARMAX, joint wargaming between the Air War College and the Army War College, begins.

1983   The Army establishes a School of Advanced Military Studies (SAMS) at Fort Leavenworth to provide the Army with officers specially educated and trained for military operations. The Advanced Military Studies Program provides selected students attending the Command and General Staff Officer course, who display an acumen for tactics and operations, an intensified course on the art of warfighting. Following graduation, students serve a mandatory eighteen-month internship at a division or corps level staff. Both the Marine Corps and the Air Force have established similar programs. The initiation of these programs had a major impact on improving the quality of the entire military in preparing for and conducting military operations.

1986   A new edition of the Operational Doctrine manual is published for the Army (Field Manual 100-5, 1986 edition) and reaffirms the doctrine published in 1982. It emphasizes the importance of the operational level of warfare.

1986   The Goldwater-Nichols Department of Defense Reorganization Act of 1986 is passed after almost four years of work, study, and deliberation. This act strengthened the authority to the Chairman of the Joint Chiefs of Staff, gave clear authority to senior commanders on how to work with different services in order to accomplish their missions, and also clearly improved civilian involvement in contingency planning. The act also gave authority and responsibility for developing joint doctrine to the Chairman of the Joint Chiefs of Staff.

1986   The Joint Warfare Center (JWC) is established at MacDill AFB, Florida, under the command of the U.S. Readiness Command with one of its missions to assist the CINCs in exploring the applicability and feasibility of integrating computer simulations in exercise and training events.

1987   The Chief of Staff of the Army approves the concept of a Battle Command Training Program (BCTP) to train senior commanders in warfighting skills. The BCTP featured a seminar at Fort Leavenworth, Kansas, followed by a computer-driven wargame-based command post exercise. The BCTP provided special support to divisions deploying to Saudi Arabia, and members of the BCTP staff were also sent to Saudi Arabia to help Central Command perfect battle plans for the ground phase of the war.

1987   The Chief of Staff of the Army approves the establishment of a Joint Readiness Training Center (JRTC) at Fort Chaffee, Arkansas, to provide tough realistic training to light, airborne, air assault, rangers, and special operations forces—training similar to what the NTC was providing heavy forces. The 82nd Airborne and 101st Airmobile divisions along with special operations forces (SOF) received extensive training at the JRTC prior to deploying to Saudi Arabia.

1987–1989   CENTCOM creates the JTFME (Joint Task Force Middle East) to spearhead efforts of the U.S. reflagging of eleven Kuwaiti oil tankers (Operation Earnest Will) during the Iran-Iraq War.

1989   CENTCOM conducts the CINCCENT Wargame to review and examine the newly revised Operations Plan (OPLAN 1002) for Southwest Asia (and particularly the Persian Gulf).

1989   CENTCOM revises its OPLAN 1002, based on the perceived need for a contingency plan to counter an Iraqi attack on Kuwait and Saudi Arabia without Soviet involvement.

1989   Beginning of the end of the Cold War. The Berlin Wall comes down.

1989   Just Cause: The United States invades Panama and ousts General Noriega. Six years after Grenada, the services achieve much better coordination.

1990   The Combat Maneuver Training Center (CMTC) at Hohenfels, Germany, begins providing U.S. Army forces in Europe the same realistic training that the NTC provides. The CMTC would provide tailored training to VII Corps units immediately prior to their deployment to Saudi Arabia.

1990   Iraq invades Kuwait. U.S. forces and their coalition partners quickly, decisively, and with minimum casualties obtain the UN objectives and force Iraq out of Kuwait. Only because of approximately two decades of preparation is the United States able to break the mold and have a military trained and ready for the first battle.

1991   A failed right-wing coup in the Soviet Union triggers the breakup of the Soviet Union and an end to the Cold War. Senior U.S. commanders realize they must now disband many of the forces they so carefully built up in the 1980s.

EVOLUTION OF ARMY DOCTRINE IN THE UNITED STATES

FM 100-5 (Army Field Manual 100-5, 1986 edition) defines Army doctrine. That is, FM 100-5 is a condensed description of how Army commanders should fight, as well as conduct campaigns, major operations, battles, and engagements. It is essentially a guide for action and a common way of thinking. There are dozens of other field manuals that go into greater detail. But all other Army manuals on ''how to fight'' must use FM 100-5 as a general guideline. Because of this, FM 100-5 is called the capstone manual.

Doctrine must be up-to-date and flexible enough to facilitate adaptation once military forces are actually committed to battle and the unexpected occurs. Doctrine facilitates training, weapon and equipment development, tactics development, communications, coordination, and organization development. The development of doctrine is influenced by many factors including technological advances, changes in threats, international issues, wartime demands, national security policies, improved weapons, rivalries between branches, rivalries between services, domestic issues, availability of resources, and personal wishes of military and government leaders. The following are some of the highlights in the evolution of military doctrine in the United States:

1700s: Frontier Improvisation

The American colonies fought their first wars in frontier areas, and under the supervision of British officers. The formal, European-style warfare espoused by British officers was not effective in the wilderness. The first truly American military doctrine developed as wilderness fighting techniques were merged with European weapons and organization. By the time of the Revolution, American troops were masters on the frontier, but still had to learn European ways for battles in the heavily populated coastal areas. French and other European advisers taught American troops how to fight set-piece battles. Much was learned, but there was no attempt to preserve this knowledge in any systematic way. The frontier fighting style did survive in the outlying areas, and has influenced American military thinking to this day.

1803–1812: In Search of a Doctrine

The American Army was essentially disbanded after the American War of Independence. The Army went into the War of 1812 with no approved doctrine.

1812–1861: The Shadow of Napoleon and Baron Jomini

Wary of large standing armies and isolated and protected from potentially hostile nations in Europe by the Atlantic Ocean, the United States did not emphasize its military forces, and development of a military doctrine was a low priority. From the War of 1812 to the American Civil War, America employed its Army primarily in the westward expansion and the protection of the frontiers. During this period, the major influences guiding military action were the concepts of General Winfield Scott and lessons derived from the Napoleonic Wars as interpreted by the Swiss theorist Baron Antoine Henri Jomini. Napoleon's concept of warfare as seen through Jomini's eyes had been integrated into the American military to a great extent by Dennis Mahan. Mahan, who was a follower of Jomini, was a tactics instructor at the United States Military Academy at West Point. Dennis Mahan was the father of a future naval strategist, Alfred Thayer Mahan, who would apply

Jomini's concepts to naval warfare. Jomini stressed mobility and concentration and battles of annihilation by attacking the hostile army at the decisive point and at the proper times.

1861–1865: The Civil War

The concepts of Jomini were modified by the experiences of the Civil War. The development of the railroad, steamboat, and telegraph made major changes in warfare. General Grant exploited these technologies and other developments of the Industrial Revolution to modify Jomini's guide for warfare to include the requirement to destroy the hostile army's supply and support system. Grant would foster a doctrine that relied on overwhelming the enemy with greater numbers of men, guns, and equipment and with relentless attacks and pursuits.

1865–1898: The Prussian System/Industrial Revolution

In the span of only a few years, Prussia decisively defeated the Danes in 1864, the Austrians in 1866, the French in 1871, and unified Germany. These remarkable accomplishments made Prussia the leading military power in Europe. With the ascension of Prussia, the military concepts of the Prussian theorist Major General Carl von Clausewitz began to have a major influence on the development of doctrine in most Western nations.

In addition, Field Marshal Helmuth von Moltke, a former student of Clausewitz and Chief of the General Staff of the Prussian army, as well as architect of German unification, would have a substantial influence on the doctrinal development of other nations. The link between political and military objectives was emphasized by both men. Military men from most Western nations including the United States went to study and learn the German military system. Among the Americans who went to Berlin were Emory Upton, Joseph P. Sanger, Tasker H. Bliss, Arthur L. Wagner, Theodore Schwan, and William Ludlow. When these officers returned to the United States, they wrote about the improvements in the German system and many of them were adapted and integrated into the American military. These reforms included the "estimate of the situation" to solve problems, the operational level of war (more emphasis on campaign planning), a general staff, an integrated educational system to include a war college, the role of the political and economic dimensions of war, and an effective and efficient mobilization system.

The evolution of doctrine during this period was also greatly affected by the Industrial Revolution. The capability to mass-produce large amounts of weapons and equipment very rapidly at relatively low cost was key to developing a modern Army. But the Army was so strapped for resources that it had difficulty taking advantage of the new methods. Only a few years after the Civil War, the Army was reduced to a strength of some 28,000 soldiers. Most of these soldiers were assigned to small outposts on the frontiers as constabulary forces controlling Indians and assisting with maintaining law and order. The rest of the Army was primarily involved with coastal artillery at key harbors. The Navy, however, began to implement a doctrine of offensive sea control. As the nation expanded its horizon toward the end of the nineteenth century, and with the support of the administration and Congress, the new Navy doctrine was developed primarily by Admiral Luce and Mahan at the Naval War College.

1898–1920: Reform

The poor performance by the American military in its mobilization planning, logistics system, and deployment during the war against Spain in Cuba created a demand by the public for major reforms. In responding to the criticism of its performance in the Spanish-American War and the demands of World War I, the Army adapted and integrated into the American Army many aspects of the Prussian system. All of these changes would have a profound impact on doctrine. In 1902, a General Service and Staff College opened at Fort Leavenworth to provide the Army with staff training.

In 1903, a General Staff and a War College were created by the passage of the General Staff Act in 1903. One of the first tasks of these new organizations was to develop an effective mobilization plan that would adapt the German system to the uniqueness of the American situation. When the mobilization plan was implemented for World War I, the 100,000-man Army mobilized over four million troops in nineteen months. This mobilization experience would be one of the major factors shaping U.S. doctrine until 1976.

Another experience of World War I that would influence future doctrinal development was the use of American forces in coalition warfare. Relying on large-scale mobilization fit well into America's traditional dislike for large standing armies, its preference for a civilian militia, and the underlying belief that wars are won by overwhelming the enemy with masses of equipment and men. Mobilization was institutionalized in America with the passage of the National Defense Act of 1920 that called for an Army of the United States that consisted of a Regular Army, a National Guard, and an Organized Reserve Corps.

1920–1940: Overcoming the Stalemate of World War I

The devastating experiences of World War I led to a major thrust during this period to find an approach to warfare that would overcome the stalemate of trench warfare. Advocates of air power put forth the theories of the Italian General Giulio Douhet and the American General Billy Mitchell, who called for strategic bombing against the homelands of hostile nations. The key doctrinal manual for air power during this period was "Fundamental Principles for the Employment of the Air Service, War Department Training Regulation (TR) 440-15, 1926," which placed aircraft units under Army commanders. Other reformers pushed the theories of the British strategists Major General J.F.C. Fuller and Sir Basil Liddell Hart and French strategist General Charles de Gaulle for mechanization and motorization.

1940–1941: Expanding into Armies

In the 1930s, the Army lacked practical experience and effective doctrine for the employment of large combat units. Although corps and armies were employed during the Civil War, the Army had been unable to stage large-scale maneuvers since 1865. Most of the World War I troops were used as part of coalition armies. To provide operational guides and to test the readiness of its leaders, forces, and equipment, the Army conducted in 1941 a free-play maneuver between two armies consisting of over 400,000 soldiers and 1,000 aircraft operating in an area covering over 30,000 square miles. The exercise was given the name Louisiana Maneuvers and the forces were Third Army being opposed by Second Army. Third Army had two corps with ten divisions. Second Army consisted of two corps and only eight divisions. Many of the lessons derived from the Louisiana Maneuvers would help guide the Army through World War II. These lessons included experiences in integrating combined arms, coordinating air and ground operations, and the critical importance of logistical support. Out of this period would come General George C. Marshall's doctrine manual, which would be noted for its clarity. These maneuvers were the largest peacetime training exercises the Army was ever to stage.

1941–1945: Global Doctrine

During World War II, with some modification, the Army doctrine remained essentially Napoleonic. Naval doctrine remained essentially Mahan with emphasis on sea control, and the Air Force doctrine remained Douhet/Mitchell with emphasis on the bomber and strategic bombing and air control. The key doctrine manual for aviation during this period was FM 100-20, 1943. This manual stated that land and air power were coequal and interdependent forces. It called for gaining air superiority as the first requirement for the success of any major land operation. The doctrinal system for World War II was dominated by the offense and primarily designed to conduct battles of annihilation by overwhelming the enemy with masses of combat power concentrated at the decisive place and time. Coordination of mass artillery was critical. The key was to effectively and efficiently use the tools of the Industrial Revolution to outproduce the enemy in the weapons and equipment of war.

1945–1950: Nuclear Monopoly

The doctrine during this period was a reflection of World War II, but with an intent to perform better. The United States was the only nation with nuclear weapons, but it was understood that there would still be a need for nonnuclear forces. The emphasis was on conventional warfare, improving coordination of fire support including close air support, offensive action, and the infantry division. A study of World War II operations convinced many military men that the best antitank weapon was another tank. This attitude toward tanks would be a premise in U.S. doctrine for many years to come. Density of forces was relatively high; it was expected that an infantry division of forces was relatively high; it was expected that an infantry division of 13,000 soldiers would defend a front of approximately 7,000 meters. Field Manual (FM) 31-35, Air-Ground Operations, 1946, and FM 100-5 (1949 edition) were the two key doctrinal manuals written during this period. As the decade came to an end, the stage was set for major changes in doctrine with the Soviets obtaining the atomic bomb, the Berlin Blockade, and the victory of the communists in China.

1950–1960: Massive Retaliation

Nuclear weapons were now seen as the key to stopping aggression. Nukes would be used quickly if the Soviets made a move. The emphasis on doctrine moved to the defense with the mobile defense being added to the doctrine. Tactical use of nuclear weapons to compensate for lack of numbers of forces became a central theme of the Army. The Army also placed greater emphasis on armor, which was a direct response to the large number of Soviet armor formations facing allied forces in Europe and the success of North Korean armor forces in the Korean War. The underlying principle of the doctrine was the national policy of massive nuclear retaliation should the Soviets attack. With improved mobility and range of weapons, density of forces was reduced. A division of 17,000 men was expected to defend a front of about 21,000 meters (depending on terrain) and the new Pentomic Division of about 12,000 men was expected to defend a front of over 24,000 meters. Key document on Army doctrine during this period was FM 100-5 (1954, 1956, and 1958 editions). The key doctrine document for the Air Force during this period was Air Force Manual 1-2, USAF Basic Doctrine, published in 1953, 1954, 1955, and 1959. All versions stressed the lessons of World War II. The 1959 version recognized the importance of missiles and space by replacing the words *air power* with the words *aerospace power*. As the decade came to an end with the Soviets obtaining the H-bomb, the launching of Sputnik by the Soviets, the perceived missile gap, and the Berlin Crisis, the stage was set for another major change in doctrine.

1960–1970: Flexible Response and Nuclear Parity

With the realization that Soviet nuclear weapons were now numerous enough to make U.S. use of nukes the equivalent of mutual suicide, the Army adopted a flexible-response concept as its doctrine. In addition, there was a major interest in counterinsurgency. At the national level, emphasis was on separating strategic nuclear warfare from all other kinds of warfare. With flexible response, there was now a clear difference between nuclear and conventional operations. During this period, mechanized infantry at battalion and division level was introduced into the Army, although the infantry still dismounted from their vehicles to fight. The offense received greater emphasis with improvements in mobility and better command and control and improved communications. The introduction of airmobility (helicopters) with vertical envelopment added a new dimension to warfare. Divisions were more flexible and balanced, using a concept of a common base and creating infantry or armor divisions by adding different combinations of armor and infantry battalions. Density of forces continued to decrease on the battlefield.

Some of the key Army doctrinal documents were FM 31-15 (Operations Against Irregular Forces, 1961 edition) and FM 100-5 (1962 edition). The Air Force in 1964 changed its basic doctrine manual from AFM 1-2 to AFM 1-1. This edition introduced the concept of flexible response; however, this was the first edition to omit the Principles of War. For the Army, as the decade came to an end, the stage was set for change, not only in doctrine but in almost every dimension. The Vietnam War had revealed to the Army a number of fundamental problems in training, morale, doctrine, and leadership. The war had broken the noncommissioned officer corps and had almost broken the officer corps. For the Air Force, an entire new family of weapon systems, munitions, and platforms was under development using smart-weapon technology and stealth technology which would have major implications for future doctrine.

1970–1980: Competence and "Come As You Are"

Army doctrine development and coordination among the services was greatly aided with the reorganization and demobilization of the Continental Army Command (CONARC) in 1973. CONARC was divided into two major commands: the Training and Doctrine Command (TRADOC) and the Army Forces Command (FORSCOM). Now the Army had a command headed by a four-star general with the priority for dealing with doctrine and training. Locating TRADOC close to major Air Force and naval commands helped the coordination of doctrine. Doctrine would also be greatly affected by lessons learned in Vietnam and in the 1973 Mideast War. Doctrine during this period concentrated on Europe and returned to the first principles (the fundamentals of military operations).

The underlying assumption of the doctrine was that the United States could no longer depend on having time to mobilize or time to make up for being unprepared at the initial stages of a conflict. Mobilization, which had dominated U.S. Army doctrine since 1916, was no longer the driving force. It was therefore essential that U.S. forces be competent and equipped and ready to fight outnumbered and win from the very first engagement until the last battle. The doctrine included concepts that employed an active defense that forced the enemy to mass most forces forward. This approach to fighting called for limited or no reserves and utilizing mobility to concentrate combat power to defeat the enemy at the right place and time while employing the natural advantages of the defender.

The doctrine during this period was a balance of both the offense and the defense and included discussions on maneuver. But the active defense received most of the attention from officers commanding combat units. Also stressed was firepower, especially the effective employment of weapon systems to obtain their maximum capability utilizing increased range, rate of fire, probability of hit, and killing power. The goal was to develop a doctrine that would cope with the massive number of Warsaw Pact forces facing NATO in the Central Region of Europe. The underlying emphasis was on exploiting the capabilities of the antitank weapons that were so effectively used in the 1973 Mideast War to multiply the combat power of the defender. All of this work on combat techniques was greatly influenced by the lessons derived from the Vietnam War and the Mideast War. Also taken into consideration were the limited terrain in Germany to maneuver and the political problems of the Germans which required them to defend well forward. The major doctrine document during this period was FM 100-5, 1976 edition. As the decade came to an end, the stage was again set for major changes in doctrine with the Soviet invasion of Afghanistan, the Iranian hostage taking, the Carter Doctrine, and the formation of the Rapid Reaction Force.

1980–1990: AirLand Battle and Extending the Battlefield

During this period, three things forced a change in Army doctrine:

1. The increased lethality and range of battlefield weapons.
2. The small number of available divisions to maintain a cohesive front line in Europe.
3. The requirement to have doctrine applicable to global threats.

Army doctrine moved to a more offensive orientation with a concept of nonlinear warfare. This meant units mixing it up with the enemy without bothering to form the traditional ''front line.'' At the same time, there would be attacks on the enemy's rear areas by Army and Air Forces operating in close cooperation. Studies conducted by the Army clearly indicated that to defeat the Soviets the Army required a doctrine that would enable U.S. forces to win its early battles as well as its succeeding battles. At the same time, U.S. forces had to keep their own losses down. U.S. forces had to maintain the initiative by attacking deep into the enemy rear area with missiles, helicopters, and Air Force jets. To seize the initiative, the Army had to find a way to reduce the number of Soviet troops U.S. ground forces had to fight.

In the past, U.S. doctrine encouraged getting a lot of enemy forces close to U.S. ground units. The idea was to then use superior U.S. firepower to smash these enemy units. But in the process, there would always be U.S. casualties. This was known as "attrition tactics" and it worked as long as the enemy lost a lot more than you did. But modern weapons are a lot more lethal, and the new doctrine proposed methods for finding and hitting enemy units before they could tangle with friendly ground units. This is precisely what U.S. forces did to the Iraqi army in the Gulf War. The new doctrine moved away from battles of annihilation and brute force by balancing attrition with maneuver. It also added the operational level of war to its doctrine with increased emphasis on campaign planning and improved coordination of the increasing number of weapons, units, and support systems found on the battlefield. The key doctrine document during this period was FM 100-5, 1982 and 1986 editions. The 1984 edition of AFM 1-1 for the Air Force added increased cooperation with ground forces and included a discussion of battlefield air interdiction. As this decade came to a close, the stage was again set for major changes in Army doctrine. America became a debtor nation, the Soviets withdrew from Afghanistan, the Berlin Wall opened, and dissolution of the Warsaw Pact and the Soviet Union was put in motion.

1990s and Beyond

The end of the Cold War has brought with it the departure of one monolithic foe (communist armies) and the appearance of a longer list of potential villains. Doctrine has to be a lot more flexible and the troops will need a lot more training to prepare for the wider array of foes and battlefields they may encounter.

Meanwhile, technology marches on. We now have the dawn of the Robotic Battlefield. Weapons that think (or rather, calculate) by themselves and roam the battlefield seeking out the enemy are becoming more common. Cruise missiles were the most notable example in the Gulf War. The Army has developed, and is about to deploy, a series of robotic mines. You turn them on and you command and control them with a new generation of information technology (computers and radio gear). Advances in this technology allow these robotic systems to communicate and coordinate their actions, operating very much like a platoon of troops. It is now possible for these robotic systems to operate as independent units under distant human control, performing many of the functions that are normally performed by manned units (reconnaissance, conducting ambushes, etc.). The challenge will be in developing the doctrine and tactics to fully exploit the capabilities of these new systems.

The growing complexity of functions on the modern battlefield is another problem for doctrine development in the 1990s. Computers are commonplace on the battlefield, as is a new generation of communications and navigational gear. Units can now move rapidly at night and in unfamiliar territory. The major impact of this information revolution will be on command and control.

The Air Force published new doctrine in 1992 and the Army followed with its own updates in 1993. Both the Air Force and the Army changed their combat techniques to reflect lessons learned in the Gulf War. The Navy has established a new Doctrine Command to write up new procedures to reflect the changes required by the demise of the Soviet Union and its navy. The Chairman of the Joint Chiefs of Staff has also issued new doctrine to reflect the new emphasis on joint and combined operations. As new national-security strategy evolves under the Democratic administration, many more changes to both the joint and service doctrines will be required. The 1990s will be interesting times for doctrine writers, and for the troops who depend on doctrine for battlefield guidance.

THE HACKWORTH ISSUE

David Hackworth served in the Army for over twenty years, entering as a private and leaving as a colonel. He spent his entire career in the infantry, and had a chestful of medals and a body full of scars to show for it. He had a knack for leading troops on the battlefield, and writing about it for a broad audience. He is currently a columnist for *Newsweek* magazine. He has also written a book about his career (*About Face*). The book, and Hackworth's attitudes toward and perceptions of the Army, caused a curious division of opinion regarding his message and how he delivered it. On one side are his supporters, primarily civilians. On the other side are his detractors, for the most part serving Army officers and even some of the men who served with Hackworth.

While Hackworth was still in the Army, he was considered one of the bright lights and sure to become a general before long. Hackworth wrote extensively for military publications on the need for better training and improved doctrine. Toward the end of the Vietnam War, Hackworth was also put to work by the Army in the initial efforts at reform. But Hackworth had one trait that turned from asset to liability. Hackworth was impatient and fearless. On the battlefield, this had caused the enemy much grief and saved many American lives. But after three tours in Vietnam and increasing frustration at the way the war was being fought, Hackworth did what an officer was not supposed to do. He washed the Army's dirty laundry in public. He went on network television and said what the troops in the field already knew. He pointed out that training was insufficient, tactics unworkable, and leadership lacking.

Hackworth didn't know the Army would reform itself after Vietnam, and there were no indications that it would. So Hackworth went to the media with his complaints and the Army hierarchy came down on him. He managed to retire in 1971 without getting court-martialed, but it was a close-run thing. Hackworth broke the rules on and off the battlefield, as most successful combat commanders do. The Army could have nailed him if it had really wanted to. But many 1971 officers agreed with Hackworth's message, even if they loathed the way he delivered it in public. In 1989, Hackworth's book *About Face* was published and the wounds were reopened. The Army officer corps was still not, as a group, willing to forgive Hackworth. But the Army had reformed, Dave Hackworth recognized and praised that, and all that was left was the bitter taste of old memories.

MILITARY ORGANIZATION, ETC.

Throughout this book, reference is made to various ranks—what they do, what they get paid, and so on. This can be confusing, so we have added this section to explain the military rank system and what it means to the average soldier.

All soldiers are identified by two primary items: rank and job specialty. The rank system is the simpler of the two. From the new recruit to the Chief of Staff (senior officer of the Army), there are but twenty-four ranks. Job specialties are more complex, there being several hundred for each service. A job specialty identifies what a soldier has been trained to do and, in most cases, what the soldier actually does from day to day. Job specialties are called MOS, or Military Occupational Specialty, for Army enlisted personnel. Officers have a different buzzword, as do sailors, Air Force officers, and so on. As with most things, a handful of job specialties comprise the bulk of the troops. For example, some 50,000 Army soldiers have the MOS 11B, which indicates they are infantrymen. Another 9,100 are 11C, which means they operate mortars in infantry units, but can also take their rifles and work with the 11Bs. In all, there are about 80,000 soldiers with the "11" series MOS. This is about 12 percent of all troops. There are several MOSs held by only a few troops, like the four hundred 84Bs (still photographers, as opposed to the two dozen 84Cs, or movie photographers). The Air Force has nearly 20,000 pilots of all types (over fifty), nearly 50,000 aircraft maintenance people, and over 40,000 security police. The Navy has 20,000 Electrical Technicians (plus 14,000 Electrician's Mates), and 12,000 Hull Technicians.

The list below shows the "24 ranks" as they are called in the Army. There are variations in names within the services (particularly the Navy), but all services use the same "pay grades" (E-1 through E-9 for enlisted personnel, O-1 through O-10 for officers, plus the five grades of Warrant Officers in between).

At the bottom of this rank structure we have the enlisted personnel. These are so called because they "enlist" in military service.

Enlisted Personnel

We have divided the enlisted ranks into the three broad levels that are often referred to in military (and civilian) publications. These are "the troops," junior NCOs, and senior NCOs.

Privates (the "Troops")

E-1 Private Recruit
E-2 Private
E-3 Private First Class
E-4 Specialist

Junior NCOs (Noncommissioned Officers)

E-4 Corporal
E-5 Sergeant
E-6 Staff Sergeant

Senior NCOs

E-7 Sergeant First Class
E-8 Master Sergeant
E-8 First Sergeant
E-9 Sergeant Major
E-9 Command Sergeant Major
E-9 Sergeant Major of the Army

Officers

Warrant Officers

There are five grades of Warrant Officer, although not all services use all the grades. In fact, not all services use Warrant Officers. The Army is the biggest user, particularly for helicopter pilots. Most Warrants (as they are called) are NCOs who have become very knowledgeable in their MOS and are simply promoted to Warrant rank. Technically, Warrants are not officers in the traditional sense, as they are not expected to ''command'' troops. Warrants do supervise troops, and these are always noncombat troops. Think of Warrants as the military equivalent of long-term and very expert clerks who are promoted to ''supervisor'' rank but can never become (or be considered) ''executives.'' That said, Warrants are generally exceptionally competent people. They are key personnel who make things happen in their specialties, whether it be vehicle maintenance or administration.

Commissioned Officers

These are what we normally consider ''officers.'' In parenthesis is the abbreviation you will often see in military publications, as a space-saving alternative to spelling out the rank.

O-1 Second Lieutenant (LT)
O-2 First Lieutenant (LT)
O-3 Captain (CPT)
O-4 Major (MAJ)
O-5 Lieutenant Colonel (LTC)
O-6 Colonel (COL)
O-7 Brigadier General (BG)
O-8 Major General (MG)

O-9 Lieutenant General (LG)
O-10 General (GEN)

Distribution of Ranks

Conventional wisdom thinks of an Army as a bunch of privates, with a smaller number of NCOs and a still smaller group of officers. The reality is a bit different. About 50 percent are privates to one degree or another (ranks E-1 through E-4). The junior NCOs are grades E-5 and E-6. The key (or "senior") NCOs are grades E-7 through E-9. These are the NCOs who run the platoons and companies. Each unit of battalion and larger size has an E-9 Sergeant Major who acts as the commander's conduit to the troops and NCOs. A good Sergeant Major can be critical to the success a commander has in running his unit. This is especially true at the battalion level, where the Sergeant Major knows all the units' twenty or thirty senior NCOs personally. The battalion Sergeant Major usually has more time in the service than anyone else in the unit, and more experience in getting things done.

Rank	Percentage of All Army Personnel
E-1 Recruit	6%
E-2 Private	6%
E-3 PFC	12%
E-4 Corporal	26% (most are "Specialists," or glorified PFCs)
E-5 Sergeant	15%
E-6 SSG	11%
E-7 SFC	7%
E-8 MSG	2%
E-9 SGM	1%

Officers are not a pyramid either. The "company grade" officers (O-1 through O-3) are the ones who run the company-size units. Majors (O-4) rarely command battalions except in wartime and are largely occupied with staff work. Lieutenant Colonels traditionally command battalions. But there are nearly ten LTCs for each battalion in the modern Army, so most of them are in staff jobs. The same ratio applies for Colonels (who command brigades) and Generals (who command divisions, corps, and armies). The Warrant Officers are technicians, although most Army helicopter pilots are Warrants.

Rank	Percentage of All Army Personnel
WO	2% (all Warrant Officers, five grades)
O-1 2LT	1%
O-2 1LT	2%
O-3 CPT	4%
O-4 MAJ	2%
O-5 LTC	1%
O-6 COL	1%
GEN	.05% (all General Officers, four grades)

Ratios Between Officers and Enlisted Men (U.S. Army)

Rank	World War II 1945 ratio	Korea 1953 ratio	Vietnam 1971 ratio
General	1:4916	1:2953	1:1952
Colonel	1:672	1:274	1:163
Lt. Colonel	1:258	1:108	1:67
Major	1:118	1:77	1:44
Captain	1:42	1:42	1:20
1st Lt.	1:35	1:44	1:41
2nd Lt.	1:76	1:45	1:71
Warrant Off.	1:242	1:105	1:52

These changing ratios show how the Army had to inflate rank in order to stay competitive with the civilian labor market. Education levels of military-age men rose considerably from 1945 on. The Army introduced larger amounts of increasingly complex weapons and equipment. The result was more officers, and more senior NCOs also.

Reenlistment Rates

About half the first-term enlistees in the U.S. armed forces reenlist for a second term. Not everyone who wants to reenlist is allowed to. The military raises and lowers the standards for reenlistment depending on how many volunteers they are getting and/or how many people Congress allows them to have on active duty. In this way, personnel strength can be maintained by raising or lowering the criteria for reenlistment. This means that when there are a lot of volunteers, the overall quality of the troops goes up because the standards for reenlistment are higher. The Air Force has the highest reenlistment rate, over 60 percent, followed by the Navy, with over 50 percent, and the Army, with about 40 percent, while the Marines trail behind with only about a third reenlisting.

Among career enlisted personnel (those who have served two or more enlistments), the reenlistment rate is over 80 percent. The Army leads with about 90 percent, followed closely by the Air Force, while the Marines and Navy get only 75 to 80 percent of their career people to reenlist each year. This is largely due to the frequent long periods at sea. Since most career people are married, career sailors and marines often have to choose between the service and a stable marriage. Nearly all of those who reenlist a second time will stay for twenty years and thus qualify for a pension equal to half their active-duty pay. Many are allowed to stay in for thirty years, which increases retirement pay to two thirds of active duty pay. These long-term volunteers must maintain a record of good duty performance and are expected to maintain their technical skills. These skills are tested periodically. They are also expected to qualify for promotion after a certain number of years in each grade. Promotions are based on the number of open slots in each grade and how well qualified the candidates are. To stay in for twenty years, an enlisted soldier has to reach at least E-6, midway up the NCO ladder.

The ratio of troops to officers varies from service to service. Overall in the U.S. armed forces, the ratio is 6:1 (six troops for every officer). In the Marines the ratio is 8.8:1; the Navy is close behind at 7.0:1, trailed by the Army's 6.1:1, and the Air Force, with an extraordinarily low ratio of only 4.4:1, just half that of the Marines. The low Air Force ratio is due to the large number of pilots and the high proportion of very technical jobs.

Pay and Benefits

It's difficult to discuss military pay because the troops are not paid the same way civilians are. The biggest difference is the "benefits." Unmarried troops live in dormitory accommodations, and get their meals along with the housing. All troops get their military clothing, although officers must pay for much of theirs out of a clothing allowance and all troops must pay for dress uniforms. Married troops get a housing and meals allowance, which varies with rank. Higher-ranking officers also have a lot of troops who act, for all intents and purposes, as personal servants. As one general commented, "The pay isn't much, but the fringe benefits are great." That said, this is an approximate civilian equivalent (benefits translated to cash equivalent) of what soldiers at each rank make. Included are adjustments for time in the service. That is, an E-7 with five years' service makes less than an E-7 with ten years' service.

Rank	Annual Compensation
E-1	$19,000
E-2	$20,000
E-3	$21,000
E-4	$24,000
E-5	$26,000
E-6	$28,000
E-7	$33,000
E-8	$38,000
E-9	$45,000
Warrants	$32,000–$50,000
O-1	$30,000
O-2	$34,000
O-3	$38,000
O-4	$46,000
O-5	$52,000
O-6	$60,000
O-7	$85,000
O-8	$88,000
O-9	$92,000
O-10	$115,000

There is additional pay for combat duty, peacetime hazardous duty, and special skills (pilots, physicians, and scarce technical specialties). These can add anywhere from $1,000 to over $10,000 a year to compensation. Active-duty officers and troops may quibble with some of the above numbers, but that's what happens when so much compensation is paid in kind rather than in cash.

Two Armies in One, and the Problems Created

Throughout this century, armies have been evolving into a pair of quite different organizations. First and foremost, there are the combat troops. In the armies of industrialized nations, combat troops rarely comprise more than 20 percent of troop strength. The remaining 80 percent are there for support. The increasing use of technology has created the need for all this support, and enormous numbers of technicians and other staff are needed to keep the gadgets running. But the difference in service conditions between the support and combat troops has also been widening. The combat troops operate in appalling conditions and get shot at. Most of the support troops live much more comfortably, and don't get shot at nearly as much. Even in peacetime, the lot of the combat soldier is more dangerous and less comfortable. Combat troops spend a lot of time out in the field, and in close proximity to large and dangerous equipment. Accidents happen, fatigue is a constant companion, and it is not unusual for combat soldiers to have their health damaged sufficiently to make them ineligible for combat duty. Such troops customarily transfer to a noncombat job to serve out the twenty years required for a pension. All military personnel are eligible for the half-pay pension after twenty years of service. This pension system was first introduced when most troops were in combat jobs and military life was a lot more dangerous than it is today.

In most cases, pay and benefits for combat and noncombat troops are identical. Combat troops get a bonus when they are in a combat zone, but so do many combat support troops who are not in nearly as much danger as the infantryman or tank driver. Paratroopers, sailors at sea, pilots, and a few other holders of nasty jobs also get a "hazardous duty" bonus. This extra pay doesn't add more than a few thousand dollars a year to the soldier's pay. The military tries to use badges to let everyone know who is a combat trooper. The warriors are recognized as a breed apart, and a group that pays a much higher price in blood for their service. But more and more, the many who are basically civilians in uniform get the same compensation as the few who really stick out their necks in war and peace.

This becomes a problem whenever there are calls to cut benefits for military personnel. The twenty-year pension is a regular target, if only because its cost grows enormously decade by decade. No one really wants to broach the subject that perhaps two classes of troops should be recognized: combat and noncombat. One major problem is that this isn't all black and white. Some combat support troops spend a lot of time at the fighting line, and cries would go out about the injustice of it all. However, it is a fact that the infantry and pilots take over 80 percent of the casualties. In peacetime, the grunts and pilots incur a disproportionate amount of the injuries. Expect this issue to become more prominent in the future.

Family Life

Before the volunteer army, only the career personnel tended to be married. Those draftees who were married generally did not have their families nearby while they did their two years' service. With the coming of the volunteer army, the number of married troops increased and most of them wanted their families around.

By the time they reach E-5 rank, an average of 68 percent of enlisted men are married, a higher rate of marriage than that for all civilian U.S. males of comparable age (early and mid-twenties). Figures for the individual services vary greatly. Only 54 percent of Navy E-5s are married and only 59 percent of those in the Marines, in contrast to 70 percent in the Army and 82 percent in the Air Force. Overall, 78 percent of officers are married, which is comparable to the rate for NCOs as a whole.

There is a reason for the low marriage rate for sailors and marines. About 15 percent of married enlisted personnel and 10 percent of married officers in the U.S. armed forces experience protracted separations from their spouses due to service in foreign nations or at sea. The lowest rate is for the Air Force, where only 8 percent of enlisted personnel and just 4 percent of officers are sent off for months of duty without their families. The Marines have the highest rates, 23 percent for enlisted personnel and 10 percent for officers. The Navy has a rate only slightly lower than the Marines. Naturally, the Air Force has the fewest of its members spending protracted periods away from the wife and kids.

While about 17 percent of all Americans change residence each year, some 28 percent of those on active duty with the armed forces do so. Since frequent change of residence is a disincentive to military service, Congress is rather generous in providing relocation allowances to military personnel. For enlisted personnel, this ranges from $1,500 for a recruit without dependents to as much as $14,500 for an E-9 (sergeant major or master chief petty officer) with dependents. Warrant officers get between $10,000 and $17,000, depending upon rank and dependent status. The figures for officers are comparable, with lowly second lieutenants and ensigns getting $10,000 without dependents and $12,000 with, while those ranking O-6 (colonel or captains in the Navy) and above get $18,000 regardless of dependents, though this compensation is rolled into their overall pay and is subject to legislation that caps military and bureaucratic remuneration at somewhat less than the $125,000 earned by members of Congress, the service secretaries, and federal judges. Despite these generous allowances, the military is trying to cut down on the constant personnel movement, to make units more effective by reducing personnel turnover and thus improving morale. Another reason is, of course, to save money.

WOMEN SOLDIERS

As of the early 1990s, each service had female personnel in the following percentages:

Air Force	14%
Army	11%
Navy	10%
Marines	5%

Women were first accepted as regular members of the U.S. forces in 1942, although "uniformed auxiliaries" served during World War I. The change was made largely because an increasing number of jobs no longer involved combat. Women could fill many of these positions and free men for combat duty. There were still restrictions on the military jobs women could perform.

But as women demonstrated ability to perform a wide variety of assignments, the number of occupations open to them gradually increased. Then, as now, they were barred from jobs that would be likely to expose them to combat.

When the draft was eliminated in the 1970s, and the all-volunteer armed forces were introduced, more women were welcomed into uniform. The reason for this was practical. The volunteer armed forces got off to a shaky start and the military could not get sufficient quantities of qualified males. This was particularly true of noncombat specialties. It was a perfect opportunity for women, as the generally better qualified women volunteers filled an even larger selection of military job specialties than before. Women were even allowed into the military academies during this period.

But at this point, in the late 1970s and early 1980s, serious controversy arose over women in the military. As has often been the case in the past, the problems were primarily a result of political pressures on the military to adopt unrealistic policies. The issue of women in combat became a political football, with members of Congress and feminist groups pushing for the elimination of all restrictions on women in military jobs. This, in turn, created some serious problems in the military. Ever sensitive to congressional criticism, the military complied with nearly every congressional suggestion except allowing women into combat jobs.

There were five very real problems created by this highly politicized movement to get women into combat situations:

1. Standards were lowered for many jobs to accommodate women, which caused problems in the units women were assigned to.
2. Double standards were adopted when even lowered standards would not do the trick. This was particularly the case in the service academies, producing class after class of cynical male officers and chagrined female ones.
3. Because of the first two items, considerable morale problems were created within the ranks.
4. Combat, even in combat support units, requires the troops to concentrate on the life-or-death mission at hand. Under combat conditions, the troops will seek out alternative activities (usually alcohol, drugs, or sex) if they have the opportunity. These alternative activities cause

more harm than good. It is bad enough when the sexual activities are with civilian women; it becomes worse when it occurs among the troops of the same unit. This situation was put to the test in the Gulf War and proved to be a major problem. Not much was made of it by commanders, for fear of the political backlash. But the problem remains, and will only get worse in future wars.

5. There is a substantial difference of opinion on this issue between enlisted and commissioned women. Female officers are more inclined to want access to all combat jobs because, ultimately, promotion favors those with command experience in the combat arms. Enlisted women are much less likely to prefer jobs in the combat arms for the same reason many men also shun those jobs. Combat arms' jobs are more arduous and dangerous.

The issue of women in the military faced its first serious challenge when the MEPSCAP program was introduced during 1981. MEPSCAP was a series of physical tests to be administered to all troops coming into the Army. MEPSCAP had previously calculated the minimum strength requirements for all Army MOSs (Military Occupational Specialties). MEPSCAP recognized that while many military jobs were no more strenuous than office work, most required varying degrees of physical ability.

Aside from the heavy physical demands of most military jobs, there was also the strenuous nature of field operations. Most Army troops are expected to serve as part of a field army at one time or another in their careers. That is, they will serve with units that must become mobile. This means everyone must pitch in and put all the unit's equipment on trucks and armored vehicles, and then unload it all after the movement is completed. Under combat conditions, such movements are normally conducted every few days. These moves take place in all types of weather, usually at night. Speed is essential, as the purpose of moving is often to avoid being located and attacked by enemy artillery and aircraft. The creators of MEPSCAP thought this would be a straightforward, militarily sound way to address the question of which military jobs women would be permitted to hold. The MEPSCAP crew was mistaken. The following data show that because of the differences in raw physical strength between men and women, far fewer women would be qualified for many MOSs.

Troops Passing MEPSCAP Tests

Physical Requirement	Number of MOSs	% of Women	% of Men	Jobs (in thousands)
Very Heavy	132	3	80	368
Heavy	48	8	82	71
Moderately Heavy	64	26	100	44
Medium	65	74	100	42
Light	42	100	100	47

Although the number of MOSs available to women was still far greater than the 10 percent of Army strength women comprised, it did bar most women from over half of all Army MOSs. This was political dynamite in Congress, where several members had made complete access for women to all military MOSs a major issue.

Rather than resist and face the real possibility of legislation telling them how to employ their personnel, the armed forces tried as much as possible to accommodate the senators and representatives making the most noise about giving women complete access to all military jobs.

Because nearly all of the pressure for complete access to military jobs from within the military was from female officers, there was intense pressure on the military academies to ensure the success of female cadets and mid- shipmen. Typical of the headlong manner in which the peacetime armed forces deals with political pressure, the service academies went to extremes to accommodate female cadets.

Officially, the military was simply being "fair." However, stories were soon circulating about cover-ups and poor morale among the staff and cadets at the academies. None of this was officially acknowledged until the state- supported Virginia Military Institute (VMI) was sued to force the accep- tance of female cadets in the heretofore all-male student body. In defending itself, VMI called as witnesses officers from West Point to explain, under oath, how the acceptance of female cadets at West Point worked in practice.

What follows is excerpts from the transcript of trial (Civil Action No. 90-0126-R) in Roanoke, Virginia, on April 8, 1991, in United States Dis- trict Court for the Western District of Virginia, Roanoke Division. The witness (A) is Colonel Patrick Allen Toffler, Director, Office of Institutional

Research, U.S. Military Academy, West Point. The cross-examining attorney (Q) is William A. Clineburg, defending VMI.

Q There is turnover every year in the cadet corps, correct, Colonel Toffler?

A Yes.

Q And because of that turnover, it's necessary to educate the incoming cadets about these physiological differences, and in your judgement the integration of women has been a success?

A That's right.

Q It's fair to say so far the cadets have not bought your argument?

A No, that's not fair to say.

Q It's not true that there are studies which show that the male and female cadets at West Point believe that integration has not been a success?

A The current information we have comes from a survey that we do of first classmen just prior to graduation, and that survey indicates that there are substantial portions of the corps, both men and women, who do not view the integration of women as having been fully successful.

Q So, that's a yes answer?

A That's my answer.

Q This is a memorandum about cadet perceptions on quotas. Correct?

A That's right.

Q And one of the things it talks about down at the bottom under 2-B is the issue of proportional representation?

A Correct.

Q And it states in there that in an effort to achieve proportional representation, we may well place a lesser but fully qualified cadet ahead of another fully qualified cadet. Correct?

A That's what it says.

Q And this is a memorandum to the superintendent of West Point. Correct?

A It's by the current, by the then chief of staff, Colonel Derring.

Q Over on page two it gives examples. Some examples of some other impacts of the quota system, correct, specifically under paragraph two about engineer branching. Do you see that?

A Yes, but what quota system are you talking about?

Q Well, let's look at the specific issue that he addresses. I think that will be clear. He indicates in the last sentence of subparagraph two that, "Five of six women who went engineers stood lower in the class than any of their 107 male counterparts." He says that probably contributes to the cadet perception of bias. Does that help you with respect to your statement you were unaware of any quota system?

A No, because the Army sent to the Military Academy a set of quotas for each branch that has a gender difference, so there is a set of quotas, if you will, for engineers that are for men and a set of quotas that are for women. And those quotas have got to be met, and so when the women are going for the engineer branch quotas, they are being compared with the performance of women, and the men are going for the men. It has nothing to do with the Military Academy and it has nothing to do with any specific unit.

Q But in the judgment of Colonel Derring, at least, or Deering, excuse me, that may contribute to the perception of cadets, that there is some bias operating. Is that right?

A That's right.

End of Transcript Excerpt

Colonel Toffler admitted that West Point has a gender-based quota system for the admission of women cadets and for their assignment after graduation. "Those quotas have got to be met," Colonel Toffler said. The females do not compete with men but only against other female cadets for designated female quota slots. Colonel Toffler admitted that to accommodate the women who cannot perform as well as men, West Point has changed from equal training of all cadets to "comparable training." This is a concept whereby if men and women appear to exert equivalent effort, they will be considered to have achieved equal performance. One typical example is pull-ups. Men are to chin themselves a certain number of times. The females need only hang from the bar a set number of times. Colonel Toffler eventually admitted that "no free speech is allowed at West Point concerning the performance of women."

What the cadets and midshipmen resent is that women are admitted to the academy on an equal basis, but once there, the rules are changed, and the standards lowered, for the women. This is the essence of the problem and the cause of the disrespect and contempt toward military women that is increasingly found among the ranks of male soldiers.

The number of female graduates of West Point who would want to become infantry officers is apparently small. Most female graduates prefer just about any branch except infantry, armor, and artillery. The most popular combat position sought by female graduates is helicopter pilot. These pilot jobs are, in most cases, technically not a combat role. But try telling that to the bad guys on the ground shooting at our helicopters without first checking the gender of the pilot.

That some women could be good at leading infantry units is a historical fact. There have been competent female leaders of guerrilla infantry units. But the proportion of women who could become good infantry officers versus the proportion of males is quite lopsided. The problem is not so much females being placed in charge of infantry units, it's more a matter of how infantry leaders are selected in general. The female combat leaders of the past earned their positions by demonstrating superior ability in the field. The favoritism and quotas at West Point besmirch the reputations of all female graduates. Moreover, any female graduates selected for infantry would have to be trained to the same standards as male cadets or face being killed or injured by their own troops. This has happened in all wars when the standards for new infantry officers were allowed to decline.

Vietnam was a vivid case of this. For example, between 1969 and 1972 there were 788 officially reported fraggings (attempted murder of officers and NCOs) resulting in 88 deaths and 714 injuries. It was known that not all fraggings were reported, as the perpetrators did not want to get caught. Those that occurred in the field were least likely to be reported and it is thought that as few as 10 percent of fraggings were recorded. This meant that as many as a thousand officers and NCOs were killed in this fashion. That's out of an "eligible" population of some 12,000 infantry officers. The troops have to get pretty angry before they will take such drastic steps, so you can imagine how many inept infantry officers were simply tolerated.

Even the civilian press has noted the problems of women in the military. One civilian publication, *Parent's Guide to the Five U.S. Service Academies,* devoted a full page to explaining the resentment of women at the academies. One of the examples they gave was the female cadet who avoided the required tower jump every year. She was too frightened of the height to jump. This continued until her last year at the academy even though the jump was a requirement to graduate. The female continued to refuse, claiming a fear of heights. The academy stood firm until the political pressure started and the female cadet was allowed to graduate without doing the jump. The *Parent's Guide* warned that female cadets face hostility from the male cadets because of the favoritism toward female cadets.

The Navy has its own special problems. More and more support ships have large portions of the crew positions filled by female sailors. There are above-average pregnancy rates while these ships are at sea and the wives of sailors have been pressuring their husbands to leave the Navy because of the presence of female sailors on ships during cruises that last several months.

Aside from the domestic fallout, the crucial problem for the Navy is the ability to perform damage-control jobs while trying to save a damaged ship (either because of combat damage or a peacetime accident). To assure the crew's ability to deal with battle damage, tests are given to recruits before basic training, and after. Sailors who cannot pass these physical tests are not allowed to hold most jobs on a ship, unless they are female. The results of these tests with male and female recruits explains why.

Task	Standard (seconds)	Recruits Capable of Performing Task (percent)			
		Females		Males	
		Before	After	Before	After
		Training		Training	
Stretcher Carry Up/Down Ladder	150	6%	12%	100%	100%
P250 Pump Carry	45	1	1	91	96
P250 Pump-Start	16	10	25	100	100
Torque Bolts 90 Lb. Pull	22	53	100	100	100

Some 84 percent of all shipboard duties involve heavy lifting, carrying, or pulling. Four of the most common jobs on board ships (boatswain's mate, gunner's mate, hull technician, and machinist's mate) are among the most physically demanding jobs in the military. In recognition of the need for physical strength among sailors, the Navy developed a program of shipboard weight training called SPARTEN. An example of SPARTEN involved the installation of Nautilus equipment on ships that have space for it. The above tasks reflect a recruit's ability to perform the basic life-and-death jobs that must be done when trying to control battle damage during combat. Naturally, far more women than men do not have the physical strength to perform these tasks. The fewer people on board who can perform these jobs, the larger the number of deaths and injuries that will result from battle damage. One can ignore this situation in peacetime, although there are accidents that call for the very same damage-control capabilities. But that means that it will take a lot of dead sailors before anyone will even address this issue.

SEXUAL HARASSMENT AND HOMOSEXUALITY

The wide-scale introduction of women into the military also reintroduced the "camp follower" problem, a problem that had largely disappeared with the development of modern armies. In times past, women (including some wives) would accompany the troops on campaign. These were the "camp followers" (which included men and some children) frequently mentioned in historical accounts. Camp followers would often number more people than the combat troops. The function of camp followers was to provide domestic (including sexual) services for the troops. The presence of women in an army on campaign was not without its problems. The troops, then as now, were largely young, unmarried men. Disputes over women were common and a good commander was one who made sure this disorder did not get out of hand. What we now call sexual harassment was taken for granted, and considered one of the fringe benefits of being a soldier.

The introduction of large numbers of women in uniform changed the situation somewhat. The military is a very macho organization. Macho is a lifesaving state of mind in combat, and the military tries to inculcate its troops with an ultra-macho attitude. However, an ugly side effect of macho is a very superior attitude toward those who are not macho. Generally, women are not considered macho (although many can be, and some definitely are). The standard male-female relationships found in civilian life did not disappear when the men and women put on uniforms. If anything, these relationships deteriorated. Men would take advantage of women, and women would take advantage of being women. One aspect of this became highly visible in the Gulf War when many women used their sudden pregnancy to get sent home from the desert. Some of these pregnancies were intentional, as it was military policy to send any pregnant soldier out of a war zone. Women soldiers would also use their femininity to their advantage in "office politics" in much the same way men would use their macho. The military was accustomed to dealing with macho; it had several thousand years of experience. Dealing with femininity was another matter, and everyone is still trying to sort out the new situation. Moreover, few are willing to wait a few centuries for these issues to be resolved.

Homosexual soldiers are also a growing source of debate. Homosexual soldiers have also existed since the dawn of time. In some cultures, homosexual soldiers were formed into all-homosexual units, although this was rare. Among the male population, those with homosexual tendencies comprise less than 5 percent of the population. Many of these are bisexual. Some homosexuals have always been attracted to the military life.

One of the attractions of warfare has been the free rein it gives to man's combative and sexual urges. Throughout history, soldiers have made the most of combat and sexual opportunities when campaigning. "Rape and Pillage" is an ancient rallying cry for troops. Many of the sexual victims of this were male, particularly young males and prisoners. Because of religious prohibitions against homosexuality, and the fact that clerics were often writing the histories of campaigns, you don't hear much of this unsavory side of warfare. But it was very common. You don't have to dig too far into the historical record to discover this.

One of the differences between males and females (of most species) is the female preference for one mate, and the male preference for many. Because of this, homosexuality did not lead to as many conflicts among troops as did the squabbles over women, partially because there were not as many homosexuals in the ranks. The number of homosexuals was lower in armies than in the general population because many homosexuals identify with females, and their less warlike nature. Many cultures that tolerate male homosexuality do so as long as the homosexuals dress as women and spend most of their time with women. But even premodern armies had less than 5 percent homosexuals and bisexuals in the ranks (and possibly more among sailors). Because these men were a distinct minority, and often living in a culture with religious prohibitions against homosexuality, they were low key in their sexual practices. Moreover, combat troops have always been the epitome of macho. Warfare is the one place where a macho attitude is a positive thing. Even nonhomosexual troops would sodomize enemy prisoners as a way to further humiliate the enemy. Generally, homosexuality in the ranks was something that was known, but not much talked about.

Until late in the twentieth century, there was no need for commanders to pay attention to "the homosexual problem," because there wasn't one. Homosexuals in uniform were discreet and were generally not bothered by their comrades because of this discretion. When civilian attitudes toward homosexuals began to change, there was concurrent pressure to show similar tolerance in the military. The problem was that there was still the ancient "understanding" in the military regarding homosexuals. The "understanding" was that homosexuals would be tolerated in this most macho of organizations as long as everyone pretended there were no homosexuals. Well, it wasn't that simple. The troops knew what homosexuals were, and that they existed in the ranks, but it was a case of out of sight, out of mind. Indeed, the conventional wisdom among the troops was that homosexuality was found among medical orderlies and similar noncombat positions. There was a definite antihomosexual attitude among the combat troops. Like so many unspoken understandings, this one caused an uproar when it was suggested that it be changed.

What has changed so much in this century is the creation of two very different, and disproportional, groups in the armed forces. At the turn of the century, the majority of soldiers in an army were combat troops. The noncombat troops were doing essentially civilian jobs and many nations freely mixed hired civilians (often in some kind of uniform) into these jobs. As technology and logistics became more of a factor, the proportion changed. In the last decade of this century, combat troops are usually less than 20 percent of most armies. Air forces have even more noncombat people and navies generally have more sailors ashore (in noncombat jobs) than afloat (where the entire crew is considered a combat unit). Most noncombat troops are doing civilian jobs, under very civil conditions. They still wear uniforms and salute, but they also lead a generally civilian life-style. The combat troops are, as they have always been, highly disciplined and constantly psyched for the rigors of combat. The fighters are very macho, the non-fighters are much less so, and this difference causes, as it always has caused, a lot of friction between the two groups. The status of homosexuals has changed in many civilian populations during this century, and those same changes could probably be carried over to the "civilianized" (noncombat) portions of the armed forces. But trying to change the quite unique culture of the combat units is another matter entirely.

What worries many military leaders is the side effects of openly allowing homosexuals in the military. As the saying goes, "The devil is in the details." The first little detail to come up would be whether the Army should change its regulations, which are set by law, against sodomy. Would this make it permissible for homosexuals to have sex in the barracks? After that, following practice in some civilian jurisdictions, will the Army have to recognize homosexual marriages and give these couples quarters? Would homosexuals now have minority rights and therefore by law a homosexual general must sit on every promotion board? Will there have to be quotas to ensure that the military is not discriminating? The military is an intensely conservative organization. The desire for change has to be balanced with the costs and benefits of making the change. Only time will tell if openly acknowledging homosexuals in the military will be a benefit or a burden.

ETHNIC AND RACE ISSUES

The armed forces are the most ethnically integrated organization in the nation, if not the world.

Minority Representation in the Armed Forces (early 1990s)

	Blacks		Hispanic		Other	
	Officers	Enlisted	Officers	Enlisted	Officers	Enlisted
Army	11%	30%	2%	4%	3%	5%
Navy	4	16	2	5	3	6
Marines	5	20	2	6	2	3
Air Force	5	17	3	4	3	3

In the general population, Blacks comprise 12.5 percent, Hispanics 9.5 percent, and Others (mainly Asian) 3.6 percent, for about 26 percent total minorities. In the armed forces overall, Blacks comprise 21 percent, Hispanics and Others 4 percent each. Also, several percent of the armed forces are foreign-born (legal or illegal aliens). This gives us about 30 percent minorities in the armed forces. The overall percentage is probably 1 or 2 percent lower (about 28 percent), because the Hispanic category is often miscounted (Italian and Irish troops have "Hispanic" names) and many Blacks and Asians of Hispanic background are counted twice.

So while the armed forces are overwhelmingly comprised of European Americans (over two thirds), African Americans are by far the next largest group. The "Ethnic" or "Race" issue in the armed forces has, for the past half century, been concerned with Blacks. Ironically, during the Revolutionary War, free (mainly northern) Blacks were among the first to answer the call to arms and these troops fought in integrated units. As the slavery issue heated up in the nineteenth century, the Army gradually prohibited Black troops from serving. The Navy, however, still recruited Black sailors for integrated crews. In the Civil War, the North eventually raised segregated Black units and these units became the norm until the end of World War II. In 1944 and 1945, shortages of troops in combat units saw the use of Blacks in some integrated units. Despite the "conventional wisdom" that "Blacks could not fight," these Black soldiers performed well. White soldiers gave testimony to this and this led to the 1948 order to integrate all Black units. This was completed by the end of the Korean War (1953).

While the Navy and Air Force took over twenty years to fully accept Black troops, the Army managed to achieve a high degree of integration by the end of the 1950s. For this reason, the word got around the Black community that you could get a square deal with the Army. As a result, the proportion of Army strength that was Black grew quickly in the 1950s and remained a common feature to the present. Many Black volunteers or draftees reenlisted and rose to comprise an even higher proportion of the senior NCO ranks. The proportion of Blacks as officers grew more slowly, mainly because of the lower proportion of Blacks who went to college and resistance in the military to Black officers. But with such a high proportion of the senior NCOs being Black, there was little opportunity for any remaining discrimination to flourish. Another item that helped matters was that many of the senior NCOs, Black and White, were war veterans. Having been in combat, or simply in uniform during a war, formed a bond that washed away much of the racial animosity the troops had been raised on. As wartime veterans put it, "The Army is an equal opportunity oppressor; it screws everybody."

Moreover, the senior NCOs were almost all married, and their seniority gave them access to family housing on Army bases. These housing communities were completely integrated, as were the schools and social facilities. While the unmarried troops would still segregate themselves when partying off base, the senior NCOs generally socialized with each other without regard to ethnicity. There was a higher rate of interracial dating and marriage among troops and dependents than in the general population. The more senior NCOs (E-8s and E-9s) found the junior NCOs quite sociable toward them, or at the very least deferential, regardless of ethnicity. The senior NCOs also tended to stick together, socially as well as on the job. It was a heady experience for a Black man who had grown up in the segregated South, or racially hostile North, to find himself in his forties, an E-7, E-8, or E-9, and getting along just fine with all those White folks. At least the ones in uniform, and their dependents.

The only downside to this remarkable bit of instant integration was that once a Black officer or NCO stepped off base, he often went right back to a very segregated and racially charged environment. But by the early 1960s, all of this began to change. The civil rights movement of the early 1960s eventually overthrew the legal aspects of segregation, and gradually began changing a lot of private attitudes on the matter. But the civil rights movement hit the Army in a different way. As the Vietnam War plunged on and garnered more unpopularity, the antipathy toward the war by the draft-age population merged with the increasing rage young Blacks were feeling. Without the Vietnam War, the Army might have slipped right through the civil rights era. The Army had achieved in the 1950s what the civil rights movement only began to move toward in the late 1960s. But Vietnam, and the breakdown of discipline in the Army that accompanied it, created a racially charged atmosphere by the early 1970s. Many of the most senior Black NCOs retired during this period, often glad to be done with arguing with angry young Blacks who never knew "how it used to be."

It took the rest of the decade for the Army to clear the air on the subject of race relations. During the 1980s, the percentage of Black officers increased, and more Blacks achieved the rank of general. One of these Black generals became Chairman of the Joint Chiefs of Staff (in civilian terms, the most senior general in the armed forces; the president is the commander of the armed forces) and won the first major U.S. war since Vietnam. This quieted any who might have complained that General Powell was appointed Chairman largely because he was Black.

While the Army has never resorted to racial quotas for promotions, there is a discreet and unofficial monitoring of the results of review boards. By law, officially recognized minorities must be represented on these boards. While minority status is taken into account for promotions, this has not become a problem. The military promotion is of the "up or out" variety, meaning that if an officer or NCO does not get promoted within a certain number of years of their last promotion, he or she must leave the service. Because of the twenty-year pension, and the arduous nature of military service, the "up or out" approach has not been seriously resisted or challenged. One side effect is that there are generally more qualified candidates for a promotion than are needed to fill the available vacancies. It's often something of a coin toss when selecting among those highly qualified candidates anyway. The Army sees to it that the qualified minority candidate gets sufficient additional consideration to ensure that, in effect, racial quotas are met. However, these quotas are not, as in the civilian sector, seen as a serious problem. Few, if any, unqualified candidates are promoted. The illusion is maintained that there are no quotas.

But a major reason for this is that there are high standards for minorities coming into the service. No quotas are allowed in this area. This in itself was an appealing feature for Blacks, as they knew the Army rank they earned would indeed be "equal" to the same rank worn by anyone else. This was clearly demonstrated in the Gulf War, where two of the three senior generals in the operation were Black (General Powell, the Chairman of the Joint Chiefs of Staff, and General Waller, the deputy commander of CENTCOM). The other general in this triad was, of course, General Schwarzkopf, the CENTCOM commander.

Hispanics, Asians, and other minorities never had it quite as bad in the Army as Blacks did. The integration of the Army in the 1950s benefited all ethnic minorities, even those who were suffering a lesser degree of discrimination. Asians and Hispanics were also well represented in senior NCO ranks. It was something of a half-joking fear among 1950s and 1960s enlisted recruits of being put in the charge of a Hispanic (often Puerto Rican) NCO who had a shaky grasp of English. The way the Army works, the recruits had to work a little harder to understand the Hispanic NCO's orders. An NCO doesn't have to provide translations for recruits. And they didn't. The recruits adapted, and expanded their language skills.

Even at the best of times, some racial tensions remained. By comparison to civilian life, there wasn't as much racial hassle. But a minority soldier need only go off base, or turn on the TV news, to get another reality check. Some of the racial tensions from "the outside" seep into the military. There are also merely personal tensions that are magnified by ethnic differences. But military discipline, particularly for career soldiers, is all-encompassing and in force 24 hours a day, 365 days a year. The troops get along, get with the program, or get out.

SOME OF THE REFORMERS

The Gulf War was very much a group effort. Success was the result of a high degree of professionalism at all levels. For years to come, historians and military professionals will be studying the actions of Colin Powell, Norman Schwarzkopf, Chuck Horner, Hank Mauz, Stan Arthur, Walt Boomer, Gus Pagonis, Ron Griffith, John Yeosock, Garry Luck, Barry McCaffrey, and Tommy Franks, just to mention a few of the senior commanders who made their mark in Desert Shield/Storm. There were also the millions who served in the twenty years before Desert Storm, and their efforts to break with the past in the Army and create for the first time in its history an Army trained and ready to win its first battle. The following are just a few of the people who were part of one of the greatest military reform movements in history. Many of them never did, and never will, get much recognition for their efforts. These people often put their careers on the line to support reform. Many paid for their courage by taking a lot of heat from hostile seniors and this often led to having careers cut short. While the reform effort was relatively bloodless, it did involve a lot of hard work and stress. The path of reform was not always the easy way out for officers. Here are some of the people who were willing to do it the hard way, the right way.

Abrams, GEN Creighton W. Born in 1914, graduated from U.S. Military Academy at West Point in 1936. A noted World War II Armor officer (he led the first armored battalion into besieged Bastogne during the Battle of the Bulge) and Chief of Staff of the Army from 1972 to 1974, he turned the Army away from the Vietnam fixation and reoriented it to protecting the vital interests of the United States in Europe and Northeast Asia. Most important, Abrams was vital in the effort to prevent the Army from falling victim to the "scapegoat syndrome" (blaming politicians and the media for their problems rather than setting out to reform the Army). He served as the Commander, Military Assistance Command, Vietnam, from 1968 to 1972.

Ball, COL Harry P. Born in 1925, graduated from West Point and received his doctor's degree from the University of Virginia. As author of the book *Of Responsible Command* and as a soldier, scholar, strategist, and teacher on the faculty at the Army War College, he had a major influence on the strategic thinking of many of the military reformers.

Boyd, COL John. A former Air Force officer who created a military theory of warfare that influenced the movement of the Army away from attrition warfare to a balance between attrition and maneuver warfare in AirLand Battle doctrine.

Cavazos, GEN Richard E. Born in 1929, and a graduate of Texas Technological University. He served in Korea and Vietnam. He was key in making sure that the human side and moral dimension of war were included in AirLand Battle doctrine. He was the Commanding General, U.S. Forces Command, from 1982 to 1984.

DePuy, GEN William E. Born in 1919, a graduate of South Dakota State College, where he was commissioned in the infantry from ROTC in 1941. He served in World War II and Vietnam. He was a visionary who distinguished himself as a commander, trainer, and planner. He was the first commander of TRADOC, and his stamp is on almost every facet of Army doctrine, tactics, training, and combat development. He was one of the moving spirits behind the creation of the National Training Center and the 1976 edition of FM 100-5. He broke the mold.

Dixon, GEN Robert J., USAF. Served in World War II, Korea, and Vietnam. At the conclusion of World War II he was a prisoner of war in Germany. He was the commander of the Tactical Air Command from 1973 to 1978. He was awarded the 1978 Collier Trophy for achievement in creating the Red Flag realistic air-power training program. He and General DePuy forged many joint programs for closer AirLand operations.

Dunnigan, James F. Born in 1943, enlisted service in the Artillery, 1961 to 1964. He began designing wargames for publication in 1966, founded a major wargames publishing company (SPI) in 1969, and ran it until 1980. Then he went into financial modeling and writing books on military affairs. He has published over three hundred wargames, designing over a hundred himself. He was asked to help reestablish wargaming at the Army War College in 1976 by Colonel Ray Macedonia, and has continued working with military organizations on wargaming and analysis matters, usually on a volunteer basis, ever since.

Franz, COL Wallace P. Served in the War Gaming Department at the Army War College and was one of the founders of "The Art of War Colloquium" which promoted historical and theoretical discussion on the theory of war. He was a major force in the military reform movement to place more emphasis on the operational level of war.

Gabriel, GEN Charles A. Born in 1928, graduated from West Point in 1950. He shot down two MiG-15s in Korea, commanded a recon unit in Vietnam, and flew 152 missions. He became Air Force Chief of Staff in 1982 and worked with his old West Point roommate (General Wickham), who was Army Chief of Staff, to forge closer cooperation between the Army and the Air Force in doctrine and in eliminating wasteful duplication in roles and missions.

Gorman, GEN Paul Francis. Born in 1927, graduated from West Point in 1950. He served in Korea and Vietnam, and was one of General DePuy's principal assistants during TRADOC's start-up. He learned a lot about commercial wargames by playing them with his teenage son. Recognized as one of the Army's premier trainers, he was a driving force behind the improvements in the Army's training programs and the creation of the National Training Center. He was the Commander in Chief, U.S. Southern Command, from 1983 to 1984.

Hardison, David. He was Deputy Under Secretary Army, Operations Research, from 1975 to 1980, Deputy Under Secretary Defense, Tactical Warfare Programs, from 1980 to 1982, and Director, U.S. Army Concepts Analysis Agency, from 1982 to 1984. One of the leaders in the Army's efforts to upgrade its weapon systems modernization program by improving the analytical tools and procedures for evaluating requirements and alternative technologies.

Holder, COL L. D. He participated in writing the 1982 and 1986 versions of AirLand Battle doctrine, FM 100-5. He served as the director of the School of Advanced Military Studies at Fort Leavenworth. He has been a driving force in the reintroduction of the operational art into the military.

Kerwin, GEN Walter T., Jr. Born in 1917, graduated from West Point in 1939. Served as Commanding General of II Field Force in Vietnam. As the first Commander of Forces Command from 1973 to 1974, he worked closely with General DePuy to revamp the doctrine, and as the Vice Chief of Staff of the Army from 1974 to 1978, he led the way in reorganizing the Army's mobilization system.

Kidd, ADM Isaac Campbell, Jr. He became Supreme Allied Commander Atlantic, Commander in Chief Western Atlantic Area, Commander in Chief

Atlantic, and Commander in Chief U.S. Atlantic Fleet on May 30, 1975, and he retired from the Navy in 1978. He was instrumental in the reform movement to increase professionalism in the Navy. He was a major sponsor of the Naval Fleet Readiness Program that used wargaming and programmed learning to increase the expertise and professionalism of senior commanders and their staffs.

Krosen, GEN Frederick J., Jr. He enlisted in the Army Reserve in 1942, and went on to active duty the following year. He was commissioned in 1944 and served in World War II, Korea, and Vietnam. He was a major force in the reform movement in the U.S. Army. He is responsible for many of the reforms in the mobilization system in the United States and the programs for the Army to make the transition from peace to war in Europe. He served as Commander of Forces Command from 1976 to 1978 and Commander in Chief, U.S. Army Europe and Seventh Army from 1979 to 1983.

Lawrence, LTG Richard D. Graduated from the United States Military Academy in 1953 and received a doctorate in operations research from Ohio State University. As a noted military educator, analyst, and Middle East expert, General Lawrence was one of the leaders in moving the military away from a fixation on Europe, as well as being one of the leaders who increased the professional preparation of senior officers in the operational level of war. As Commandant of the Army War College and President of the Defense University, he made a major contribution to improving the professionalism of senior military leaders.

Macedonia, COL Raymond. Born in 1932, received his bachelor's degree from the University of Pittsburgh (including a commission into the regular Army), his master's from Wharton Graduate School, University of Pennsylvania, and his doctorate from New York University. He was on the faculty of the Army War College for over eight years, teaching strategy, contingency planning, and operational analysis. He was assigned the task of reintroducing wargaming into the curriculum and was the first chairman of the Army War College's Department of War Gaming. He was also on the faculty at the United States Military Academy at West Point for over four years, teaching leadership and psychology. As a member of the Joint Staff, he directed the interagency analytical study efforts that led to the negotiations with the former Soviet Union on Mutual and Balanced Force Reductions.

Merritt, GEN Jack. Born in 1930, and a graduate of the University of Nebraska. He served in Korea and Vietnam. He was a major force in leading many of the major reforms in the Army over the past two decades. The impact of this distinguished officer will be felt in the Army for years to come. He served as the chairman of the Military Professional Development Study Group for the United States Military Academy in 1977. He was the Commander of the U.S. Field Artillery School from 1977 to 1980, Commandant of the Army War College from 1980 to 1982, Deputy Commanding General of TRADOC from 1983 to 1985, Director of the Joint Staff, OJCS, from 1983 to 1985, and U.S. Representative to NATO Military Committee from 1985 to 1987.

Meyer, GEN Edward. Born in 1928, graduated from West Point in 1951, and served in Korea and Vietnam. He became Chief of Staff in 1979 and used wargames extensively for improving the way the military conducted contingency planning. He extended the Army doctrine and focus to a global orientation and pushed many reforms before, during, and after his tenure as Chief of Staff. He galvanized the Army into breaking the mold of being a ''hollow'' Army.

Morelli, MG Donald R. As the first Deputy Chief of Staff for Doctrine in TRADOC, his presentations and clear explanations of the underlying concepts of AirLand Battle doctrine were central in gaining its acceptance from industry, Congress, and the executive branch.

Otis, GEN Glenn K. Born in 1929, graduated from West Point in 1953. He served in Korea and Vietnam. As the TRADOC Commander from 1981 to 1983, he was instrumental in adding the operational level of war into AirLand Battle doctrine. As the Commander in Chief U.S. Army Europe and Seventh Army and Commanding General Army Group for Allied Forces Central Europe from 1983 to 1988, he was key in integrating AirLand Battle doctrine into the Army.

Reed, COL Robert T. Born in 1932, graduated from West Point in 1954. He served in Korea and Vietnam. As a strategy and planning expert on the faculty at the U.S. Army War College, he greatly assisted the Commandant of the Army War College in his initiatives in 1976 to increase instruction in the operational art. As one of the Army's leading experts in operations research and systems analysis, he also played a critical role in the establishment of both the organizations and the methodologies at the TRADOC for rigorously evaluating new weapon requirements and concepts.

Richardson, GEN William R. Graduated from West Point. He served in Korea and Vietnam. A brilliant and distinguished officer, as the Commander of the Combined Arms Center at Fort Leavenworth from 1979 to 1981, he was responsible for the development of AirLand Battle doctrine, an increased focus on historical study, and the reorganization of the Army's heavy divisions and the restructuring of the Command and General Staff College to meet the demands of a modernized Army. Under his aegis as the TRADOC Commander, the Army reorganized its combat and support forces into the Army of Excellence and revised AirLand Battle doctrine to more fully cover the operational level of war. He was a major force in forging closer cooperation between the Army and the Air Force.

Rogers, GEN Bernard W. Born in 1921, graduated from West Point and was commissioned in the Infantry in 1943. As the Commander of Forces Command from 1974 to 1976, he was a major player in the creation of the National Training Center. As the Chief of Staff of the Army from 1976 to 1979 he was responsible for many of the major reform movements, including the Army's Tactical Command Readiness Program to keep senior tactical commanders abreast of changes in operational developments. As the Supreme Allied Commander in Europe in 1979, he was key in creating a winning spirit in the forces in Europe and integrating the follow-on-forces attack concept into NATO.

Saint, GEN Crosbie E. He is a graduate of the U.S. Military Academy and has served in many key staff and command positions including Commander in Chief, U.S. Army Europe and Seventh Army, Commander, Central Army Group, and Commander of III Corps. He has been a major force in the reform movement to improve training and to utilize simulators and computerized wargaming models to improve the quality of the officer corps. He has also been an innovator in the development of tactics for new weapon systems, such as the attack helicopter.

Shoemaker, GEN Robert M. Born in 1924 and graduated from the U.S. Military Academy at West Point in 1946. Served as the Assistant Division Commander of the 1st Cavalry Division (Airmobile) in Vietnam from 1969 to 1970. As the Commander of Forces Command from 1978 to 1982, he played a critical role in bringing AirLand Battle doctrine into the Army. He was also one of the prime movers for improving command and control in the Army by adopting the German concept of mission orders. By nesting the commander's intent in the concept of operations, this allows the subordinate commanders to rapidly adapt their actions to unique changes in the situation in accomplishing the commander's intent.

Smith, LTG DeWitt C., Jr. Born in 1920 and a graduate of the University of Maryland. A distinguished officer who served in World War II, Korea, and Vietnam. He was the major advocate for changing the way students were taught at the Army War College. This included reintroducing wargaming and increasing the amount of instruction on the operational level of war. He was also the leading advocate of ensuring that senior officers understood their special responsibilities as military leaders in a free society.

Starry, GEN Donn A. Born in 1925, graduated from West Point in 1948. Served in Korea and Vietnam. One of General DePuy's early allies in the push for reform. A visionary with great intellect, as Commander of TRADOC from 1977 to 1981, he led the development of AirLand Battle doctrine (the intellectual foundation of the Army's current combat superiority). As the Commander in Chief of the Readiness Command from 1981 to 1983 he was instrumental in introducing major reforms in the military in contingency planning and in joint operations.

Sullivan, GEN Gordon. A college graduate (Norwich), he received his commission in 1959. In 1962 he served as an adviser in Vietnam, where he was wounded. An Armor officer, he spent the rest of the Vietnam War with Armor units in Europe and the United States, until 1970, when he was a staff officer in Vietnam for three years. He then went through a series of command and staff assignments until becoming Chief of Staff of the Army in 1991. One of his assignments was as Commander of the 4/73rd Armor Battalion in the mid-1970s. The 4/73 was one of the many units that had gone completely to pieces during this period, and it was the mark of an exceptional officer if such a battalion could be turned around. Sullivan (then a lieutenant colonel) was able to turn the 4/73 into a combat-ready unit. General Sullivan was one of the many officers who worked with General DePuy during the 1970s. Sullivan continued the ongoing reform that DePuy had started, including being the driving force in the creation of the Army's Tactical Command Readiness Program designed to improve the professionalism of senior officers.

Summers, COL Harry G. Colonel Summers taught at the Army War College in the 1970s and, while there, wrote *On Strategy,* a popular, penetrating, and controversial book about the Vietnam War and on the need for a coherent grand strategy.

Thurman, GEN Maxwell. Born in 1931 and commissioned from ROTC in 1953. An Artillery officer, he served two tours in Vietnam. As the Army's chief recruiter, as the Commander of the U.S. Army Recruiting Command, he was instrumental in turning the volunteer Army into a quality force. As Vice Chief of Staff of the Army from 1983 to 1987 and then TRADOC Commander in 1987, he continued making major reforms that improved the readiness of the U.S. Army. He personally saw the fruits of his efforts when, as the Commander in Chief of Southern Command in 1989, he led U.S. forces in Panama in Just Cause.

Tuttle, GEN William G. T., Jr. Born in 1935 and graduated from West Point in 1958. He served in Korea and Vietnam. As Commander of Army Material Command, he was instrumental in many of the major reforms in logistics in the Army. In 1972, while assigned to the Pentagon, he and Colonel Jim Edgar developed the concept that would lead to reorganization of the Continental Army Command and the creation of TRADOC, which would provide for the first time a four-star general who could concentrate on training, doctrine, and force development.

Vandiver, E. B. "Van" Vandiver ran CAA (Concepts Analysis Agency) during the late 1980s and early 1990s. CAA, while an Army simulation and wargaming organization, actually does a lot of the wargaming for the Department of Defense in support of budgeting and doctrinal decisions. Vandiver brought historical gaming to CAA and caused a lot of the older, rather murky, models to become a lot more convincing. When the older models were put to the test of history, many were found wanting, and all benefited as deficiencies suddenly became obvious.

Vessey, GEN John W., Jr. Born in 1922, graduated from the University of Maryland, and commissioned on the battlefield. He served in World War II, Korea and Vietnam. As the Vice Chief of Staff of the Army in 1979 and then later as Chairman of the Joint Chiefs of Staff, he was a key leader in revamping the Army's mobilization system to ensure that the reserve force was trained and ready to go.

Vuono, GEN Carl E. Born in 1934 and graduated from West Point. General Vuono was Chief of Staff of the Army from 1987 to 1991. Prior to that, he was the Commander of TRADOC. He led the way in establishing a truly strategic Army and in creating the Combat Centers that were so critical to the success of U.S. forces in Desert Storm and Just Cause.

Wass de Czege, BG Huba. He is a graduate of the U.S. Military Academy at West Point and Harvard University. He served in Vietnam. He was the lead author on the writing of the 1982 edition of AirLand Battle doctrine, FM 100-5. He served as special adviser to the secretary general of NATO.

Weyand, GEN Frederick C. He was commissioned through ROTC at the University of California in 1938. During World War II, he served in the China-Burma-India Theater. He was Commander of II Field Force in Vietnam from 1967 to 1968 and Commander of the U.S. Military Assistance Command in Vietnam from 1972 to 1973. As Chief of Staff of the Army from 1974 to 1975, he worked hard to ensure that the Army did not fall into the self-defeating trap of blaming the civilian leadership for a stab-in-the-back.

Wickham, GEN John Adams, Jr. Born in 1928, graduated from West Point in 1950. He served in Korea and Vietnam. He became Army Chief of Staff in 1983 and worked closely with his West Point roommate (General Gabriel), who was Air Force Chief of Staff, to increase cooperation between the Army and the Air Force, Their efforts not only improved AirLand Operations, but but also saved precious resources by eliminating duplications.

Yerks, LTG Robert G. Born in 1928, graduated from West Point. He served in Korea and Vietnam. He was a major force in the Army's reform movement to increase emphasis on the operational level of war for senior officer education. As Deputy Chief of Staff of Personnel for the Army, he was a leader in the efforts to improve the quality of the volunteer Army.

INDEX

A

A-10, 129, 201
Abrams, Creighton W., 118, 304
Achille Lauro, 205
Active component, 10
Active defense, 10, 122–124, 129, 161, 162,
    164, 168, 172, 188, 263, 276, 277
Afghanistan, 65, 79, 136, 154, 160, 163,
    189, 197, 198, 264, 277, 278
AFQT, 10, 146, 147
Africa, 27, 41, 42, 44, 45, 62
Airborne Warning and Control System, 11,
    227
Air Combat Command, 10, 36, 230
Air Defense, 13, 116, 226, 230
AirLand Battle, 10, 119, 121, 129, 139,
    161, 166, 167, 168, 226, 233, 265,
    266, 277, 304, 305, 306, 308–310,
    312
Air Mobility Command, 10, 36
Air Tasking Order, 11, 219, 229
All Volunteer Army, 170
AMC, 10
American Civil War, 25, 123, 270
American Revolution, 17, 23–25
Amphibious assault, 206
Anarchy, 97, 106
Antisubmarine Warfare, 11, 223
AOE, 10, 155, 156
Apache, 193
Arab-Israeli War, 19, 28, 65, 113, 115,
    163, 216, 261, 262
Arabs, 114–116, 141
Armed Forces Qualification Test, 10, 146
Armored divisions, 35, 166
Arms race, 108, 109, 114, 115, 159, 189,
    239, 250
Army Forces Command, 16, 276
Army Material Command, 10, 311

Army of Excellence, 10, 154, 155, 162, 309
Army Training and Evaluation Program, 11,
    262
Army War College, 11, 18, 64, 67, 110,
    134–136, 138–140, 186, 187, 217,
    263, 264, 265, 304, 305, 307–311
ARPA, 14
ARTEP, 11, 262
Assault Breaker Program, 165
ASW, 11, 223
ATO, 11, 219, 229, 235
Attrition warfare, 265, 304
AWACS, 11, 66, 168, 198, 227, 235
AWOL, 107

B

B-2, 32, 53, 169, 196, 201, 226, 229, 236
B-36, 53
B-52, 229
BAI, 11, 12
Ball, Harry, 304
Battle Command Training Program, 187
Battlefield air interdiction, 11, 278
Battlefield promotion, 102
Battle management, 219, 228
BCTP, 12, 139, 185–188, 268
BDM, 123
Berlin Wall, 268, 278
Beyond Visual Range, 12, 230
Bliss, Tasker, 271
Blitzkrieg, 10, 84, 125, 127, 162, 168, 169
Body count, 86, 87
Bombers, 43, 52–54, 56, 59, 86, 127, 200,
    201, 224, 225, 226, 228, 229, 235
Bosnia, 32, 33, 36, 246
Bounding Overwatch, 162
Boyd, John, 264, 304
Braddon, Russell, 140–142
BVR, 12, 230, 231

C

C², 12, 193
C³I, 12, 28, 161
C-130, 47
Cambodia, 33, 74, 75, 78, 79
CARMAX, 267
Carter administration, 189, 198
Carter Doctrine, 65, 264, 277
CAS, 12, 226, 227
CASSS, 13, 110, 111
Cavazos, Richard, 305
CEM, 13
Central Battle Calculation, 164
Central Command, 13, 19, 66, 268
Central Front, 1, 27, 61–63, 201
Central Intelligence Agency, 13, 38, 109
Chairman, Joint Chiefs of Staff, 13
Chief of Naval Operations, 13, 218
Chief of Staff, United States Air Force, 14
China, 33, 53, 55, 74–76, 79, 85, 160,
  249, 250, 274, 312
CIA, 13, 38, 109
CINC, 13, 133
CINCCENT, 13, 268
CINCLANT, 13
CINCSOC, 12
Citizen Soldier, 25
CJCS, 13
Clausewitz, Carl, 64, 217, 271
Close Air Support, 12, 93, 116, 226, 274
CMTC, 13, 184, 269
CNO, 13, 218
Cohen-Nunn Amendment, 94
Cold War, 16, 27, 29, 33, 35–38, 47, 49,
  58, 62, 68, 71, 79, 109, 114, 129,
  150, 155, 160, 169, 190–192, 195,
  198–202, 219, 223, 230, 237–239,
  241–243, 245, 248, 249, 251, 253–
  255, 258, 260, 268, 269, 278
Combat Maneuver Training Center, 13, 269
Combat Movement Records, 211
Combat Services Support, 14
Combat veterans, 82, 150
Combined Arms and Service Staff School,
  13
Combined Arms Team, 13, 111, 124
Combined Effects Munition, 13
Combined Operation, 13
Come As You Are, 13, 14, 161, 276
Command and Control, 12, 70, 120, 129,
  169, 172, 185, 193, 275, 278, 279,
  310
Command, Control, Communications, and
  Intelligence, 12
Commander in Chief, 13, 218

Commander in Chief, Atlantic Command,
  13
Commander in Chief, Central Command,
  13
Commander in Chief, Special Operations
  Command, 13
Commissioned officers, 9, 103, 281, 282
Communist(s), 32, 33, 53, 61–63, 71, 72,
  75–78, 83, 84, 85–92, 206, 215, 243,
  245, 278
Competitive Strategies, 169
CONARC, 14, 276
Concept of operation, 14, 129
Congress, 16, 31–34, 37, 44, 52, 55, 59,
  71–73, 94, 95, 107, 114, 133, 134,
  147, 154, 155, 168, 181, 191, 194,
  197, 202, 235, 236, 259, 272, 285,
  289, 290, 292, 308
Conscription, 26, 96, 98, 104, 143, 144,
  147, 152, 160, 216
Conscripts, 82, 98, 100, 104, 143, 144,
  149, 173, 191, 193, 194, 202
Continental Army Command, 14, 276, 311
Contingency plan, 14, 19
Contingency planning, 136–138, 140, 187,
  263, 265, 268, 307, 308, 310
Counterinsurgency, 14, 92, 134, 135, 215,
  242, 275
Coup, 77, 269
Covering force, 124, 125
CSAF, 14
CSS, 14
CVA, 14
CVBG, 14

D

DARPA, 14, 165
DAS, 14
Deep Attack, 15, 162, 167
Defeat Disease, 15, 113
Defense Advance Research Agency, 14
Demobilization, 45, 51, 160, 251, 258, 276
DePuy, William, 5, 21, 28, 113, 117–128,
  137, 161, 162, 172, 173, 186, 262,
  263, 305, 306, 311
DePuy foxhole, 162
Desert One, 15, 47–49, 65, 80, 94, 265
Desert Shield, 46, 64, 65, 68, 133, 139,
  142, 182, 184, 265, 304
Desert Storm, 30, 31, 48, 50, 68, 112,
  129, 130, 139, 169, 181, 183, 184,
  188, 219, 244, 247, 248, 265, 304,
  312
Desert Storm Equivalent, 30
Desertion, 107

Direct air support, 14
Discipline, 28, 40, 96, 106, 107, 112, 147–
151, 157, 180, 194, 215, 302, 303
Divorce, 152
Dixon, Norman, 142
Dixon, Robert, 118, 305
Doctrine, 10, 15, 16, 21, 23, 28, 36, 37,
41, 44, 45, 46, 47, 56, 57, 63–65, 73,
79, 84, 92, 112, 113, 115, 117, 119–
123, 125, 126, 127–133, 139, 142,
157, 162–164, 166–169, 172, 174,
184, 185, 188, 189, 202, 208, 216,
226, 230, 233, 234, 238, 242–244,
253, 260, 263, 264, 265–280, 304–
306, 308–312
Douhet, Giulio, 273, 274
DPICM, 15, 209
Draft dodgers, 24
Drugs, 111, 147, 148, 290
Dunnigan, James, 1, 66, 67, 123, 135,
264, 305

E

ECM, 15, 230
Egypt, 140–142, 211
Electronic countermeasures, 15
Electronic field training, 111
Electronic warfare, 15, 116, 120, 218, 225,
230
Enlisted personnel, 252, 281, 285, 288, 289
Equipment procurement, 41
Escalation, 85
Estimate of the situation, 138, 271

F

F-4, 225
F-15E, 201, 220
F-16, 201
F-117A, 201, 220, 225, 226, 236
False confidence, 1, 27, 39, 68
Firepower, 19, 21, 36, 77, 84–88, 92, 114,
122, 129, 162, 165, 166, 168, 172,
183, 229, 277, 278
First battle, 14, 22, 27–29, 39, 41, 63,
119, 120, 126, 130, 132, 133, 162,
172, 181, 186, 187, 211, 269, 304
Fleet Readiness Program, 18, 135, 185–
187, 217, 307
Flexible Response, 59, 60, 275, 276
FM 100-5, 15, 28, 64, 119, 121–123, 127–
129, 139, 162, 163, 168, 172, 188,
244, 263, 269, 274–278, 305, 306,
312
Force Planners, 257–259

Foreign policy, 71, 253
Forrestal, James, 52
FORSCOM, 16, 118, 276
Fort Irwin, 18, 177, 178, 182, 183, 265
Fragging, 87
France, 25, 62, 75, 76, 138, 211, 248, 250
Franz, Wallace, 305
Friendly fire, 12, 16, 46, 83, 87, 88, 183,
208, 227
Fulda Gap, 63, 66

G

Gabriel, Charles, 6, 233, 234, 266, 306,
312
GDP, 16
General Defense Plan, 16
Generate maximum violence, 171
German Army, 64, 109, 118
Global Positioning System, 16
GNP, 51, 239, 240, 244, 245, 248–250,
255, 260
Goldwater-Nichols Department of Defense
Reorganization Act, 16, 32, 133, 233
Gorman, Paul, 172, 173, 186, 263, 306
GPS, 16, 169, 183, 198, 208
Gradualism, 70, 71
Green Berets, 92, 94, 158
Grenada, 46, 94, 205, 246, 267, 269
Guerrilla wars, 18, 60, 78
Gulf Strike, 67
Gulf War, 9, 16, 24, 29–31, 33–38, 40,
49, 54, 66, 67, 94, 111, 124, 139,
140, 143, 152, 155, 156, 161, 165,
167, 169, 192, 195, 196, 198, 201,
203, 205, 206, 208, 209–213. 219,
220, 223–225, 227, 228, 231, 232,
235, 237, 238, 243, 247, 252–254,
278, 279, 291, 297, 303

H

Hackworth, David, 279, 280
Haiti, 33
Hardison, David, 66, 306
Hearts and minds, 69, 89
Helicopter, 47, 48, 74, 93, 94, 98, 193,
282, 284, 295, 309
Herman, Mark, 6, 66, 67
High Technology Test Bed, 166
Holder, L. D., 306
Hollow Army, 1, 16, 26, 28, 96
Homosexuals, 298–300
Hostages, 47, 65, 189, 264, 265
Huey, 74, 82, 93
Hussein, Saddam, 211

I

ICBM, 17, 169, 229, 254
Indian wars, 78
Innovative training, 1, 29, 170
Institutional knowledge, 26, 83
Integrated battlefield, 165, 166
INTEL, 17, 38, 85, 91, 229
Intelligence, 12, 13, 17, 20, 28, 33, 38,
    66, 67, 85, 88, 91, 117, 127, 161,
    186, 200, 230, 245, 263
Inventory, 137, 192, 208
Iran, 15, 17, 30–32, 47, 65, 66, 94, 136,
    189, 205, 254, 257, 259, 262, 264,
    265, 268
Iraq, 17, 30, 31, 35, 66, 67, 119, 140,
    189, 195, 207, 210, 211, 219, 225,
    238, 246, 254, 257, 259, 262, 264,
    268, 269
Israel, 48, 114, 115, 117–119, 131, 141,
    142, 211, 250

J

Japan, 33, 44, 45, 51, 52, 62, 211, 246,
    248, 249, 254, 256, 259
JCS, 17, 133
Johnson, Louis, 44, 52
Johnson, Lyndon, 70, 72, 80
Joint Chiefs of Staff, 13, 16, 17, 32, 48,
    70, 133, 233, 266–268, 279, 302,
    303, 312
Jointness, 32, 133, 134
Joint Operations, 17, 36, 219, 221, 233,
    234, 310
Joint Readiness Training Center, 17, 268
Joint Staff, 17, 67, 70, 307, 308
Joint Task Force Middle East, 17
Jomini, Henri, 270, 271
JRTC, 17, 184, 268
JSTARS, 17, 198, 227, 228, 234, 235
JTFME, 17, 268
Junior NCOs, 100, 105, 145, 281, 283, 301
Junior officers, 99–103
Just Cause, 64, 65, 269, 311, 312
Just War, 72

K

Kasserine, 41–43, 45, 261
Kennedy, John, 60, 79, 80, 158
Kent State University, 97
Kerwin, Walter, 118, 306
Kidd, Isaac, 218, 306
Korea, 26, 27, 32, 39, 41, 45, 46, 55, 56,
    62, 64, 70, 72, 79, 82, 84, 100, 104,
    105, 148, 150, 151, 173, 190, 215,
    219, 232, 257, 261, 262, 284, 305–
    313
Kroesen, Frederick, 307
Kut, 141, 142
Kuwait, 19, 35, 66, 67, 114, 140, 199,
    205, 206, 210, 238, 246, 259, 268, 269

L

Language, 74, 83, 303
Laser, 18, 176, 177, 181, 182
Laser tag, 18, 176, 177, 182
Lawrence, Richard, 307
Leadership, 21, 25, 26, 43, 45, 56, 58, 64,
    65, 69, 71, 99, 104, 113, 114, 128,
    140, 148, 160, 163, 172, 187, 193–
    195, 215, 229, 237, 245, 246, 250,
    253, 254, 257, 276, 280, 307, 312
Leshem, Moshe, 142
Lethality, 22, 28, 113, 115, 120, 131, 261,
    277
Libya, 46, 205
Liddell Hart, Basil, 273
Light Division, 166, 263
Lightning War, 10
Lind, William, 264
Little wars, 166, 224
Low Intensity Conflict, 18
Low-intensity warfare, 31, 243
Ludlow, William, 271

M

M-1 tank, 161, 193, 201
McClintic, Fred, 18, 66
McClintic Theater Model, 18
Macedonia, Raymond M., 1, 67, 265, 305,
    307
Mahan, Alfred, 272, 274
Mahan, Dennis, 270
Marine Corps, 17, 32, 54, 55, 151, 220,
    267
Marines, 15, 17, 23, 26, 29, 32, 55, 60,
    78, 81, 99, 144, 148, 159, 202, 205,
    206, 208, 214, 215, 219, 220, 235,
    240, 255, 256, 285, 288, 289, 300
Marshall, George, 51, 52, 134, 273
MEPSCAP, 291, 292
Merritt, Jack, 6, 308
Meyer, Edward, 65, 66, 136, 137, 140,
    142, 187, 265, 266, 308
Micromanagement, 70, 80, 124
MILES, 18, 42, 47, 54, 120, 140, 141,
    176, 177, 181, 182, 183, 217, 233,
    241, 273

Military Assistance Program, 71
Military history, 23, 26, 29, 49, 106, 162, 173, 186
Military Integrated Laser Engagement System, 18, 176
Military Occupational Specialties, 18, 291
Military professionals, 9, 31, 64, 90, 98, 242, 248, 256, 259, 304
Military reform, 48, 95, 129, 195, 241, 242, 261, 304, 305
Military strategy, 18, 52, 60, 138
Militia, 24, 25, 51, 55, 240, 272
Mission management, 228
Mission orders, 121, 310
Mitchell, William, 273, 274
MLRS, 18, 165
Mobility, 10, 28, 36, 66, 74, 82, 92, 120, 123, 124, 131, 161, 172, 215, 271, 275, 276
Mobilization, 32, 55, 69, 120, 131, 132, 134, 258, 262, 271–273, 276, 306, 307, 312
Mohave Desert, 177, 178
Morelli, Donald, 308
MOS, 18, 281, 282, 292
Multiple rocket launcher, 18, 165

N

National Defense University, 110
National Guard, 25, 51, 57, 101, 102, 150, 155, 156, 191, 240, 260, 273
National strategy, 18, 58, 60, 117, 135, 217, 229, 230
National Training Center, 18, 111, 175, 219, 263, 265, 267, 305, 306, 309
NATO, 18, 28, 60, 63, 94, 108, 109, 115–117, 126, 127, 128, 160, 164, 165, 170, 188, 246, 258, 277, 308, 309, 312
Naval operations, 13, 218, 220, 222
Navy Fleet Readiness Program, 18
Nazis, 61, 248
NCO, 9, 18, 98, 100, 102–107, 112, 145, 149, 258, 261, 285, 301–303
NCO training, 112
Nellis Air Force Base, 262
NFRP, 18
Nixon, Richard, 72, 97
Nuclear warfare, 27, 28, 30, 50, 52–60, 73, 79, 82, 120, 127, 131, 135, 158, 166, 169, 183, 194, 199, 220, 221, 229, 241, 245, 246, 249, 250, 256, 274, 275

O

Observer controller, 18
Office of the Secretary of Defense, 19
Officers Evaluation Report, 18, 181
Officer training, 110
One-Third Solution, 244
On Strategy (Summer), 266, 311
OPEC, 19, 262
Operational art, 19, 111, 135, 139, 266, 306, 309
Operational order, 19
Operational plan, 19
Operation Torch, 42
OPFOR, 19, 178, 179, 184
OPLAN, 19, 268
OPLAN-1002, 19
OPORD, 19
Opposing force, 178
OSD, 19
Otis, Glenn, 308
Overwatch, 19, 162

P

Panama, 46, 47, 64, 114, 205, 246, 269, 311
Patton, George, 61
Pentomic Army, 50, 57, 58, 60, 64, 73, 151, 158, 214, 238, 275
Per capita income, 239
Petty officers, 18, 145
Philippine Insurrection, 78
Potential enemies, 27, 36, 112, 123, 241, 244, 256
Potential opponents, 221, 225, 240
Powell, Colin, 302–304
Precision-guided munition, 19
Prussia, 137, 271

Q

Quakers, 24

R

Race issues, 300
Racial conflicts, 97
Racial problems, 114
RAND Corporation, 58
R&D projects, 252, 255
Rangers, 243, 255, 268
Rank inflation, 98
Rapid Deployment Force, 19, 65, 66
Reagan, Ronald, 66, 109, 194, 195, 201, 239, 265

Recession, 155, 251
Recruiting Command, 153, 311
Recruitment standards, 40
REDCOM, 20
Red Flag, 36, 174–176, 224, 262, 305
Reduction in force, 20, 28, 56, 97, 112
Reed, Robert, 308
Reenlistment rates, 107, 285
Reform, 1, 9, 16, 21, 25–28, 36, 38, 45,
    47–51, 95, 112, 113, 118, 129, 130,
    149, 157, 170, 189, 205, 213, 214,
    216, 217, 223, 224, 237, 241, 242,
    261, 272, 280, 304, 305, 307, 309–
    311, 313
Regulars, 10, 24–26, 57
Research and development, 19, 37, 53, 92,
    191, 195, 196, 197, 199, 225
Reserves, 12, 57, 69, 101, 102, 104, 126,
    127, 150, 164, 165, 191, 203, 276
Retirement, 98, 100–102, 145, 151, 190,
    258, 285
Review of Education and Training for offi-
    cers, 20, 187
Revolt of the Admirals, 52, 53
Richardson, William, 137, 309
RIF, 20, 28, 56, 97, 99, 101–103, 112
Rogers, Bernard, 135, 309
Rotation policy, 83, 88, 99
ROTC, 100, 110, 305, 311, 312

S

SAC, 20, 36
Saint, Crosbie, 309
SAMS, 20, 139, 267
Sanctuaries, 78, 79, 84
Sanger, Joseph, 271
Satellite, 59, 80, 108, 185, 222, 235, 256
School of Advanced Military Studies, 20,
    267, 306
Schwan, Theodore, 271
Schwarzkopf, Norman, 133, 304
SDI, 20, 169, 195, 196, 199, 254
SEAL, 20
Search and destroy, 84–86, 88
SECDEF, 20
Secretary of Defense, 19, 20, 44, 52, 94
Secret projects, 235
Senior NCOs, 68, 99, 100, 103–105, 202,
    281, 282, 283, 284, 301
Senior officers, 31, 101, 103, 106, 109,
    112, 118, 130, 134–136, 139, 140,
    142, 149, 172, 186, 187, 307, 310,
    311
Sensors, 85, 169, 176, 193, 214–216, 219,
    223, 231, 232

Sergeants, 9, 18, 99, 103–105, 107, 112,
    145, 149
Sexual harassment, 154, 297
Shake 'n Bake, 100, 101, 104, 105, 145
Shoemaker, Robert, 310
Sidra, 205
SIMNET, 20, 184
Simulation Publications, Inc., 20
Simulations, 12, 66, 67, 171, 183, 185–
    187, 209, 253, 263–265, 267, 268
600-ship Navy, 196, 201, 223
Smart munitions, 20, 32, 165, 169, 197
Smith, Charles, 45, 46
Smith, DeWitt C., Jr., 263, 310
Somalia, 18, 32, 33, 36, 166, 243, 246, 247
Soviet menace, 257
Soviet Union, 27, 31, 33, 35, 56, 61, 62,
    73, 85, 92, 108, 123, 188, 196, 245,
    248, 249, 252, 257, 259, 269, 278,
    279, 308
Spanish-American War, 26, 240, 272
Special Forces, 13, 32, 158, 256
Special operations forces, 20, 92, 94, 243,
    268
Special Operations Review Group, 48
SPI, 20, 67, 305
Standing army, 50
Starry, Donn, 119, 137, 167, 172, 173,
    263, 266, 310
Stealth, 169, 201, 225, 226, 229, 236, 276
Steuben, Wilhelm von, 64
Strategic Air Command, 20, 36, 230
Strategic Bombing Survey, 21, 54
Strategic Defense Initiative, 20, 195
Strategic weapons, 191, 195
Strategy, 18, 50, 52, 53, 57–60, 72, 117,
    135, 138, 139, 195, 217, 220, 221,
    224, 229, 230, 265, 266, 279, 307,
    308, 311
Strike packages, 228
Sullivan, Gordon, 6, 47, 136, 264, 265,
    310, 311
Summers, Harry, 262, 311
Synchronization, 9

T

TAC, 21, 36
Tactical Air Command, 21, 36, 118, 230,
    233, 305
Tactical Command Readiness Program, 21,
    136, 138, 187, 263, 309, 311
Tactics, 21, 23, 37, 41, 45, 46, 70, 84, 86,
    88, 94, 115, 117, 119, 125, 127, 130–
    134, 138, 139, 161–163, 169, 172,
    174, 179, 208, 215, 224, 244, 265,

267, 269, 270, 278, 279, 280, 305, 309
Tailhook scandal, 40
Target servicing, 21, 162
Task Force Smith, 27, 41, 45, 135, 212, 244, 260, 261
Taylor, Maxwell, 59, 60
Taylor, Zachary, 25
TCRP, 21, 187, 263
Terrorists, 243, 244
Tet Offensive, 90, 91
Third World, 30, 79, 134, 238, 252, 254
Thurman, Maxwell, 153, 311
Ticket punching, 96
Toffler, Patrick, 292–294
Top Gun, 174, 176, 216, 219, 224, 262
TRADOC, 18, 21, 28, 37, 117–119, 123, 132, 161, 167, 172, 173, 177, 262, 276, 305, 308, 309–312
Troop quality, 103, 106, 112, 146, 194, 255
Truman, Harry, 44, 50–52, 55, 149
Tuttle, William, 311

U

U-boats, 42
Unmanned aerial vehicle, 21
Unpreparedness, 27, 41, 44–46
Untested weapons, 253
Upton, Emory, 138, 271
U.S. Army War College, 263, 309
USSTRATCOM, 36
U.S. Strategic Bombing Survey, 21, 54

V

Vandiver, E. B., 311
Vessey, John, 312

Victory Disease, 21, 29, 30, 33–35, 47, 244, 260
Vietcong, 76–79, 84–86, 91
Vietminh, 75–77, 84
Vietnamization, 69
Volunteers, 1, 28, 104, 106, 143, 144, 148, 149, 152, 153, 154, 191, 210, 223, 285, 290, 301
Vuono, Carl, 312

W

Wagner, Arthur, 271
War Academy in Berlin, 137
WARFIGHTER, 187
Warfighting, 10, 16, 21, 47, 136, 139, 186, 267, 268, 310
Warfighting skills, 21, 186, 268
Wargaming, 18, 21, 67, 135, 137, 164, 184–186, 217–219, 265–266, 268, 305, 311
War of 1812, 25, 130, 261, 270
Warrant officers, 98, 281, 282, 284, 289
Warrior Preparation Center, 140
Warriors, 39, 40, 57, 59, 138, 287
Warsaw Pact, 28, 63, 94, 109, 115, 126–128, 132, 165, 246, 258, 259, 277, 278
War to End All Wars, 26, 241
Wass de Czege, Huba, 312
Weyand, Frederick, 262, 312
Wickham, John, 66, 233, 234, 266, 306, 312
Win the First Battle, 22, 120
Women soldiers, 289, 297

Y

Yerks, Robert, 313